Writing with W

TITLES OF RELATED INTEREST

College Writing Basics: A Progressive Approach, Third Edition,
Thomas E. Tyner (1993)

Composing Through Reading, Second Edition,
Peter Elias Sotiriou (1994)

*Critical Thinking and Writing: A Developing Writer's Guide
with Readings*, Kristan Cavina (1995)

Developing Writers: A Dialogic Approach, Second Edition,
Pamela Gay (1995)

Inside Writing: A Writer's Workbook, Form A, Second Edition,
William Salomone, Stephen McDonald, and Mark Edelstein (1993)

Inside Writing: A Writer's Workbook, Form B, Second Edition,
William Salomone, Stephen McDonald, and Mark Edelstein (1994)

The Language of Learning: Vocabulary for College Success,
Second Edition, Jane N. Hopper and JoAnn Carter-Wells (1994)

Making Connections Through Reading and Writing,
Maria Valeri-Gold and Mary P. Deming (1994)

Patterns and Themes: A Basic English Reader,
Judy R. Rogers and Glenn C. Rogers (1993)

Right Words, Right Places, Scott Rice (1993)

Texts and Contexts: A Contemporary Approach to College Writing,
Second Edition, William S. Robinson and Stephanie Tucker (1995)

Variations: A Rhetoric and Reader for College Writing,
Judy R. Rogers and Glenn C. Rogers (1991)

Writing as a Life-Long Skill, Sanford Kaye (1994)

*Writing Paragraphs and Essays: Integrating Reading, Writing,
and Grammar Skills*, Second Edition, Joy Wingersky, Jan Boerner,
and Diana Holguin-Balogh (1995)

Writing Voyage: A Process Approach to Basic Writing,
Fourth Edition, Thomas E. Tyner (1994)

Writing with Writers, Thomas E. Tyner (1995)

Writing with Writers

Thomas E. Tyner

Kings River College

Wadsworth Publishing Company
Belmont, California
A Division of Wadsworth, Inc.

English Editor: Angela Gantner Wrahtz
Assistant Editor: Lisa Timbrell
Editorial Assistant: Kate Peltier
Production: Johnstone Associates
Designer: Christy Butterfield
Print Buyer: Barbara Britton
Permission Editor: Robert Kauser
Copy Editor: Judith Johnstone
Cover: Vargas/Williams/Design
Compositor: Thompson Type
Printer: Arcata Graphics/Fairfield

*This book is printed on
acid-free recycled paper.*

INTERNATIONAL THOMSON PUBLISHING
The trademark ITP is used under license.

Printed in the United States of America
1 2 3 4 5 6 7 8 10–99 98 97 96 95

Library of Congress Cataloging-in-Publication Data

Tyner, Thomas E., 1944–
    Writing with writers: Thomas E. Tyner.
        p.   cm.
    Includes index,
    ISBN 0-534-23616-2
    1. English language—Rhetoric.   I. Title.
PE1408.T97   1995
808'.042—dc20   94-12902
                                                             CIP

Contents

vi CONTENTS

Preface

Since I wrote *Writing with Writers* in the first person, let me introduce myself. My name is Tom Tyner, and I teach college writing classes and write an occasional textbook. I'm also a failed inventor, which you'll read more about later. I'm married, have two grown children, and live in a small town in central California.

I enjoy watching sports, going to movies, composing songs on the piano, lifting weights, eating junk food, and teaching small classes. I don't enjoy getting up early, working in the yard, jogging, waiting for anything, or teaching large classes. On the positive side, I like people, follow through on most tasks, have a decent sense of humor, and don't mind taking risks. On the negative, I tend to procrastinate, am impatient and impulsive, and don't mind taking risks.

Speaking of risks, I took one by putting a lot of myself in this book, beginning with this introduction. As you read and work through the book, you will get to know me better as a person and a writer. The risk lies in my exposing more about myself and my life than you may care to read about, and in believing that sharing my writing process with you will in some ways benefit your own writing.

I hope you enjoy using this book as much as I enjoyed writing it. It was fun to come out from behind the omniscient "textbook voice" and speak for myself. I tried to write to you much as I would talk to my students about writing. While we can't carry on the same dialogue, I can "talk" to you through my writing, and you can respond through your journal entries. More about journal writing in the first chapter.

However, I go beyond just talking with you about writing. I also work through the book with you and your instructor, doing the same writing activities that you do. As you work through various writing assignments, you will also see and hear what I am doing: how I decide on a writing topic, my "prewriting" plans for a particular draft, my first drafts with handwritten revisions, reflections on my drafting process, and examples of my final drafts.

For me, doing the writing activities was the most enjoyable part of writing the book. However, that's not why I did them. First, I wanted you to see how much we as writers have in common—the time spent coming up with a good topic, the struggle to express our ideas so others can understand them, the discovery of new ideas as we write, the constant need to revise, and the satisfaction of seeing others enjoy what we have written.

Beyond that, I think that you will benefit from my experience as a writer, as well as from your instructor's. As you read how I come up with writing topics, work through a first draft, think through my revision plans, consider my reading audience, and so on, you may find things to apply to your own writing processes. Finally, I hope you enjoy reading some of my essays, and that as you get to know me better through my writing, you will find the text reasonably interesting.

Along with my own writing, I have also included the writings and reflections of student writers throughout the text. While you may find some of my essays interesting and benefit from what I have learned, you may find the student writers' entries even more interesting and helpful. As students, they are at similar stages in their writing development—and their lives—as you are, and you will probably relate well to some of the things they write about.

My purpose in writing this book was getting writers together as equals to write, talk about writing, share our work, and learn from one another. Of course, your reading about my writing process and those of other student writers isn't the same as our being there, but it's the closest I've gotten through a textbook.

However, with the help of the text and your instructors, you can create you own classroom writing "community," perhaps with your instructor as a writing participant. That is how I got the idea for this textbook—writing along with my students and discovering their interest in what I had to write, and seeing how their perspective of me changed from an English teacher to a real person. That is how I am writing to you—as a fellow writer and real person. I hope you enjoy the approach and that you become an even better writer through using this book.

Tom Tyner

ACKNOWLEDGMENTS

As always, I am deeply indebted to the reviewers whose responses helped to shape this book: Harry Moore, Calhoun Community College; Linda Findley, Draughons Junior College; James Stowe, El Paso Community College; Kathryn Swanson, Augsburg College; Carole Lundeberg, Hartford State Technical College; Steven Katz, State Technical Institute at Memphis; and William Hodgkinson, Penn Valley Community College.

Chapter One
Thinking About Writing

Writing is discovering. Although I had given this textbook a great deal of thought, I had to sit down at my word processor and start writing to find out exactly where I was headed. My goals were to write a book that would help you to develop your writing potential, and I wanted to provide plenty of writing opportunities for you to do so. For me, as well as for most writers, writing is a process of "making meaning," or discovering how I think and feel about a variety of things. I write, read what I am writing, write some more, reread everything, and move from words to sentences to paragraphs, carried by the momentum of what I have already written. I don't know what my next sentence will contain, because it depends on how this sentence ends and on everything else in the paragraph.

Even as I wrote the last paragraph, I rediscovered something fundamental about my writing process: how I gain momentum by rereading sentences and paragraphs. During this course, you too will make discoveries about your writing that will help you build on your strengths as a developing writer.

WRITER'S JOURNAL

Three purposes of this text are to have you write regularly, reflect on your writing, and respond to the writings of others. One way to accomplish these goals is through regular journal writing.

Throughout the text you will respond to a number of writing situations: things you've written, things others have written, and activities you've done. Your journal writing will be for yourself, your instructor, and occasionally for your classmates. Through your journal writing, you will learn more about your own writing process and share what you learn with others.

Journal Entry 1

Write a page about your previous writing experiences: how much writing you have done, whom you have written for, what kinds of writing you've done, and how you feel about your writing. Keep your journal entries in a notebook.

STUDENT WRITER

Rebecca

Most writing I've done was in school years ago, and I didn't do a lot of that. I remember writing some short pieces for English in high school, but all I did was knock out the assignments as fast as I could. They weren't something that I put any real effort or enthusiasm into, and as I remember them, the assignments were pretty dumb, like "One day in the life of a paper clip." I also remember writing a lot of long essay tests for a history class, page after page of information I regurgitated from the textbook. That was more reporting what I read than actual writing.

I've written very little outside of school, other than a few brief job applications and a couple thank you letters here and there. I'm not a letter writer. So I haven't done much writing and have little opinion about it. It's not something I dread or something I look forward to. I've just never had much reason to write or anything that I cared to write about. Maybe that will change in the future, but I have my doubts.

GETTING STARTED

Aside from journal writing, you will also write one main paper for each chapter. Before you begin your first writing assignment, let me share with you something about how I write and how other student writers get started. I'm back on my word processor for a new day. My goal in the summer—and it's now early June—is to write at least five pages a day on my manuscript. This is how I try to keep my writing going.

1. I usually write in two-hour blocks. Then I take a break (eat something or read the paper) before getting back to work. Without those breaks, I get bogged down and lose my writing energy.

2. When I write, I think in increments—write down an idea, build a paragraph, finish a page—without looking too far ahead. When I think of writing many pages, or an entire manuscript, I am overwhelmed. It seems an impossible task. So I take it little by little, and eventually it gets done.

3. When I've finished writing for the day, I'm seldom finished thinking about it. Whether watching TV, driving to work, or reading, I have an occasional thought about how I want to continue writing the next day. That way I don't come to the word processor cold. I usually have some ideas to begin working on, which helps motivate me to write.

4. I try to write almost every weekday. If writing wasn't a regular part of my routine, I'd never finish anything. I set aside some time each day, and I stick with it. It's not that I'm a diligent person. Writing is something I can always put off for a more leisurely activity, so I must set a schedule and stay on it. Most of the time, it works.

STUDENT WRITERS—HOW I WRITE

Shara

I do most of my writing in the library computer room on campus. In the late afternoons the room is relatively vacant, so I can usually plop down at my favorite computer station, which is in the far corner away from student traffic, and work a couple hours. I've nicknamed my computer "Mabel" because it balks like an old horse when I don't give it the right commands. I talk to my computer while I'm writing, trying to get all the cooperation from it that I can.

I need a real quiet place to work, and the computer room provides that. I also like to get my work done in the afternoons because it's so noisy around my house at night. Once I start typing, I work pretty much nonstop until I've written what I want to for the day. If I take a break, I'm usually a goner. It's hard for me to sit down and get going again. So I block out everything but my writing, and sometimes I forget the time and where I am, and before you know it, I look up and it's dark outside. Past time to go home.

Tomas

The kitchen table is my writing area. I usually write fairly late at night when everyone is in bed: no TV, no screaming kids. Just me and my yellow writing pad. The kitchen is well lit for writing, and it's close to the food. Writing and eating go hand in hand with me. I'm not in love with writing but I am in love with eating, so if I do the two together I can hang in there for awhile.

I like to write fast and not think a whole lot about what I'm putting on the yellow pages. I don't sit and analyze every word because I know that this is just a start. Knowing that nothing I'm putting on paper is permanent lets me write freely. I can write a couple hundred words on a topic pretty fast. The faster I write the faster I eat!

We're lucky to have a computer lab at school where I write my final drafts during writing-class time. I take in my pages of yellow paper filled with scrawling and get to the business of turning them into what I hope becomes a good paper. I make lots of changes from my yellow paper as I type on the computer, but for me it all starts there in the kitchen late at night with some nachos and cheese dip, my yellow pad, and my chewed-up pencils.

Journal Entry 2

Write what you know of your own writing patterns: where you write, when you write, how you keep yourself going. Then exchange entries with classmates to get other ideas.

CHAPTER WRITING ASSIGNMENT

Some things are basic to most writing we do:

1. having something to write about
2. having someone to write to
3. having a reason for writing

For your first paper, write about an experience you had, recent or past, from which you learned something: something about yourself, about life, about values, about other people, or about right and wrong. The experience could be associated with school, work, family, friends, or whatever. Here are some suggestions for getting started.

1. Think of a number of things that have happened to you at various times in your life. Consider writing about one that stands out as particularly interesting or important.

2. Once you select a particular experience, reflect for a while on why it is memorable to you: Why does it stand out, and what effect did it have (or does it continue to have) on you?

3. Think about why you would want to relate this experience to someone else: What purpose would there be? What would someone else get out of reading about this experience?

4. Think about whom you would like to read your paper: the person or people who might be interested in it (a classmate or classmates? your mother, brother, husband, wife? a friend? young adults? teenagers?).

5. Write the first draft of your paper, relating the experience and what you learned from it. Since you will be *revising* your draft later, don't worry about its being "perfect." You can change anything you want when you revise.

6. Before doing items 1–5, read the following section on my writing plans and those of a student writer.

As a fellow writer, I'm going to do the writing assignments along with you to gain a sense of what you are going through, and to show you my own struggles as a writer. You will also be reading the drafts of other student writers.

What I will try to do, in this rather artificial world of classroom writing, is to make my writing as real as possible: to write honestly about things that matter to me, in ways that I hope will have some effect on my readers. That seems a worthy goal, and one I hope you will share.

As I write my drafts, you'll be seeing some of the results. Please don't think I'm trying to impress you. I'm writing for other reasons: first, to experience the challenge of writing enthusiastically for a class, and second, to document my struggles and occasional successes so that you understand the common bonds that unite all writers, beginners and experienced alike.

As I analyze my writing, I will also provide some tips on getting started, revising, and editing that should be helpful to you. Since I'm more experienced, I won't pretend that some things won't come more easily for me than you, and my drafts may be longer and more polished than yours. However, you will be surprised at the similarity of the problems we wrestle with.

Finally, in writing along with students in my own classes, I find that many of them are as curious about what I've written as I am about their papers. They enjoy learning something about my life and interests beyond the classroom. Perhaps some of you will have a similar interest, and your instructor might occasionally write along with you.

AUTHOR'S TOPIC SELECTION THOUGHTS

For the first writing assignment, I thought about a number of topics before deciding on one. Recent experiences came to mind more readily than those long past. Some were exciting, like seeing my Alma Mater beat USC in a bowl game, watching my daughter's college graduation, and finally recording on tape some fifty melodies I'd composed on the piano. Some were real downers, like tearing a shoulder muscle while bench pressing, losing money on my one-and-only invention, and burning holes in the new carpet in front of my fireplace.

As I debated writing about this experience or that, I asked myself three questions:

1. Did I learn anything from the experience that's worth passing on?

2. Would my writing audience—the college students reading this book—have any interest in it?

3. Would I enjoy writing about it?

Based on these questions, I decided to write about my experience in leasing a pick-up truck. It was definitely an eye-opener for me, and one from which some of my readers might profit. It was also something that's been on my mind lately, so I feel ready to write about it.

STUDENT WRITER—TOPIC SELECTION

Elia

It seems all I've had on my mind the past year was the problems I had with my boyfriend, who got heavily involved in drugs. I really thought I could help him and that he'd come around. I believed all of the lies that someone on drugs tell themselves and other people.

I learned a lot from my experience and I think I can look at the situation clearly enough now to write about it and maybe let some other people know what I learned. I'd write this for just about any student, since drugs are something that are out there everywhere, and since we never know for sure what kind of relationship we're getting into with a person.

Journal Entry 3

As Elia and I did, write about your topic selection process: how you came to decide on the topic you chose and why you picked it.

AUTHOR'S FIRST DRAFT

(The handwritten notes in this draft are revision ideas that came to me while rereading the draft.)

Leasing My First Pick-Up

About six years ago, I was going through the classified section of the newspapers looking for a pick-up truck to buy. *For some time* I'd ~~always~~ wanted my own truck because ~~too often~~ I would have to borrow a friend's truck ~~in order~~ to take trash to the dump or ~~to~~ move my son or daughter into an apartment. Having my own truck would really *come in* ~~be~~ handy.

Looking through the newspaper, my eyes zeroed in on ~~an ad for~~ *a* *add no down payment* new Toyota pick-up with monthly payments of only $99, ~~a month.~~

Being ~~the~~ *a* pretty cheap guy, ~~that I am,~~ that low monthly payment

~~really~~ excited me, particularly since most of the ads ~~in the section~~

showed ~~monthly~~ payments of $150 and higher, ~~for similar trucks.~~ I

did ~~happen to~~ notice that the Toyota ad read $99 a month to "lease"

rather than buy, but that didn't dampen my enthusiasm ~~at all.~~

went   *talked*   *drove*
So I ~~go~~ to the dealer, ~~talk~~ to one of the ~~many~~ salesman, and ~~drive~~

off in ~~my choice~~ a brand new dark red five-speed Toyota pick-up, the

(leased, that is)
first new vehicle I'd purchased, ~~or should I say leased,~~ in over fifteen

years, ~~of car buying.~~ The details of the lease were still a bit vague to

me, but I knew that after 60 months of $99 payments, I had the

option of buying the pick-up outright or refinancing it. ~~Right?~~ The

was
main thing ~~that stuck in my head were~~ the five years of $99 a month

add no down   payments, ~~Okay,~~ I'd worry about the other stuff later. I'm good at
payment

blocking out the negative when I want something badly.

I really enjoyed my little pick-up. It had plenty of power and a

nice air conditioner, and I used it regularly to haul things. I'd even

put my full garbage bags in it and drive them to the alley rather than

off topic—   walking them out the back. ~~I'd also drive around to city dumpsters~~
delete

~~around town and deposit my trash bags when the cans in the alley~~
add trips to
coast & mileage ~~were full.~~

As you might imagine, I started thinking of that pick-up as my

treated   *as*
own, ~~rather than as a lease,~~ and I ~~started treating~~ it ~~like~~ a pick-up

should be treated. I didn't wash it much, I bumped it against a wall here and a parked car there, and the bed and walls ~~of the pick-up~~ got plenty scratched up from all the hauling. No one keeps a pick-up looking new for five years, right?

The years passed pretty fast, and one day I got a letter from the leasing company giving me my options: ~~to~~ buy the pick-up outright, ~~to~~ refinance it, or ~~to~~ return it to the company. I called the company and talked to some woman who asked me about the condition of the truck*(and the mileage⊙)*, I told her about ~~what I presumed to be~~ *the* "normal" wear for a pick-up, and she said, "If you turn in the truck, it will cost you at least $1000 based on ~~the~~ *its* condition ~~you described.~~ *and 65,000 miles⊙* If you buy the truck outright, it will cost you $3000, and if you refinance the $3000, you can keep the $99 a month ~~truck~~ payments for three more years." That sound of $99 ~~which was so appealing before~~ had suddenly lost its magic.

Talk about three lousy options! "No one ever told me I'd have to pay ~~you~~ just to give back the truck," I said angrily. "Well, sir," she said calmly, "if you read section 4A on your lease, you will see that any kind of excessive wear *or mileage* on the truck will result in a payback by the leasee." Well, I'd never read section 4A of the agreement or section 1, 2, or 3A either. That agreement was ancient history to me.

I also knew I wasn't going to pay another $3000 to buy a truck I'd paid on for five years, and I sure wasn't going to make another 3 years of $99 refinancing payments. I was stuck! "One other thing, sir," said the ~~kind voice~~ *woman* on the phone, "is you could try selling the pick-up for the $3000 you owe ~~on it~~ and then pay us ~~the~~ $3000 rather than turning it in and paying ^*an additional* $1000. You'd break even that way. You have two weeks before either the truck or the $3000 is due."

Selling the truck was my only out, I decided, so I set to work fixing it up: washing, waxing, vacuuming, getting a tune-up and paint touch-up, and having some minor body work done. I did more for that truck in a week than I'd done in five years. Then I put it on the market for $3500, and luckily sold it within two weeks for the $3000 I needed, which I mailed to the lease company. I still was out about $300 for the tune-up and body work, but that was better than $1000. *new paragraph* Out from under that situation, I proceeded to *buy*, not lease, a new Mitsubishi pick-up, which was a couple thousand dollars less expensive than the new Toyota. The payments are only $115 a month (yeah, I'm still cheap), and in forty-five more months it will be all mine—dents, scratches and all.

Never again will I lease a pick-up. I was lured in by those great

= =   *and no down payment,*
$99 a month payments‸but after five years, it wasn't my truck. Had

I gone ahead and paid $125 a month, I could have bought the pick-up

in sixty months and paid considerably less than if I'd leased and

then bought it for $3000. The five-year lease plus $99 payments for

the remaining $3000 for another three years would have cost me

delete—too many figures, extraneous

over $11,000 to finally call the truck my own; on the other hand,

had I bought it outright, it would have cost me about $7500 with the

$125 a month payments, a savings of $3500. Turning back the

truck to the company would have been a bad deal whether I would

have had to pay the $1000 or not. I only had 65,000 miles on it, and

I could easily have gotten another five years of transportation out of

it. Instead, now I'm paying for another 60 months on the Mitsubishi.

Leasing is a bad deal any way I look at it.

Having said that, I know there may be people who feel that leas-

ing a car or truck is the way to go. In fact, many people lease expen-

sive cars for no down payment and drive them two or three years

delete—not important to college audience

before trading them in on another new car. They always have a rel-

atively new vehicle, and the trade-off is paying $250–$300 a month

year after year, like long-term rent. Of course, if you are in that

situation, my leasing concerns probably would never affect you. But

if you do decide to lease a new car or truck, please do the things I

add option of
buying used car

didn't do: Understand well the terms of your lease agreement; accept

that you must keep the car in great condition and the mileage rela-

tively low in order to avoid a payback charge when the lease expires;

and realize that after 60 months (or whatever your terms), it will

still cost you a few thousand dollars if you want to keep the vehicle.

FIRST-DRAFT REFLECTIONS

Writing this first draft was relatively easy because the experience was fresh in my mind, and I knew well the order of events in which it occurred. I didn't have to stop much to consider what I thought or how I felt about the situation.

As I wrote, I would go back and reread sentences and parts of paragraphs to keep my train of thought going, but otherwise there was little writing hesitation. I wrote straight through without taking a break, and it took me a little over an hour to write. I did pause before I wrote the last paragraph because I hadn't planned to write about leasing cars, but I added the paragraph and I'll decide whether to keep it when I revise.

Journal Entry 4

As I did, describe your writing process for the first draft: how you began putting your thoughts on paper, how much difficulty you had, the kinds of things that made you stop or hesitate, how long it took you; and so on. Share your entry with a classmate.

WRITING AND REVISING

Revising is a critical part of my writing process. I revise my writing for four reasons.

1. I want to write what I believe is true. On rereading a first draft, I look for any dishonesties, exaggerations, or questionable assertions. I revise anything that I feel will mislead readers or present an inaccurate picture.

2. I want to write for my readers. When I first write something, I write mainly for myself to get my thoughts on paper. Then I revise with readers in mind: Will they understand what this means? Will they identify with that example? Is the tone conversational enough? Will

they be confused by the organization (or lack of it)? Will they find the essay interesting enough to read on?

3. I want to accomplish my purpose. I read each paragraph of my first draft with the thought "Does this help keep me on track?" or "How could this better help accomplish my purpose?" I revise the draft so that every paragraph serves my general writing purpose in some way.

4. I want my draft to be highly readable. My first-draft sentences are seldom acceptable. I usually revise every sentence in some way: deleting unnecessary words, replacing a questionable word or awkward phrase, and moving phrases around for smoother wording. Sentence revision is a major part of my writing process.

For me, revising isn't the most enjoyable part of writing. It's more fun to create something than to improve what I've already written, and I sense this is true for most writers. However, revising is an essential part of my writing process, and I rely heavily on revisions to get a manuscript in publishable form.

In addition, revising is often hard work. Writing something the first time, I phrase my ideas however they come to mind. I can write rather quickly because I'm not concerned how my sentences sound. Turning this personalized style of writing into "public" prose is the work of revision, and I must weigh the value of every word and thought I've written.

Revision is the craftsmanship of writing. It is putting forth your ideas in the best possible form for your readers. It means working over a sentence until every word carries essential meaning; organizing your ideas in their most logical and effective order; adding the explanation, detail, or example that helps readers understand a particular concept; inserting a new thought that comes to mind as you revise; or deleting something that would be better left unsaid.

Author's First-Draft Revision Plans

The notes leading to the following revision plan are handwritten on the first draft (see pages 7–12).

1. The first paragraph starts at a good point: when I first looked in the classifieds for a pick-up. A common problem in relating an experience is beginning far back before the experience gets going, which I consciously avoided doing. The second sentence in the paragraph is too wordy and repetitive, and the *always* isn't true, so I'll revise the sentence.

2. The next few paragraphs need revisions to eliminate wordiness, but they convey what happened and how I felt about it pretty accurately. I'll get rid of informal words like *so* and *okay* and *right*, which don't sound good when I'm thinking of my reading audience. They crept in as I "talked to myself" in my first draft.

3. In the fourth paragraph, I start getting off track towards the end. The purpose of the paragraph is to show how I'm using and enjoying the truck, but the business of taking bags of garbage to the city dumpsters is something I threw in because I thought it was a clever way to dispose of trash. It doesn't further my purpose, so I'm going to delete it.

   As I was reading the paragraph, I remembered I also took trips in the pick-up, and the mileage on the pick-up was another factor in returning it, so I added that to paragraph 4 and will also tie it into later paragraphs. (Much later, I remembered something else that I should add, which I will mention in number 9 of this list.)

4. In the fifth paragraph, I continue to tighten up the language, but I keep the question at the end with *right* in it, as if I'm talking to my readers and hoping they'll agree with me.

5. Paragraphs 6, 7, and 8 form the climax of the experience: here the reader discovers my problem. My earlier paragraphs lead to this climax and my later paragraphs reveal what I do as a result. I need to include the mileage problem throughout the paragraphs following paragraph 4, and I need to improve a lot of wording. I like using phone dialogue between myself and the woman at the lease company rather than telling about the conversation. I'll keep that in for reader interest.

   I will move the last part of paragraph 8, about buying the Mitsubishi, to a new paragraph because it doesn't tie in well with the rest of the paragraph about selling the Toyota. This is a new incident that belongs in a new paragraph. It is also too important to stick at the end of a paragraph; it shows that I learned my lesson about leasing pick-ups.

6. The tenth paragraph is the beginning of my conclusion: It sums up my attitude about leasing a pick-up, my purpose being to share what I learned with other potential truck buyers. I need to reword the paragraph so that it shows clearly why I think leasing a vehicle isn't a good deal. The way it reads now, the figures and differing situations may confuse readers, so I'll make things clearer. I've de-

cided not to tell my readers what I think *they* should do. I think it's more effective to tell them how I feel and let them decide whether it makes sense for their situation.

7. I debated about keeping the last paragraph, and I'm still debating. It introduces a somewhat different kind of leasing concept, and perhaps it has no business in this essay. On the other hand, I wanted to show that there are people who feel differently than I do about leasing, and to generalize the leasing situation beyond pick-ups. I'm going to leave it in for now, and then make a final decision when I reread the essay.

8. I think the paragraphing of the essay is okay except that I will divide paragraph 8 into two paragraphs. Basically, I changed paragraphs as I moved to different parts of the experience. Paragraphs 6, 7, and 8 all cover parts of the same incident (my phone conversation with the woman at the leasing company) but I didn't want to put it all in one huge paragraph, so I divided it up into her talking in paragraph 6, my responding in paragraph 7, and her final response in paragraph 8.

   Paragraphs 9 and 10 are my conclusion: 9, summarizing why I won't lease a pick-up again, and 10 (if I keep it), telling about leasing luxury cars. I think the paragraphing helps readers follow what's going on.

9. It's about three hours later, and I've eaten lunch and run some errands. A couple new things occurred to me about my draft. First, I remembered that with a lease there is no down payment, another reason I went for it. I need to include that in the draft. Second, that idea helped me solve my problem with the last paragraph. Most people reading the draft (generally college students) aren't in a financial position to consider leasing luxury cars, so why should I mention such leases? However, my readers who are short on money may be interested in the no-down-payment aspect of leasing, so I'm going to talk to these people in the last paragraph.

My final draft, with all of the revisions just mentioned, appears at the end of this chapter. I have placed all of my final drafts at their chapter's end so they don't take up space within the chapters but are available for you to read and compare to my first drafts.

Specific Revision Suggestions

Based on the revisions I made, I suggest you consider the following when revising your first draft.

1. Keep your readers and your purpose in mind as you revise. Consider everything you write from the standpoint of the other people who will read it.

2. New things might come to your mind as you reread the draft. Add anything—some new information, an example, detail, or explanation—anywhere in the draft that you feel will improve your essay.

3. As you read, if you find a sentence or a paragraph that gets off the track of your experience or purpose, consider deleting it or changing it so that it is relevant to what you are trying to accomplish.

4. If you are like most writers, you will find a number of first-draft sentences that aren't worded as well as you want. If any sentence seems a bit wordy, awkward sounding, or confusing, consider how you might improve it.

5. End your essay in a way that helps readers to understand why you are writing about this particular experience. If you don't feel that your draft has a strong conclusion, you will want to change, or add to, the ending.

6. Your paragraphing should help move readers clearly from one part of your experience to the next. Do you have any particularly long paragraphs that might be effectively divided? Do you have any really short paragraphs (a sentence or two) that might be developed further or added onto the previous, or following, paragraph?

7. Have you accomplished what you wanted to in the essay? Can you think of anything else you'd like to add or change before turning it over to your readers?

 **REVISION ASSIGNMENT**

Read and evaluate your first draft with the help of the revision suggestions. Note the kinds of revisions you want to make for your next draft.

SECOND OPINIONS

During the process of writing a textbook, I get plenty of second opinions from people. I call them *second* opinions because I consider my own opinion the first, last, and most important.

I get opinions from my editor and a number of college teachers around the country who read and critique my manuscripts. They respond to questions posed by my publisher, and they tell me what they like, don't like, or don't understand. They also advise me on how to improve the manuscript.

When I first read these critiques, I am happy about the positive comments, but I sometimes bristle at the negative. I've put a lot of work into the manuscript, and in truth, I'm looking more for praise than criticism. So I set them aside for a day.

When I return to them, I evaluate the criticism and suggestions more objectively. After all, these people are trying to help me write a better textbook. Once I put my ego aside, I see that they make some good points. On the whole, the reviews are constructive, and they help me make revisions that strengthen the manuscript.

At the same time, if I accepted every criticism and suggestion, I'd twist into a pretzel trying to please everyone. I weigh the comments carefully and respond to two types: those that I agree have definite merit, and those that are repeated by a number of reviewers. I retain what I feel is important and make changes where I agree with reviewers' suggestions or where a number of reviewers cite a similar problem.

Second opinions are invaluable to me in the writing process. I, along with my publisher, need to get other instructors' opinions on the manuscript before it becomes a textbook. I think you too will find such opinions valuable to your writing process.

Peer Review of Drafts

Before you revise your first draft, get at least one classmate's opinion on what you've written, and do the same for him or her. Like my manuscript reviewers, you will be able to respond most helpfully by answering some specific questions regarding the draft.

1. What do you like (or find interesting or thought provoking or informative) about the draft? Give specific examples.

2. In what ways can you relate to what is being said? Give specific examples.

3. What questions do you have that you wish the draft would have answered? (What would you like to know that isn't clearly revealed in the first draft?)

4. What do you find confusing in the draft? Give specific examples.

5. Does the paragraphing help you follow the writer's thoughts? Do any paragraphs present problems for you? Give specific examples.

6. Are there any sentences that seem overly wordy or awkward or confusing? Give specific examples.

7. What do you think the writer's purpose was in writing about this experience, and whom do you think was the audience? How well did the writer accomplish his or her purpose, and what might accomplish it better?

PEER EVALUATION ASSIGNMENT 1

Before exchanging papers, read the following student first draft and, with a classmate, answer the seven revision questions. Be prepared to discuss your responses with the class. This activity will give you some practice responding to a draft before helping your classmate.

STUDENT WRITER—FIRST DRAFT

Lydia / A Problem at Home

Ever since I lived with my adopted mother, my life has changed in a way I could never have imagined. I was only fifteen years old when I came to America. My adopted mother was very excited because she never had any children of her own. It was sort of a dream come true for her.

She changed me totally and completely by telling me what to do, what to wear, how to act, and how to respond to people, and so on and so forth. At first, I thought it was really nice of her to care so much about me, and for the whole two years I put up with it. I also went through my freshman and sophomore years with straight A's, although I remember when I got a B in one of my classes, she told me that I was no good. I started to feel the pressure, but I took what she said as a challenge though it hurt me badly.

When I was in my junior year, I started making friends and I also had a boyfriend at that time. Only the biggest problem that I had was she never I mean never let me go out with either my friends or boyfriend. So I began to sneak out, ditch school, even lie to her and make up excuses. It was pretty hard for me as a teenager not to have the freedom other teenagers had. We started getting into fights and constantly we would be yelling at each other. I had to drop out of school and took a vacation for four months. When I came back, it was okay again, but everytime I would come home late from work, she would be mad and say "If you can't follow my rules, the door is wide enough for you to get out of." Over and over I heard her say that although I ignored her most of the time. Within a couple of months, we were at each others' throats again. I went back to the island and decided to stay there forever, but I couldn't.

When I came back for the second time, she clearly pointed out all the rules that she wanted me to follow. It was tough but I agreed. I enrolled here at college and at the same time I'm trying to get my high school diploma. We were getting along pretty well until recently. For the first time, I got a 72 percent grade on my history test and I told her about it. Guess what she said? She said, "Only 72 percent? That's not good. You're no good." I felt like crying but I didn't although that really hurt me the most. I told myself, never again will I tell her anything about me or my grades. My best friend told me to let it go, so I did. It didn't bother me anymore. Two weeks ago, she kicked me out. Why? Because of the 89-cent phone call to Fresno that I didn't even make. Now I am staying in the dorms and I will show her that I'll make it without her or her support.

My point is that when I become a mother I will never ever be like my mom. I will try my very best to be not like her. I will give my children all the love, care, and mostly understanding that they need. And if anyone has gone through what I have gone through, have faith in yourself and don't let anyone make you feel like you're not worth anything, not a mother or a father. I'm going to succeed in spite of my mom, and so can you.

PEER EVALUATION ASSIGNMENT 2

Exchange papers with a classmate and apply the revision questions to your classmate's draft as you did to the sample draft in the text. Then discuss your responses. Finally, considering your classmate's responses to your draft, along with your own revision plans, write the second draft of your essay.

Journal Entry 4

Comparing your first draft to your second one, describe the revisions you made and why you made them. How do you feel about your second draft compared to the first?

FINAL EDITING

The last thing I do with a draft is check it over for any errors in spelling, grammar, or punctuation. Actually, I usually catch and correct most of these errors as I am revising, so my final editing check is a proofreading of the draft to see if I have missed anything. The following are corrections I made in my first draft.

1.   In paragraph 1, I wrote "newspapers" when I meant *newspaper*.

2.   In paragraph 3, I started off with the present tense: "So I *go* to the dealer, *talk* to a salesman, and *drive* off in a . . ." I am writing about something that happened six years ago, but I put this sentence in the present tense, perhaps to make it sound more immediate. However, I decided the paragraph sounded better with everything in the past tense, so I changed "go," "talk," and "drive," to *went, talked,* and *drove.*

As in paragraph 3, in paragraph 6 I shifted to the present tense for a while: "So I *give* her a call and *talk* to a woman who first *asks* me the condition of the truck," and so on. I decided it sounded best to keep everything in the past tense, so I changed the verbs to "gave," "talked," and "asked." I also made a typo, writing "it sound" rather than *it sounds.*"

4.   In paragraph 7, I wrote "I also *new*" instead of *I also knew,* another one of those sound-alike word errors.

EDITING ASSIGNMENT 1

With my writing experience, I have fewer problems with punctuation errors than most of my students, so initially you may need to pay more attention to your use of commas and periods than I do.

To get a feel for punctuation usage, review my "Leasing" draft with a classmate, and discuss why I put commas and periods where I did. Then write a few rules for when to use commas, based on the usage in the essay. Be prepared to share your guidelines with the class.

EDITING ASSIGNMENT 2

Now proofread and edit the following student writing sample, correcting errors in punctuation, spelling, and grammar. Two punctuation errors to be aware of that the writer occasionally makes are running sentences together without a period and separating sentences with a comma instead of a period. You'll need to put in a few more periods to end sentences. Then compare your corrections with a classmate's.

STUDENT WRITER—FIRST DRAFT

Daniel / The Apple Falls Close to the Tree

Many years ago when I was only eight years old my father and I were walking trough are orchard, I remember saying to him, when I grow up I want to be just like you. He began to tell me that about the time he was my age he and his father had this same talk.

My fathers father was a farmer all of his life and my dad farmed a little to help his parents out when he was living at home. However my dad didn't want to farm all of his life, so at the age of 18 he went into the army. There he learnred to be a D.D.S., and moved to California. After a few years pasted he bought sixty acres of almonds for a hobbie.

As the years past along came one at at time us four kids two girls and two boys. On weekend and after school almost every day I was the only kid right behind dad all the time, checking water looking for pests and sitting on his lap on the tractor. This went on for years until poor market prices for almonds made it hard to farm anymore, so he sold the almond orchard.

As for myself I didn't I wanted to farm ether, but Im right back into it today with oranges and hay Im going back to school to maybe gain more of what dad already has.

When I was about sixteen years old or so I didn't want to be anythjing like my father because he didnt know the right way to do things or run them but I did. However as the years past I was able to see that he did know a little about what he was doing. My life as I see it now is very much the same as my fathers has been, you can say I followed in his footsteps. The saying, fruit doesn't fall too far from the tree has some truth to it. The impact my father had on me and his father on him shaped the direction our lives took. Knowing this I hope to have a good influence on my own sons and daughters life.

EDITING ASSIGNMENT 3

Now proofread your own draft, checking your punctuation, spelling, and grammar. If you'd like a second opinion, exchange drafts with a classmate.

At this point it is between you and your instructor what happens to your draft, depending on your instructor's system for dealing with drafts. Your instructor may have you write a final draft now, or put your draft aside in a folder to return to later. Finally, your instructor might have you "publish" your draft in some form (for example, copies given to your intended audience of readers, a copy put up in the class-room, or an oral reading).

Journal Entry 5

Relate the kinds of errors you corrected on your draft and the reasons you think you made them. Do you see any pattern in your errors (certain error tendencies that repeated themselves in your paper)? What did you learn from your editing that might help you in writing your next paper?

EDITING GUIDELINES

The last chapter of the text, Chapter 9, deals with most of the grammar and sentence-structure problems that writers have. It contains a number of exercises to give you practice in using the correct grammatical forms and sentence punctuation.

If you have identified in your writing particular errors that give you trouble, you can refer to the editing chapter for help in those specific areas. Your instructor might also assign you particular sections or exercises based on a diagnosis of your writing.

I would suggest using the editing chapter at the time you are proofreading your drafts for errors, near the end of your writing process for a particular paper. That way you can apply what you learn through the exercises to your final editing of your draft. Studies suggest that working in isolation on grammar or sentence-structure exercises is of little benefit in improving your writing. However, if you work on specific problem areas as you are editing your draft, what you learn through the exercises can transfer successfully to your correcting and eventually eliminating those errors in your papers.

AUTHOR'S FINAL DRAFT

Leasing My First Pick-Up

About six years ago, I was going through the classified section of the newspapers looking for a truck to buy. For some time I'd wanted my own truck because I would always have to borrow a friend's truck in order to take trash to the dump or move my son or daughter into an apartment. Having my own truck would really come in handy.

Looking through the newspaper, my eyes zeroed in on a $99 a month/no down payment ad for a new Toyota pick-up. Being a pretty cheap guy, I found that low monthly payment exciting, particularly since most of the ads showed $150-and-up payments. I did notice the Toyota ad read $99 a month to "lease" rather than buy, but that didn't dampen my enthusiasm.

I went to the dealer, talked to a salesman, and drove off in a brand new, dark red, five-speed Toyota pick-up, the first new vehicle I'd purchased ("leased", that is) in over fifteen years. The details of the lease were still a bit vague to me, but I knew that after 60 months of $99 payments, I had the option of buying the pick-up outright or refinancing it. The main thing was five years of $99-a-month payments, and I hadn't paid a penny down. I'd worry about the other stuff later. I'm good at blocking out the negative when I want something badly.

I really enjoyed my little pick-up. It had plenty of power and a nice air conditioner, and I used it regularly to haul things. I'd even put my full garbage bags in it and drive them to the alley rather than walking them out the back! My wife and I would also take it on occasional trips to the coast or mountains to keep the mileage down on our car.

As you might imagine, I started thinking of that pick-up as my own, rather than a lease, and I treated it like a pick-up should be treated. I didn't wash it much, I bumped it against a wall here and a parked car there, and the truck bed and walls got plenty scratched up from all the hauling. No one keeps a pick-up looking new for five years, right?

The years passed pretty fast, and one day I got a letter from the leasing company giving me my options: buy the pick-up outright, refinance it, or return it to the company. I called the company and talked to a woman who asked me about the condition of the truck and the mileage. I told her about the "normal" wear and the 65,000 miles, and she said "If you turn in the truck, it will cost you at least $1000 based on its condition and mileage. If you buy the truck outright, it will cost you $3000, and if you refinance it, you can keep the $99-a-month payments for three more years." That sound of $99 had suddenly lost its magic.

Talk about three lousy options! "No one ever told me I'd have to pay you just to give back the truck," I said angrily. "Well, sir," she said calmly, "If you read section 4A in your lease, you will see that any kind of excessive wear on the truck, or mileage beyond 50,000, will result in a payback by the leasee." Well, I'd never read section 4A of the agreement—or sections 1, 2, or 3A for that matter. That agreement was ancient history to me.

I also knew I wasn't going to pay another $3000 to buy a truck I'd paid on for five years, and I sure wasn't going to make another three years of $99 refinancing payments. I was stuck! "One thing sir," said the woman on the phone. "You could try selling the pick-up for the $3000 you owe on it and then pay us the $3000 rather than turning it in and paying an additional $1000. You'd break even that way. You have two weeks before either the truck or the $3000 is due."

Selling the truck was my only out, I decided, so I set to work fixing it up: washing, waxing, vacuuming, getting a tune-up and paint touch-up, and having some minor body work done. I did more for that truck in a week than I'd done in five years. Then I put it on the market for $3500, and luckily sold it within two weeks for the $3000 I needed, which I mailed to the lease company. I still was out about $300 for the tune-up and body work, but that was better than $1000.

Out from under that situation, I proceeded to *buy*, not lease, a new Mitsubishi pick-up, which was a couple thousand dollars less expensive than the new Toyota. The payments are only $115 a month (yeah, I'm still cheap), and in forty-five more months it will be all mine—dents, scratches, and all.

Never again will I lease a pick-up. I was lured in by those great $99-a-month payments, but after five years it still wasn't my truck. Had I gone ahead and paid $125 a month, I could have bought the pick-up in sixty months and paid considerably less than if I'd leased and then bought it for $3000. Turning back the truck to the company would have been a bad deal whether I had to pay the $1000 or not. I only had 65,000 miles on it, and I could easily have gotten another five years of transportation out of it. Instead, now I'm paying for another sixty months on the Mitsubishi. Leasing is a bad deal any way I look at it.

Having said that, I know there may be people who feel that leasing a car or truck is the only way they can afford one. If you can't afford a $1500 or $2000 down payment, or more than the most minimal monthly payments, you might view leasing as the only way to go. I would suggest that one option is to settle for buying a decent used vehicle with a low down payment and reasonably monthlies. But if you do decide to lease a new car or truck, please do the things I didn't do: Understand the terms of your lease agreement; accept that you must keep the car in great condition and the mileage relatively low in order to avoid a payback charge when the lease expires; and realize that after sixty months (or whatever your terms) it will still cost you a few thousand dollars if you want to keep the vehicle.

Chapter Two

Selecting a Topic

When I am writing a textbook, I have to come up with a number of topics. In the first chapter, I knew I wanted to write about the experience of writing, to have you think about how you write, and to establish the process approach on which this book is based. I had some definite topics to develop.

For this chapter, I needed to come up with new topics. Two considerations helped me make choices: first, my ongoing concern with "What will help students continue developing their writing potential?" and second, "What topic should be explored at this stage in the text?"

I decided one of the most important writing considerations—perhaps the most important—is selecting a topic. Like you, I do a kind of writing that requires completing an essay on a different subject every couple of weeks. The teachers' association at my college puts out a regular newsletter for which I write. Rain or shine, I fill a column twice a month with something that I hope will interest faculty.

My main concern each time is coming up with a decent topic. Once I decide what to write about, I am greatly relieved. The actual writing isn't a problem; in fact, it's the pleasurable part.

TOPIC CONSIDERATIONS

The following considerations help me and my student writers come up with topics to write about.

1. *What do you want to write about*? It's hard for me to write in an interesting way about something I'm not interested in. I know it's certainly not enjoyable. While it's important to consider your readers, it's equally important to consider your own interests, because your motivation to write is based on enjoying what you are doing.

2. *What do you know that your readers don't*? (Or what do you probably know *more* about than most of your readers?) People aren't greatly interested in reading something that they already know all about. Explaining how to change a tire on a car would bore readers who have changed many tires. However, there are topics about which you have special knowledge, based on your experiences or background, that would interest many readers.

3. *What perspective do you have on a topic that may interest readers*? For example, there are always topics that stir up faculty interest: tenure, class size, merit pay, a national standardized curriculum, and so on. While many teachers are knowledgeable about the topics, they have differing viewpoints on them, and if I have a perspective that

I think is worth sharing, I do so. Even when your readers may have the same information as you, your particular viewpoint on the topic may interest them.

4. *What can you write about in a relatively short essay?* Like you, I write my essays within certain length limits, so I don't take on broad topics that I can't handle in a few hundred words. For example, I won't write a column on college educational reform in the 80s and 90s because I would have to fill many pages to do justice to the topic. However, I might write a column on course content reforms to meet state critical-thinking mandates, a narrow topic within the broader area of college educational reform.

   By the same token, while you would have trouble writing on the broad topic "My High School Experience" (or military experience or secretarial experience) in a short essay, you might write a good paper on a narrower school-related topic like "An Unforgettable Teacher," or "The Great Cafeteria Food Fight of 1986."

DECIDING ON A TOPIC

By way of example, I'm going to "talk myself through" coming up with a writing topic for the semester's final edition of the newsletter.

"Okay, the semester's almost over, so there's no point in getting into something controversial because no one's going to be around to talk about it in a week anyway. I don't think faculty feel like hearing anything really negative at the end of a semester either, so I won't attack the administration on not providing raises for part-time faculty this semester. Why not end on something upbeat so that folks will go into the summer break with some positive thoughts about the teachers' association and their profession? This is a time for happy thoughts. School's almost over!

"Let's see, this last article should concentrate mainly on faculty. How about the outstanding new faculty hires we have on campus this year? Trouble is, I'd have to single out some individuals, which is difficult. Maybe I don't really know enough about those people anyway. I don't want to research this one.

"Maybe some sort of a summary article is appropriate for the end of the year, a compendium of positive things that occurred during the school year. Some good things did happen: increased enrollment, reduction in the freshman dropout rate thanks to the early-intervention program, a decent raise negotiated by the teachers' organization, a reduction in class size for writing courses, and a new shared-governance policy that will provide for increased faculty input in decision making. That's surely plenty to write about in my column, and I know other things will come to me as I write.

"So my topic will be a summary of the good things that have happened in the district this school year, and I'll use the following theme to tie everything together: When faculty and administration put aside differences and work together for the good of the college and the students, great things can happen."

STUDENT WRITERS' RESPONSES

Here are ways that the following student writers select topics to write about, some of which may interest you.

Amanda

I always start with what I'm interested in. I want to enjoy my writing, and I can't do that unless I please myself. Sometimes I start my thinking with the school: What's going on these days? What are students interested in? How are the sports teams doing? Are people concerned about the increase in tuition? What about the earlier final drop date being proposed by faculty senate? What about all the part-time faculty the school's been hiring? They have no offices or office hours so they're impossible to get ahold of.

After I come up with some possible topics, I decide what interests me the most and go with it. If nothing connected to school clicks with me, I'll see what's going on on other fronts: movies, local politics, my family, my friends, etc. I like to write about things that are pretty current, things that people are talking about or concerned over or excited about. Luckily, I'm interested in lots of things, so I seldom have trouble coming up with something to write about.

For example, my friend from high school recently had twins. Here she's twenty years old with a husband, a two-year old girl and twin boys, and I can't even imagine getting married for four or five more years. I'd like to compare different perceptions on marriage and family that young women have, and where those perceptions come from. How could my close friend from high school and I have such different viewpoints?

Malcolm

My writing almost always involves sports in some way. That's what I'm most interested in, and I know a lot of other people are interested too. However, my instructor doesn't like me just to write about my favorite sports' stars over and over, so I've had to think about different topics.

Sometimes I'll read the paper and find a hot topic on the sports page to write about, like Michael Jordan's retirement or whether the Dallas Cowboys are the team of the 90s. Sometimes I'll want to write a technical paper for knowledgeable sports fans on something that interests me, like the best defensive strategy for holding "Shaq" under twenty points and beating the Magic, or why Bobby Bond's presence will not provide the San Francisco Giants with what they hoped for: a World Series victory.

I've got a vivid imagination, and sometimes I like to write fantasy papers on topics that put me in the middle of the action, like "Malcolm's Fabulous Final Quarter in the Super Bowl," or "Malcolm and Riddick Go Toe to Toe," or "The Dream Outfield: Bonds, Griffey, and Malcolm." Once I get going, I can always think of some fantasy topic. I've dreamed of those situations all my life.

Sara

I usually start off with a broad topic and move in from there. I'm a fashion merchandising major, so say I want to write something about fashion. Recently I read in the paper about a guy named Blackwell who lists famous people who are the worst dressed in the world. Looking at the outfits some of these people wear, I have to admit I agree with him to a large degree.

So here are these famous, wealthy ladies who can afford anything—like Madonna or Julia Roberts—and they end up looking ridiculous. Then I see women on campus who look terrific in what I know aren't designer clothes. So I feel myself moving in on a possible topic (women's taste in fashion), my point being that fame and money have nothing to do with taste, and that any woman with a sense of taste can look good.

TOPIC ASSIGNMENT 1

For practice generating potential writing topics (some of which you might use later), come up with possible topics for the following scenarios. Consider the four points I mentioned and the student writers' responses, as well as your own ideas for generating topics.

1. You have been invited by your ten-year-old sister (or daughter or granddaughter) to speak for five to ten minutes to her fifth-grade class. You can choose any topic you want.

2. You have been asked to write an article in the school newspaper about one particular college experience that stands out in your mind. What might you write about?

3. You are to write a paper for your classmates to read. You can write about whatever you want.

4. You are going to write a paper that only your instructor for this course will read. What might you write about?

Journal Entry 6

How did you decide on potential topics? On paper, "talk through" your decision-making process in coming up with a topic for one of the four scenarios as I did on my article for the newsletter. When you finish, you might also share your writing with classmates so you can get some ideas from each other on how to generate topics.

TOPIC ASSIGNMENT 2

Beginning with the following broad subjects areas, narrow each subject until you come up with a topic that you could handle well in a type-written one-and-a-half to two–page essay:

1. college
2. employment
3. music
4. famous people
5. gangs
6. relationships

STUDENT WRITER RESPONSE

Samuel / Relationships

I have relationships with all kinds of people: my parents, brothers and sisters, other relatives, friends, people at work, my boss, some of my teachers, my girlfriend, her friends, people at the gym where I work out, etc. What comes to mind first is a fun relationship I've developed with a few guys I didn't know until about a year and a half ago when I joined the Fitness Quest gym. Now there are four of us, of different ages and backgrounds, who work out together on the bench press two or three times a week. We're like a little club, and we have a ball together. I think I'll write about this relationship.

WHAT TO WRITE ABOUT A TOPIC

Coming up with a topic is one thing. What to do with it is another. Sometimes my topic and how I am going to approach it come together quite naturally. Other times, I have something I want to write about, but I'm not exactly sure what I want to do with it.

For example, for one newsletter article, I decided I wanted to write on the new college reform law AB1725. It mandated a few important changes for our college system, so I felt I should write about it. I knew I needed to present the reform items in the article to inform my readers, but I wanted to go beyond presenting information—they could look that up in the educational codebook in the library.

I needed to take some type of a position on the reform act, so I reread the law carefully and talked to people at the college whose departments or divisions would be affected by specific reforms. After talking to people and rereading the law, I reached a surprising conclusion: The reforms weren't any big deal. They sounded impressive, but they would have very little effect on how we educate students within the system. So I had a definite approach to take on the reforms, one that would surprise and interest my readers (as well as upset a few).

Approaching Your Material

In deciding what to do or "where to go" with a topic, you are coming up with a tentative *thesis* for your writing, that is, the main point that your essay is supporting. The following queries help me, and may help you, consider possible approaches to a topic.

1. *What do you want to say about the topic*? What point do you want to make or what ideas do you want to get across? For example, in the paper I wrote in the first chapter, my topic was leasing pick-up trucks. The point I wanted to make was that, for me, leasing wasn't a good way to go. That viewpoint influenced everything I wrote in the essay.

2. *What's your purpose in writing about this topic*? Why write about it at all? Following the same example, I figured many of my readers might be as ignorant about leasing conditions as I was originally. I wanted to let them know the negatives so that they would think twice before leasing a vehicle, or at least understand the terms of the lease before making a decision. Had I felt my readers already knew as much about leasing as I'd learned the hard way, I wouldn't have written the paper.

3. *Does the approach you are considering make sense for your audience*? For example, let's say I decided to write something about microwave ovens, since I think they're a marvelous cooking device. I could

write a short paper from the approach that heating leftovers in a microwave is simple and effective, explaining how to use the microwave and the kinds of things a person can heat. That may have been an informative paper ten years ago, but today most people know all about heating leftovers. Readers would be bored and get nothing from it.

So, if I wanted to write about microwaves, I'd need an approach that might stimulate reader interest, like "beware the dangers of microwave cooking," which would go into the dangers of radiation exposure from microwave ovens. Your approach to a topic should provide readers with something new to think about.

As an example of deciding on an approach for a topic, I'll "talk through" my thinking for deciding what to do with the topic, *large composition classes*, to be written for English-teaching colleagues.

"This (large composition classes) is something many of my English colleagues have to deal with, so it's worth writing about. My initial reaction is that I should write an anti–large class paper: that it's unfair for teachers and students to have thirty or more enrollees in a composition course, and here is the evidence teachers need to convince their administration to lower those numbers.

"The problem with that approach is that I'm not addressing the practical needs of many teachers who must labor with those large classes whether it's educationally supportable or not. So, while I want the anti–large class message in the paper some way, I also have to focus on the needs of teachers who have no choice but to teach large classes. Perhaps my best general approach is something like this: What can you do with large composition classes to help your students and to survive yourself?

"I still want to lobby for smaller class sizes and discuss ways to go about getting them, something I think I'll do in the conclusion of the essay. Now I've got a basic approach (there are things we can all do to help students learn in large composition classes) and a secondary agenda (lobbying for smaller classes), which I think I can work together in the paper."

STUDENT WRITERS' RESPONSES

The following are responses of student writers to the question "How do you decide on the approach to take with your topic?"

Maria

I knew that I wanted to write about my brother who had come home from the service. I hadn't seen him in two years, and he'd really changed. He was like a different person in some ways—more confident, nicer to me, nicer to my folks, more interesting to be around, and happier, it seems—like he knows who he is.

I looked around at his friends who had stayed around the neighborhood the last two years, and they hadn't changed, and my brother seemed different from them now. I knew that the change in my brother was more than just getting two years older; it had to do with his getting out of the area, joining the service, and gaining some confidence in what he could do. I tentatively decided to take the approach that, for someone like my brother, joining the service can be a very good thing to do with your life.

Todd

I enjoy going to car races, anything from go-carts to Indy-type racers. But I really like going to drag races. What is it about drag racing that makes it more exciting than other kinds of racing? That would be the approach I'd take in my paper: analyzing why, for me, drag racing is the most exciting kind of car racing. Until I start writing and analyzing, I'm not really sure what that special excitement is all about.

Candice

I think I'll write a paper about my new job, because it's taking up so much of my time these days. A lot of people think I was lucky to get on with this big discount store, but they don't know. It's to the point that I dread going to work in the afternoon. The money's pretty good, but I don't know how long it will keep me going.

My approach to my topic is to open people's eyes about what it's like to work for this discount store chain, to let them know that it's not what it's cracked up to be. If my readers still want to work there after reading my paper, then at least they won't go in all naive like me.

TOPIC ASSIGNMENT 3

Pick three of the topics from Topic Assignment 1 and decide on a tentative approach to each that you might take in an essay. Use the three considerations presented and the student responses to help you make a decision, and consider different options before deciding what to do. Then write down the topics, your approaches, and why you decided on them.

Journal Entry 7

How did you make a decision on what approach to take for a particular essay topic? On paper, talk yourself through your thinking process as I did mine. This could be interesting to share with classmates.

CHAPTER WRITING ASSIGNMENT

Using the guidelines for choosing a topic and a possible approach to it, select any topic you find appealing for your next paper. Decide on the following:

1. your specific topic
2. your reading audience
3. your tentative approach to the topic—your thesis (This may change as you get into your writing. It gives you some direction for getting started.)
4. your purpose for writing

AUTHOR'S TOPIC DECISIONS

Sometimes I enjoy writing about people I find interesting, or people who have had some influence on me. I'll begin by thinking about different people I've known fairly well who stand out in my mind.

It's been about four hours since I first started thinking about people (of course, I did other things during that time), and I thought about my mom, dad, sister, wife, children, various friends, colleagues, neighbors, old college friends, and people from high school and earlier.

There are lots of people I could write about, but I decided on a boy I got to know back in junior high, where our friendship both began and ended. Ours was a rather complicated relationship, and I thought I might learn something by writing about it.

I hadn't given this person much thought in over twenty years, but when I thought back on my earlier years, he was the first person who came to mind. I figured there must be a good reason for that, so I decided to write about him and our relationship to each other.

My reading audience, of course, is college students, and I think you may relate in some way to what I'm going to write. My tentative approach (thesis) is rather hazy. Thinking about my friend and myself,

I know that our life circumstances dictated to a great extent how things went for us, and I know that peer pressure was a strong influence on both of us. I think the way I write the essay may reveal those things.

As to my purpose, I hope to reveal some things through the essay that will make readers look at how *they* relate to others, or that might help them teach their children how to relate to people different from themselves. I'm going to try and recall situations, thoughts, and feelings from nearly three decades ago. I'll think a lot about my friend, our relationship, and what I can remember before I start writing.

STUDENT WRITER RESPONSE—TOPIC DECISION

Alicia

School is really hard for me now because I'm still struggling with learning to speak and write English. Sometimes I feel pretty dumb compared to other students in my classes. I often think back to my school days in Mexico and how in the eighth grade I ended the school year with the top award in my class for the best grades. I felt so proud then and my family was proud of me, and I think back on that—so I remember that I can be a good student.

I think I will write about my school experience then (in Mexico) and now, and what it was like for me to learn in Mexico and here. My approach to my topic, I think, is that it is so much more difficult to go to school and learn and do well when you are trying to learn a new language and learn new subjects at the same time.

I think I would write this mainly for students like myself. We have students from Mexico, the Philipines, and China in my classes, and I feel many of them may be going through the problems that I am going through. I'd like American students to read my paper also, because sometimes I think they feel we are dumb in our classes when we are still slow in English but maybe smart in our own language.

I guess my purpose would be to make people like myself see that they are going through the same struggles that I am and that many others are, and that they shouldn't feel dumb or feel bad about themselves, and that they should keep trying.

TOPIC ASSIGNMENT 4

Write down your topic decisions for this chapter's writing assignment: the specific topic you selected, how you decided to write about it, the audience you are going to write to, the tentative approach you may take, and what your purpose may be.

PREWRITING CONSIDERATIONS

Writers do a number of things to help them prepare to write a first draft. I give my topic a lot of thought before writing. This is my main prewriting activity: thinking about things I might include and thinking in a general way about how I might organize them in my paper. However, I am not one to write things down before beginning my first draft. Part of my writing enjoyment is not having a definite map to follow. I like to see where my writing leads.

However, some writers put their ideas on paper before drafting, and some develop precise plans for their essays before they begin. In fact, there are a variety of prewriting strategies that help writers generate ideas. They will be covered in the next chapter.

For my upcoming essay about my junior-high classmate, I asked myself prewriting questions like the following to help me think about the experience.

1. Why am I writing about this particular person? Why does he seem important or special to me?

2. What was he really like? Why do I remember him so well?

3. What was our relationship like? What examples can I recall that reveal the nature of the relationship?

4. How did this relationship compare to others I had with friends at the time?

5. How did our relationship change, and why? Who was involved, or what forces were at work?

6. What happened as a result of that change? How was I affected? How was he affected?

7. What did I learn from the relationship and the changes? What can I pass on to my readers?

Journalistic questions of "what," "why," and "how" helped me to think about my topic in some depth before beginning the first draft. I looked at my friend and examined our relationship in a way I had never done.

PREWRITING ASSIGNMENT

Before beginning your first draft, ask yourself some questions that may help you get started on your paper. Either write down your responses or think them through, whichever is most helpful. Not only will you generate some ideas for your essay but you may also come up with a good approach to your topic (if you haven't settled on one yet), a clearer purpose for writing, and some sense of how to organize your draft—what might come first, next, and so on.

After you have done the prewriting activity and considered how you might use some of the ideas in your essay, write your first draft.

STUDENT WRITER RESPONSE

Alicia

Topic: Writing about my school experience in Mexico and today.

Questions:

1. What are the biggest differences between my schooling then and now?

2. What are the biggest problems I face in school?

3. How do they affect me in class? Out of class?

4. What can I do to keep going despite the difficulties?

5. How can I make others like myself feel better about their situation?

6. How can I make American students see what it is like for people like me?

7. How can I draw on my school experience in Mexico to help me in school now?

AUTHOR'S FIRST DRAFT

Jessie and I

In junior high we were first thrown together with kids from all parts

of town. This was the first time I went to school with the Mexican

kids from the east side of town, and on the whole they seemed like a

pretty rough, mature, and threatening bunch. A few of them even

drove old cars to school and parked them a block away~~ from school.~~

The only ~~times~~ *places* we had contact ~~was~~ *were* in the classroom and on the athletic fields. Most of them didn't go out for sports, but there was one kid named Jesse Sanchez, nicknamed "Wadda," ~~for who knows what reason,~~ who did everything. He was slightly built and not very tall, but ~~he was very~~ *well* coordinated. He ~~was the guy with~~ *had* the hand-eye coordination to be the pitcher on the softball team, the quarterback in football, and the point guard in basketball. We saw a lot of each other in sports and slowly got to know each other a little.

Jesse was a real character. He was kind of a goofy looking guy with sleepy, hooded eyes, bad teeth, and a greasy flat-top with "fenders" and a ducktail. In class, he was always cutting up and driving the teachers crazy. As soon as one turned her back, *give example* — Jesse would be imitating her in some way, and he was a natural comic.

I was attracted to Jesse first because he was a good athlete like myself, but also because he was such a "bad" dude: cutting up in class, never doing his homework, making out with his girlfriend behind the library, being a *Mexican* ~~"cholo"~~ from east Sanger. He was an exotic ~~and dangerous~~ character for a middle-class white boy like me whose dad was a school principal and who got straight A's and had never *delete— not needed* — ~~even gone with~~ *dated* a girl. When Jesse would talk about taking Celia out

delete—
not needed into the vineyards after school, I hung enviously on every word, hoping at least some of it were true.

Jesse and I became pals ~~of sorts~~ during sports and in homeroom, but outside of those times he'd hang with his Mexican buddies out by

wordy—
revise the wood shop and I'd be with my white middle-class friends who like me held all the class offices and decorated the gym for the noon dances. One day, however, I decided to break with tradition. After homeroom there was a fifteen-minute break, and one day I told Jesse "Let's go hang out at the snack bar. I'll buy you an Abba Zabba." That sounded okay to him, so we walked to the snack bar together, bought our Abba Zabbas and sat at one of the outdoor tables until the break was over. No big deal.

too slangy As you probably remember, junior high is one of the "cliquiest" times of a kid's life, so Jesse and I hanging out together had an im-

reword pact I hadn't even considered. My friends teased me a little about it in typically crude terms like "Is Wadda gonna let you watch him and

delete! Celia do it?" or "Why don't you invite Wadda home for dinner tonight? Your dad'll *love* that." Jesse's friends, however, must have been a lot harder on him because the next day he'd hardly talk to me. I remember asking him "What's up, Jesse?" but he didn't say anything. He just stayed away from me.

I never knew what went on between Jesse and his eastside buddies, but from that day on he wasn't my friend. Apparently it wasn't enough that he didn't hang around with me—he had to be my enemy. He started giving me dirty looks and saying things under his breath that I couldn't catch. In sports class, he quit passing me the basketball, which started getting me mad. What had I done to be the focus

stuffy
sounding   of his abuse?

One day I was walking near the wood shop and I heard someone say, "Hey asshole. F_____ you." It was Jesse, slumped against the shaded side of the building with about ten of his cholo buddies,
all dressed in white tee shirts, *and* black khakis, ~~and shiny black spit-shined shoes.~~ I stopped, shocked and embarrassed, and said what every kid said when he was called out, "What did you say?" "F_____ you, you white kissass," Jesse hissed. No question about it, it was a call to fight, so I said "After school, asshole. Behind the backstop. You'd better be there." Then I walked off before any more could be said.

I didn't want to fight Jesse. First, I figured he could beat me up, because I'd never been in a fight before and I was sure he'd been in many. Getting beat up was the worst thing for your reputation. Second, I wasn't even mad at Jesse, just hurt. I still didn't know what was going on. I determined to ~~somehow~~ get him aside ~~from~~ *for* a minute during the day and have a talk.

My one chance ~~during the day~~ was to follow him into the bathroom between classes. When I went in and he saw me, he got his fists ready and flared his upper lip. I put my hands up, palms open, and said "Jesse, I don't want to fight you. You were my friend until two weeks ago. Let's just forget everything. I'm not going to fight you, man. What the hell did I do wrong?" Jesse relaxed and then looked real sad. "Nothing, white boy," he said. "Nothing." Then he walked out.

too much dialogue— sounds unreal

We were never friends again. A certain respect developed between us, and he started passing me the ball again and quit the *hostile looks.* ~~phony hostilities.~~ Basically, we were back in different worlds, and that was the way he wanted it, or felt it had to be. But ~~I think~~ it hurt us both. Jesse~~, it seems,~~ lost some of that light spirit and playful michievousness. He didn't smile as much and acted tougher. I was saddened by losing a friend and losing my window on what I thought was Jesse's exciting, dangerous, sensual world. I think we both felt a loss.

wordy— revise

I have three more memories of Jesse after that. One was his standing outside the door of the gymnasium with his girlfriend at the eighth-grade graduation dance. He hadn't graduated, just passed on without a diploma, so they weren't letting him in. He wasn't causing trouble, just standing there in a white shirt and black tie with Celia, who wouldn't go in without him. Looking back, I can only imagine what a hard moment that must have been for Jesse, and I wonder how many moments like that had made up his young life.

reword

The second thing I remember was my freshman year in high school. It was during the second week of football practice, and Jesse had showed up in his street clothes, asking if he could try out for punter. Practice went on and I saw Jesse booming some spirals off of his black spit-shined right shoe on a side field. He never came back after that day, and I never saw him at school.

The last time I saw Jesse was some years later at a local bank. He was sweeping up and I was depositing my monthly teaching check. I recognized him immediately and went up and introduced myself. "How ya doing, Jesse?" I asked. "Not bad, Tom," he smiled, a mouth full of new teeth. In that moment all the petty eighth-grade bullshit was behind us and we were a couple of old friends. He told

too slangy

me about marrying Celia and about their two daughters, and I told him what I was doing. We didn't have much to say, and when we

we'd

parted, I doubted ~~we~~ see each other again since I was moving to a new job in another town. But that was a nice moment in my life, shaking Jesse's hand and seeing that smile again. ~~I don't remember ever feeling closer, to a friend than then.~~

exaggerated—reword

Times have changed in the thirty years that have passed, and the stricter racial and ethnic boundaries of my childhood have fortunately blurred. Yet I know the junior high cliques are still out there, and kids still hang out primarily with kids who look, act, and dress like them. Jesse and I tried to make a small statement long ago—crossing the boundaries of color, background, and economic class—and were reeled back in by friends who defined who we were. I can imagine now the kinds of things Jesse's friends must have said to him to change his behavior, and they were, after all, the people he lived with then and would probably be with forever. But the chances for change are always there, and if Jesse and I had been a little stronger or braver than we were, we might have made a little difference in a few people's lives, at least for a while.

divide into 2 paragraphs

reword—make clearer and stronger

FIRST DRAFT REFLECTIONS

This was not a difficult draft for me to write since I had thought a lot about it and asked and answered questions before writing. As I wrote, I frequently reread sentences and paragraphs to help me figure out what to write next, but I wasn't stumped for long periods of time until I got to the ending. I did make some discoveries as I wrote, recalling incidents to add that I hadn't remembered previously, and also recalling some feelings that I hadn't thought about in thirty years.

Here are the things I tried to accomplish in my draft, as well as some of the things that occurred as I wrote.

1. Bring Jesse to life for readers by describing him and revealing his personality. I wanted to do this early so they could picture him as they read.

2. Reveal my interest in Jesse based on our obvious differences as well as our similarities. Readers need to understand our differences in order for the paper to work.

3. Dramatize for readers the most dramatic moments for me: my first confrontation with Jesse by the wood shop and the second one in the bathroom. I used direct quotations to make the incidents vivid, and provided some setting for visual effect.

4. Relate how I felt about various things throughout the paper. I tried to reconstruct my thoughts and feelings back then at key times in the relationship: watching Jesse act up in class; listening to him talk about his girlfriend; hanging out with him at break; having him "cuss me out" in front of his friends; confronting him in the bathroom; seeing him outside at the graduation dance; seeing him years later at the bank. I wanted to get in tune with what went through my mind thirty years ago for both myself and the readers.

5. I didn't really know how far I was going to take the draft until I wrote it. The things that came to mind as I wrote were the graduation dance, the high-school football incident, and the bank encounter years later. I added one, then the next, and then the next, and they fit well and brought me to the end of my knowledge of Jesse. I enjoyed writing those last three memories more than anything.

6. I still didn't know how I was going to end the paper when I finished the bank encounter. I thought about writing about Jesse's being the janitor and my being the school teacher, and how the two situations may have been reversed had I been the poor Mexican and he the well-off white boy, but I felt that was getting off the basic topic of our friendship.

    I reflected back on that relationship and thought about what significance it had and what might have happened had we continued our public friendship despite what people thought. I knew it wouldn't have been anything earth-shaking, but I felt there was something there to write about, and that change often starts with individual acts of will that don't seem like a big deal at the time.

7. As I wrote, I felt emotional about my friendship with Jesse and the things that happened, so I had to guard against getting sappy and sentimental. It's not that I didn't want my emotions to come through, I just didn't want to sound melodramatic, which could seem corny rather than sincere to readers.

    For example, I wrote and immediately deleted the following sentence at the end of the bank encounter paragraph: "Never in my life had I felt closer to a human being than at that moment." That was an overstatement, and written from the emotion of reading over the paragraph rather than from a true recollection of the experience.

8. Paragraphing the essay was pretty easy. After I introduced Jesse in the draft, a number of incidents followed, each of which I paragraphed separately. Then I put each the three final memories in separate paragraphs. Looking over the paragraphs, none appears long enough to bother readers or so short that it disrupts the flow. I know I'm going to rework the final paragraph because I'm not satisfied with it, and it may end up being two paragraphs.

Journal Entry 8

How did your first draft go? Relate your own writing process for the draft, how you moved through the paper, any problems you encountered, what your thinking was as you wrote, and what you accomplished in the draft.

REVISIONS

Since I had thought this paper through in my mind for days before writing, I was pretty satisfied with what I had in my first draft. As I revised, I didn't come up with much to add or change in the way of content. Here is what I did.

1. My revisions focused primarily on wording, and I reworded almost every sentence. I have absolutely no talent for writing good first-draft sentences, and knowing that, I have to work hard on sentence revision.

    If you compare the following paragraphs in the two drafts, you can see the things I did to improve the sentences: deleted repeated words and phrases, deleted unnecessary words, replaced some words with more appropriate ones, and replaced some sentences with completely different wording. Overall, I think my new sentences are stronger, clearer, and smoother.

First Draft:	*Second Draft:*
In junior high we were first thrown together with kids from all parts of town. This was the first time I went to school with the Mexican kids from the east side of town, and on the whole they seemed like a pretty rough, mature, and threatening bunch. A few of them even drove their old cars to the school and then parked them a block away.	In junior high I went to school with kids from all parts of town. For the first time I was in school with the Mexican kids from the east side, and on the whole they seemed pretty tough, mature, and a bit threatening. A few of them even drove old cars to school and parked them a block away.

2. I used direct quotations to bring the confrontation scenes alive, including keeping the obscenities, because they were an important part of the incident. I can't recall the exact things I said in the bathroom, so I replayed the scene in my head, with Jesse and me standing there as fourteen-year-olds, and put in quotes that sounded real to me.

3. I read through the draft to detect any of the "stuffy" language that I have a tendency to use, and I revised or eliminated phrases (underlined) such as "Jesse and I hanging out together had an impact I hadn't even considered" and "What had I done to be the focus for his abuse?" and "No question about it, it was a call to fight" and "He started passing me the ball again and quit the phony hostili-

ties" and "I was saddened by losing a friend and <u>losing my win-</u> <u>dow on what I thought was Jesse's exciting, dangerous, sensual</u> <u>world</u>" and "<u>I wonder how many moments like that had made up</u> <u>his young life.</u>" When I catch myself writing things that I would never say in conversation, I revise them. They didn't sound natural or interesting to me when I reread the first draft.

4. I worked on the last paragraph (now two paragraphs) for quite a while, although I didn't change the basic content. I didn't want to make Jesse's and my hanging out together look like a big, conscious effort to change the status quo; my social conscience wasn't that developed then. At the same time, we knew what we were doing and that we'd surprise some people, but we didn't know how they would react. I wanted readers to see that something almost happened back then that could have been positive, and also that it takes a lot of courage to go against the social grain—more than we probably had.

The final draft of "Jesse and I" is at the end of the chapter.

Journal Entry 9

Write your reaction to the "Jesse and I" draft: what you liked or disliked, what you found interesting or boring, what if anything you could relate to your own life, what suggestions you'd make to improve it. Share entries with a classmate.

REVISION ASSIGNMENT 1

Before reviewing your own draft for possible revisions, read the following student draft and then discuss it with a classmate. Use the following revision guidelines to help evaluate the draft:

1. What do you like (find interesting, thought provoking, funny, or touching) about the draft? What specific things would you compliment the writer on?

2. In what ways, if any, could you relate your own experiences or relationships, or those of people you know, to the draft?

3. What specific questions would you like the draft to have answered? (For example, "What does your boss look like?" "Why did you stay with the job if you hated it so much?" "Why did you write about this relationship?")

4. What things does the writer describe in the draft? What effect do the descriptions have? What other things might the writer have described that would have been interesting to readers?

5. What if anything did you not understand or find confusing in the draft? Give specific examples.

6. Could any sentences be reworded to make them clearer and smoother? Give specific examples.

7. How effective is the paragraphing of the draft? When does the writer move from one paragraph to the next? Are there any overly long or short paragraphs that may bother readers, or any confusing paragraphs that jump around to different points?

8. What did you get out of the draft? What do you think the writer's point was in sharing the relationship with readers?

9. What other suggestions might you give the writer to make his draft more effective from a reader's viewpoint?

STUDENT WRITER—FIRST DRAFT

Working at the Laundry

I badly needed a summer job to get some money for college, so I looked in the paper and saw a "help wanted" ad for a laundry worker. Working for a laundry didn't sound too bad, so I applied over the phone and got the job.

Driving to the laundry's address, I pictured a family-owned business in a small building. What I found was a large building full of workers and noisy machines. The foreman, a no-nonsense woman, immediately put me to work with another worker who showed me what to do.

Our job was to dry the towels and sheets that came to us from the washing machines. First, we would dry them partially in a large, round spinning machine and then transfer them to huge hot-air dryers that could hold a ton of towels and sheets.

When the foreman came around, she'd stand over us, her arms folded across her chest. If things were going right, she'd say nothing and move on, but other times she'd say "Move faster, you're not keeping up." Never a pleasant word, and never a hint of a smile.

The work was rough. The wet towels and sheets were heavy, and we'd have to load and unload them twice because of the two different dryers. Sometimes the spin dryer would start kicking and making a racket, so we'd have to rebalance the load, losing precious time. When I'd open the door on the hot-air dryer at the end of a cycle, I'd get a blast of hot air in the face, making it stiflingly hot in the already warm, humid building.

Before we'd complete one drying cycle, another huge basket of wet laundry would be wheeled to us, and sometimes a couple baskets would back up. This is when the foreman would appear out of nowhere yelling "Faster! Keep it moving! You're getting behind." I thought I was moving as fast as I could, but I'd shift into an even higher gear, brushing back the sweat and tears of frustration.

By the end of that first day, I was exhausted and my arms, back, and feet ached. Before I left, the foreman came over and said, with her stone face, "You're going to have to do better tomorrow, Susanna. You college kids have to learn to work." That really made me mad, but instead of telling her to shove her job, I decided to stick it out and show her.

I did learn to work more quickly as I grew accustomed to the routine, so the foreman wasn't on me as much. Her silence was as much of a compliment as I ever got. When she did say something, it was always to lecture me about moving faster or not dropping anything on the floor, or to make snide comments like "I have more trouble with you college kids than anyone."

If I thought I'd ever please her or earn her grudging respect, I was wrong. I worked my tail off for two months, and when I left to return to school, all she said was "Well, now at least you know something about what work is." I think she resented me or anyone else who was getting an education, knowing that we could escape from that hellhole, and that she never could.

I did gain respect for people who labored in jobs like mine year after year, but I was even more determined to finish college so I'd never get stuck permanently doing physical labor. I also learned that how a supervisor treats you can make a big difference in your attitude. I hated the foreman and that hate carried over to the job. As a business administration major, that's a good lesson for me to learn.

REVISION ASSIGNMENT 2

Now review your own draft for possible revisions, using the revision questions as guidelines. Once you have a good idea of what you want to change, exchange drafts with a classmate and get a second opinion before writing your second draft. Review and discuss each other's drafts as you did the student draft in the book.

When you write your next draft, keep an open mind on making changes that you hadn't considered before beginning your rewrite. Even if I have a good idea of the basic revisions I plan to make, I always discover other things I want to include or change as I work through the draft.

The longer I wait between writing drafts, the less "sacred" my original draft ideas and wording appear. When I write my second draft immediately after the first, I still have an emotional attachment to what I've written, and it is harder to evaluate the content or wording objectively. This attachment, however, fades with time, so revising is easier and more effective for me when some time has passed between drafts.

Journal Entry 10

Relate the kinds of revisions you made in your second draft, why you made them, and how you feel the new draft compares to the first one. What is the purpose of the revision process for you personally? What gets done?

EDITING

The point of editing your draft is to find and correct errors in order to deliver a relatively error-free paper to your readers. By editing, you put your essay in "publishable" form, which means cleaning it up for inspection.

EDITING ASSIGNMENT 1

With a classmate, review my uses of punctuation in the "Jesse and I" draft, and make a list of my purposes for using commas, periods, quotation marks, apostrophes, colons (:), and semicolons (;). My punctuation usage is conventional, so I think the draft is a reasonable model for you to analyze. The purpose of the analysis is for you to see and understand the basic conventions of punctuation, and then to apply them in a general way to your own writing.

EDITING ASSIGNMENT 2

The following student essay contains some errors in punctuation, spelling, and grammar. Proofread the essay carefully and correct the errors. Among other things, you will find a few run-together sentences that need periods between them or joining words (conjunctions) to connect them, and a couple sentence *fragments* (incomplete sentences set off by periods and capital letters). To correct these, you can usually add the fragment to the sentence before or after it, whichever seems best.

The purpose of the editing exercise is to give you revision practice on a student paper containing typical first-draft errors. While the experience won't be the same as editing your own draft, it will be as close as textbook drafts can come, and it will help sharpen your editing "eye" for finding errors in your papers and your classmate's.

STUDENT WRITER—FIRST DRAFT

Someone Influential

The people that had such an impact on my life time is my parents. These two people taught me wright and wrong, good and bad, how to my best, and that I can accomplish anything I want, if I really want it. These two role model figures taught me mostly that being in a good state of mind and that means being happy with my self being and being happy with others equals the road to success. This thoughtful information came to my belief that laughter is the best medicine.

The times I would unfortunately run into problems and do something drastically wrong, In turn I wouldn't be in trouble but was shown the proper way to handle the situation. And I was told it was wrong and why it wasn't a good idea for it to happen again. I began to realize what things were good and what things were bad.

Mr. and Mrs. Salazar always told me all my life that to do my best at what I try to do, and go after what I really want and eventually my dreamy goal will be reached. Despite the ups and downs and the long time periods it is true and I have accomplished allot with that attitude and I possess allot of materialistic valuables that I dreamed about when I was an early teen. My mother once told me that what ever you really want, son you can eventually get it. As long as you work hard enough for it and you really want it bad enough. This statement seems true to me because they came from Mexico with little money and education and a will to succeed. Today their results are stunningly unbelievable.

But the most important moral of all is it only can be done in a good state of mind and to succeed in life one must be happy with ones self and to like your self. One can not reach far enough for what he wants if he's always depressed, take pride in all you do son. I have learned that people like to see you in a good mood and come back to be in your presents more and more. I have been asked ,"Why are you always in a good mood?"

That's probably why I think the way I think,I have the things I have, I like the things I like, and I do what I do. Also that's why Im here today in school reaching higher and higher. It's been said you learn everything from your parents.

EDITING ASSIGNMENT 3

Now proofread your latest draft for errors and make necessary corrections. Pay particular attention to any error tendencies that you have discovered in previous writing. You may want to edit your paper while working on specific sections of the editing chapter (Chapter 9) that cover your problem areas.

If you aren't confident that you have found all the errors, exchange papers with a classmate for proofreading. Write the final draft of your essay when your instructor assigns it.

Journal Entry 11

Evaluate the error tendencies in your latest draft: how much of a problem you have with errors, the kinds of errors you tend to make, what you can do to eliminate such errors, and what you have learned that will help you in future writing.

AUTHOR'S FINAL DRAFT

An Old Friend

In junior high I went to school with kids from all parts of town. For the first time I was in school with the Mexican kids from the east side, and on the whole they seemed pretty tough, mature, and a bit threatening. A few of them even drove old cars to school and parked them a block away.

The only times we had contact were in the classroom and in sports. Although most of them didn't go out for teams, there was one kid names Jesse Sanchez, nicknamed "Wadda," who did everything. He was slender and not too tall, but very well coordinated. He was skilled enough to be the pitcher on the softball team, the quarterback in football, and the point guard in basketball. We saw a lot of each other in practice and slowly got to know one another.

Jesse was a real character. He was kind of different-looking with his big teeth, sleepy hooded eyes, and flat-top with slicked-back sides and a ducktail. In class, he was always cutting up and driving the teachers crazy. As soon as one turned her back, Jesse would be imitating her mannerisms or voice, and he'd have the whole class snickering.

I was attracted to Jesse because he was a good athlete, but also because he was so different from me: always cutting up in class, never doing his homework, having a girlfriend, and being a Mexican from the east side. He was an exciting and interesting character in the eyes of a middle-class white boy whose dad was a school principal, who got straight A's, who'd never gone with a girl, and who longed to rebel a little. When Jesse talked about making out with Celia after school, I hung enviously on every word, hoping some of it were true.

Jesse and I gradually became pals during sports and in home room, but outside of those times, he'd hang out with his Mexican buddies by the wood shop and I'd be with my white friends who held the class offices and decorated the gym for the noon dances. One day, however, I decided to break with tradition. After home room there was a fifteen-minute break, and one day I told Jesse, "Let's go get something at the snack bar. I'll buy you an Abba Zabba." He said okay, so we walked to the snack bar, bought our Abba Zabbas (the best candy bar of our day), and sat at an outdoor table until break was over. No big deal.

Back then, middle-class white boys and eastside Mexicans didn't hang out together. The only Mexicans who were "insiders" were those few whose parents had worked themselves into the middle class and who dressed and talked like we did. The eastsiders called them "coconuts": brown on the outside, white on the inside.

Jesse's and my behavior caused a minor stir. My friends teased me about it, saying things like "Is Wadda your best friend now?" and "Why don't you invite Wadda home for dinner? Your dad'll love that." Jesse's friends, however, must have been a lot harder on him, because the next day he'd hardly talk to me. I asked him "What's up, Jesse?" and he didn't say anything. He just kept his distance.

I never knew what went on between Jesse and his pals, but from that day on he wasn't my friend. In fact, he became my enemy. He started giving me dirty looks and saying things under his breath that I couldn't catch. At practice, he quit passing me the basketball, which got me mad. What had I done?

One day I was walking by the wood shop and heard someone say "Hey asshole. F_____ you." It was Jesse, slumped against the shaded side of the building with about ten of his eastside buddies, all smoking cigarettes. I stopped in surprise and said what every guy says when called out: "What did you say?" "F_____ you, you white kissass," Jesse hissed. I couldn't let that pass so I said "After school asshole. Behind the backstop. You'd better be there." Then I walked off before he could say anything else.

I didn't want to fight Jesse. I figured he could beat me up, because I'd never been in a fight and I guessed he'd been in a lot of them. Getting whipped was bad for the reputation. Moreover, I wasn't even mad at Jesse, just hurt. I still wasn't sure what was going on. Since I knew I couldn't chicken out of the fight, which was worse than getting whipped, I decided to try and get him by himself during the day and talk to him.

After sixth-period class I followed him into one of those small, smelly junior-high bathrooms. When he saw me, he clenched his fists and narrowed his eyes to a deadly squint. I put up my hands, palms open, and said "Jesse, I don't want to fight you, man. I'm your friend. Let's just forget everything." Jesse relaxed his fists and stood there staring. Finally I said "What's wrong, Jesse?" He slowly walked past me toward the door, muttering "Nothin', white boy. Nothin'."

There was no fight, because I went home after school. Whether Jesse showed up or not I don't know, and neither of us mentioned it again. Although we weren't friends, a certain respect developed between us. He started passing me the ball again and quit acting hostile. But we were back in our different worlds, which was the way he wanted it, or felt it had to be. However, I think it affected us both. Around me, Jesse's playful mischievousness was replaced by a harder edge. He didn't smile that toothy grin as much. I felt the loss of a friend, and also of my window to his world. I think we were both sadder for the experience.

I have three memories of Jesse after that. One was his standing outside the gymnasium door with his girlfriend at the eighth-grade graduation dance. He hadn't graduated, just passed on without a diploma, so he couldn't get in. He wasn't causing trouble, just standing there in a white shirt and black tie with Celia, who wouldn't go in without him. Looking back, I can only imagine how hard that moment was for him, and how many other painful moments he had encountered as a poor young Mexican in a world run by white people.

My second memory was in my freshman year of high school. During the third week of football practice, Jesse showed up in his street clothes, asking if he could try out for punter. As practice went on, I saw Jesse on a side field booming long spirals off his black spit-shined shoe. He never came back to practice after that day, and I never saw him at school.

The last time I saw Jesse was years later at a local bank. He was sweeping up at closing time, and I was depositing my monthly teaching check. I recognized him immediately and went up to him. "How ya doing, Jesse?" I asked. "Not bad, Tom," he said, flashing that memorable grin. In that moment all the petty eighth-grade baloney fell aside, and we were a couple of old friends. He told me about marrying Celia and about their two daughters, and I told him what I was doing, and about my new job up state in the fall. When we parted minutes later I said "Really good to see you, Jesse," and he said "You too, Tom," and we both meant it. That was a good moment in my life, shaking Jesse's hand and seeing that smile again.

Times have changed somewhat, and the stricter racial and ethnic boundaries of my childhood have blurred. Yet I know kids still hang out primarily with kids who look, act, and dress like them, and perhaps they always will. Jesse and I made a small statement years ago, crossing in friendship those ethnic and class boundaries, but we were reeled back in by the kids who defined who and what we were.

I can imagine now the kinds of things Jesse's friends said to him to undermine our relationship, and they were, after all, the guys he would probably be with forever. I certainly don't blame him for freezing me out, and I didn't do much to save the relationship. But I still wonder, if Jesse and I had been a little stronger, whether we might not have shaken up the ethnic and social lines at school and brought some people a little closer together, at least for a while.

Chapter Three
Prewriting

Prewriting means anything writers do to prepare themselves. It includes those activities that help get you ready to write: thinking about a topic, looking at it from different perspectives, planning a writing approach, making a list of ideas, asking and answering questions, or writing freely to discover a topic. Prewriting habits vary greatly among writers.

The purpose of prewriting is to make the actual writing task easier and more productive. Anything that helps accomplish that is worth doing. Since you have been writing for years, you may already have some well-developed prewriting routines.

PREWRITING HABITS

When I first considered my own prewriting, I didn't feel I did much. However, as I gave it more thought and paid attention to what I did, I discovered the following.

1. In the summer, I prefer writing soon after I get up in the morning. If I don't get started by 8:30 or 9, I don't feel good about it. However, I almost always read the sports section of the paper before starting. I give myself that small pleasure before getting to work.

2. In the afternoon, I often return to writing for a couple hours. However, I usually do some reading before starting again. I like to get my mind away from my writing, and also to be exposed to other writers' styles. Then I'm ready to get back on the computer.

3. I like to think about what I'm going to write the day before I start a new topic or manuscript section. I want a good idea of where I'm heading so that I can get started without delay. I hate to waste morning writing time.

4. I don't make elaborate plans before I write. I'll give a topic some thought, but mainly about general things I want to accomplish. I seldom write anything down. For example, if I were to write about an inexpensive Mexican cruise that my wife and I took in June, I know I would include something about what we did, make suggestions to would-be cruisers, and emphasize that cruising isn't for everyone. With that in mind, I'd be ready to write.

   For this particular chapter, I thought about doing three things: revealing the individual nature of prewriting, presenting some prewriting options for you to try, and working through some of those options myself. With those things in mind, I was ready to get started.

5. Many of my ideas come to me as I write. I don't plan my writing elaborately because it doesn't work for me. Much of my writing

enjoyment lies in discovering ideas as I go. I know where I'm headed in general, but I don't know exactly how I will get there. That's part of the fun. It seems a bit boring to have everything charted in advance. Besides, in my experience I don't stick to a detailed writing plan very well, although some writers have great success doing just that.

6. My prewriting approach reflects who I am. I am not an organized person, as you could see from the mess on my desk or in my garage. I am organized enough for my own needs—I can find what I want—but rather messy by my wife's or office mate's standards. I don't think I could change my prewriting habits any more than the other habits of a lifetime. How I write works okay for me, but I wouldn't try to impose it on the next person.

STUDENT WRITERS—PREWRITING

Inez

I don't do a whole lot before writing my first draft because I change so much from first to second draft that my first draft is kind of like my prewriting.

I'll think a bit about my topic and my general approach, and then I just start writing longhand in pencil. My first draft is like free writing in a way, except that it's more controlled: I try to move logically from thought to thought, and I write in paragraphs.

When I finish my draft I set it aside until the next day and then type my second draft on the word processor. I always make lots of changes, like moving paragraphs around, rewording sentences, adding examples, adding a conclusion, redoing my opening, deleting things I don't like, adding new points, and so on. When I finish my second draft, it is usually very different from my first one, and I think a lot better. My first draft is starting-point A. I couldn't get to B—my improved draft—without A. For me, it's a two-step process.

Rudy

Once I have a topic, I like to make a list of things that come to my mind about the topic. This helps me think about the topic and also gets some things on paper that I can use in my writing. I try to write down at least ten items. If I can hardly think of anything, I usually forget that topic and go on to something else.

Once I have my list, I take a good look at it to see what I can use and how things might fit together. I look for some main ideas that I might develop paragraphs around, and then I look for some items that would fit under the main ideas. I highlight the main ideas and draw arrows from other items to the main ideas they come under. If some items don't fit anywhere, I cross them off, or if they seem important to include, I think about how to include them. I also add other points that come to me as I am going over the list.

Now I'm ready to write my draft because I have some main ideas to develop into paragraphs and some material to include for support. My job is to turn my list items into sentences and to tie things together. Making lists is a big help for me.

Cicily

When I have chosen a topic, I do a mapping diagram, something I learned in high school. I use it for all of my writing assignments, and for me it's the best way to get ready to write.

Let's say I'm going to write about something I really dislike doing—like cleaning the bathroom. I'm the designated bathroom cleaner in our house, and it's the pits. So I start with writing "sink" within a bubble. Then I draw a line out from "sink" and write "clogged hair and mascara marks" in a second bubble. Then I draw one line from that bubble and write "yucky to touch" in a bubble and a second line and write "hard to get off" in a bubble. Now I've got a good beginning for a paragraph on one of the worst parts of the job—cleaning the sink.

I go on and do similar mapping for the toilet, the tub, and the floor, and I'm ready to write.

Sometimes it's not as easy as the example I gave. Sometimes I'm not sure what I want to do with a topic or even what I know about it, so I do mapping to think about the topic. Here [Figure 3-1] is an example of what I did with the topic "Should Condoms Be Sold in the Restrooms on Campus?" Once I finished the diagram, I had thought about a number of things and was ready to write.

Marvin

Well, I get my topic and then I sit back and think. I talk to myself, something like this: "Let's see, I'm writing about hardwood floors. I really like their looks. That's one thing I'll write about, and include the different looks you can get with hardwood designs and finishes. What else? They're relatively easy to clean, easier than carpet. I could write about that, somewhere in the end, because maybe that's not a big deal.

"But it's the looks. That's the thing that attracts me. Maybe most of the paper would be about that. If I write about the various designs

Figure 3-1

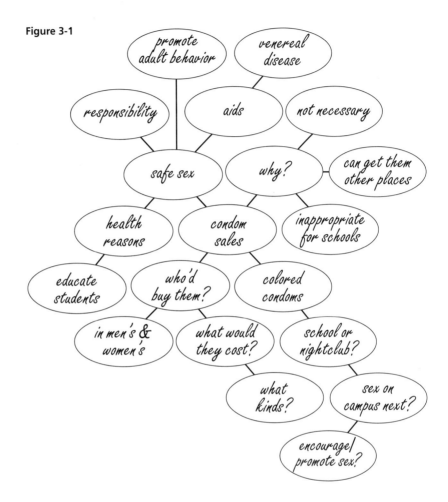

and finishes and yes, also about how certain furniture and decorating styles go great with hardwood, that would be quite a bit. It's not as if we're talking empty rooms here. Easier on the feet than concrete floor finishes too. (Something I might throw in, but like the cleaning, not the big deal.) I want readers to picture a beautifully furnished room with a terrific hardwood floor. That's the picture I'll draw for them.''

Lourdes

I use the *So what?* prewriting approach. It helps me get into a topic pretty deeply. Here's how it works for me.

"I think I'll write about the campus police. (*So what?*) Well, I think they get a bad rap from a lot of students. (*So what?*) A lot of students don't understand the need for the campus police, so they unfairly give them a bad time. (*So what?*) Well, it makes the officers' jobs that much more difficult.

"(*So what?*) It's difficult enough already with all of the things they have to do, like making sure non-college people don't take up valuable parking spaces, answering all kinds of emergency calls all over campus, and patrolling at night to keep the campus safe, especially for women. (*So what?*) Well, if they didn't do all those things, this campus would be a lot more dangerous, and the parking situation would be really impossible. (*So what?*) We'd lose students. Who wants to be on a dangerous campus where it's tough to find parking? Without the campus police around, that would be the situation here. (*So what?*) Enough already!"

Once I get to the point where the "so whats" lead to the obvious or ridiculous, I quit. For this particular topic, I've come up with a lot of stuff: important things the police do, what would happen if they weren't around, how many students feel about them, how their attitude makes it more difficult for the police. I'm going to write a paper supporting the campus police and try to convince some students to change their attitude.

Journal Entry 12

Relate your current prewriting routine, the things you commonly do before beginning the first draft of a paper. How does this routine help you get started?

PREWRITING ACTIVITIES

Writers use a variety of prewriting activities to generate ideas and plan essays. In this unit you will try out a number of strategies to see what works best for you.

Free Writing

Free writing means putting pen to paper and writing whatever comes to mind without concern for logic or order. Free writing can have at least three purposes:

1. To improve a writer's fluency by writing in a relaxed, uninhibited way. Free writing helps some writers overcome their fears and provides practice for people who have trouble putting their words on paper.

2. To find potential topics for essays. Some people discover subjects they want to write about by writing freely on whatever comes to mind.

3. To generate ideas and material for an essay. Once you decide on a topic, you may write freely to unlock ideas, discover connections between ideas, generate some details or examples, or find out how you feel about the topic. The writing flows in any directions your mind carries it.

PREWRITING ASSIGNMENT 1

Free write to generate a possible topic (or topics) for an essay. Write for ten minutes about anything that comes to your mind. Then see if you've uncovered a topic you'd like to write about.

AUTHOR'S FREE WRITING

My son will be coming by the house in an hour or so. He's teaching a summer school class in biology at the college, the first class he's ever taught. I hope it goes well for him, and so far he seems to be doing a good job. I'm always curious about how he looks when he goes to school. One day he comes in bermuda shorts and another day he hasn't shaved. He seems awfully casual for his first teaching job, but he probably dresses like his professors did at UC Santa Barbara, a laid-back school by the beach.

Clothes are going in the dryer now and I should have started a wash with the clothes sitting in the washer, but I couldn't open the new container of detergent. With all this weightlifting I should be pretty strong but I couldn't get the stupid lid off. Lori, my daughter, should be coming home some time this afternoon. I hope her friends drop her off instead of my having to drive to Visalia and pick her up—a forty-minute ride. She's just getting back from a trip, and I'm looking forward to seeing her. She's living at home this summer for the first time in five years. She's nice to have around. I think she might be able to get a summer job at the Bear Club. One of their waitresses is leaving for the month of July, so I'll have Lori go down today or tomorrow and talk to the woman who does the hiring. That would be an okay summer job until her school starts in September.

I've got to clean up the back yard this weekend. Paint the faded flower barrels, cut back the ivy and the bushes, and buy some flowers to plant and a couple hanging plants to add to the patio. It shouldn't take all that long, but I'll start early Saturday because it's going to be a hot weekend. I'd love to get away to the coast but that won't happen. That nice pool in the back yard and we hardly ever use it. What a waste. It was nice when the kids were young but now it just sits back there. I've been in once all summer.

After reading over my free writing a couple times, I've come up with three possible ideas for an essay.

1. The new division of labor around the house, where men like myself are doing more of what was once considered "women's work" to help out our working wives. While I'm proud of the help I give, I suspect first that I don't really do all that much, and second that I create problems by not doing things the way my wife would have done them. I have lots of examples I could use.

2. Grown children coming back home to live. This is a phenomenon I've read a lot about, and now it's happening in my home with my twenty-three-year-old daughter. Once I was out of the house at eighteen, I never considered living at home again. I think my interest in writing would be analyzing the reasons for adult children to return to the nest and the effects that can have.

3. Weightlifting provides people with a lot of useless strength and hurts their flexibility. I'm stronger than I've ever been, but when I try to apply that strength to opening a lid or lifting a bag of cement, it doesn't help much. In addition, when I play golf or shoot baskets, my tight muscles restrict movement. Perhaps weightlifting does more harm than good.

Of the three topics, I could have some fun writing about the first, and the second would be interesting to think about, especially its economic and psychological implications. Since I hadn't considered either topic before, the free writing did help.

Journal Entry 13
What kinds of things did you find yourself writing about in the free writing? What potential writing topic (or topics) came from it?

 **PREWRITING ASSIGNMENT 2**
Free write for a few minutes to generate some ideas for one of the topics from Prewriting Assignment 1. Write anything that comes to mind that

is related to your topic. I'll write for ten minutes on my topic of the husband helping around the house.

AUTHOR'S FREE WRITING—SHARING HOUSEWORK

When I was first married I hardly helped around the house at all. My wife cooked, did the dishes, did the wash, vacuumed, dusted, everything. I just worked for a living and took care of the yard, which was pretty easy. Today I do things that I didn't used to. I do my own ironing in the morning before school, and I always make my own breakfast and lunch. I still don't cook dinner, but I do clear the table, rinse the dishes and put them in the dishwasher, and frequently unload the dishwasher. I also carry dirty clothes out to the garage, wash and dry them, and sometimes fold and put them away.

This is all stuff I hardly ever did before. But it's not without problems. Sometimes I forget whether the dishes in the dishwasher are clean or not, and I end up putting dirty dishes up in the cupboard, having my wife discover it, and finding myself putting everything back in the dishwasher. Or my washing the white clothes with the colors and the whites coming out pink. Or my putting dishes away where no one can find what they need. Or my ironing my pants and shirt, putting them on, and having my wife say "You're not going to wear those wrinkled clothes are you?" Or my rinsing dishes but not putting them into the sink far enough and the water squirting on the counter and floor. Or my folding the clothes and my wife unfolding and refolding them the "right" way. Same goes for remaking the bed. Or my sometimes reverting back to my old ways and letting my wife do all the laundry and clean up the kitchen while I read the paper and lie on the sofa.

Maybe I really don't do as much as I think I do. I read some article that said that men who think they're a big help around the house only do about 10 percent of the actual work. And I still like to be praised for what I do—thanked for doing the kinds of things my wife has done for twenty-five years. Still, I'm a lot better than I used to be. If I learned how to cook that would be a big help. I do barbecue in the summer though, a couple times a week. And I take my wife out to eat a lot. That helps, but it doesn't really count as housework.

I wrote without stopping for ten minutes. I got out a number of ideas in my free writing and many examples of the problems I unintentionally create. I could use a lot of this in writing my first draft. I see a fuzzy focus coming out of the free writing, but I'll have to make it clearer in the draft. I even have a sense of organization, at least through the first two-thirds of the writing. The free writing was helpful.

Journal Entry 14

Relate your free writing experience for a particular topic: how easily you were able to write, the kinds of things you put down, and what you could apply to your first draft of an essay. How useful was the free writing for your particular topic?

Listing Ideas

A common prewriting practice is to list some points you may want to include in an essay. While this doesn't produce the detail that free writing does, it gives you some definite things to develop in a paper.

I often list some ideas before I write, although usually in my head. As I mentioned earlier, I came up with three main ideas to develop in this chapter: presenting prewriting as an individual act, presenting specific prewriting strategies that work for many writers, and working through those strategies to evaluate them. Those ideas came from my prewriting "list."

PREWRITING ASSIGNMENT 3

Select any three topics from the following and come up with a list of possible ideas to develop in an essay. Depending on the topic, these ideas may be supporting points, steps, incidents, reasons, or examples—whatever the topic requires. For my lists, I'll use other topics so I won't influence what you do.

Select three:

1. How to _____ .

2. _____ is a very _____ person.

3. Why students drop out of college.

4. Graduating from high school was a _____ experience.

5. Watching _____ (some sport) on television is _____ .

6. The effects of divorce on children.

AUTHOR'S LISTS

1. The drawbacks to lecturing as a teaching mode

    Supporting reasons:

    - Attention-span problem (students)
    - Feedback difficult
    - Retention poor
    - No student interaction
    - Doesn't accommodate different learning styles

2. Reformulating the welfare system

    Suggestions:

    - Encourage rather than discourage marriage
    - Encourage rather than discourage smaller families
    - "Workfare" instead of welfare whenever possible
    - Emphasis on the "temporary" condition of welfare

3. Dropping out of high school

    Examples of effects:

    - Unskilled laborers
    - Poverty
    - Large percentage on welfare
    - Cycle continues for children
    - High incidence of crime/drug use

Making lists helps me in several ways. First, it provides me with some main points I will include when writing. Second, it makes me think about the order in which I want to present them. Third, it helps me see possible connections between points, which I can write about.

The one drawback I see is that I might limit myself to writing about my list ideas. As I write, I might discover more significant things to include in the essay, and realize that some of my initial points weren't that important or relevant. If I rely only on prewriting ideas, I might write a rather shallow essay, short of the insights the writing process may help reveal.

Journal Entry 15

How useful would your lists of ideas be in helping you develop an essay? Compare listing ideas to free writing as prewriting activities. Which would you be more inclined to use? Why?

Brainstorming

Brainstorming combines listing and free writing. When you brainstorm a topic, you make a list of whatever comes to mind to get as many thoughts on paper as you can. Your list might include details, main points, and examples mixed together.

After you have done your brainstorming, you can go over the list and classify your entries, putting similar thoughts together, noting main ideas and supportive examples and details, discarding unimportant entries, and adding new ideas.

PREWRITING ASSIGNMENT 4

Brainstorm a list of twenty to thirty ideas on a topic of your choice. You may use an unused topic from Prewriting Assignments 1 or 3, or come up with a new one. When you finish, classify your entries by grouping similar ones together, indicating their relationship in some way, discarding irrelevant entries, and adding new ideas that come to you.

AUTHOR'S BRAINSTORMING

Topic: Adult children returning home to live (topic from assignment 1)
Brainstormed list:

out of money

couldn't afford rent

no job

divorced or separated

looking for security

planning on temporary stay

disrupt living pattern

three people instead of two

eating habits

privacy

need to work

contribute to expenses

no longer children

set down rules

responsibility around house

enjoy their company

help them out

extended adolescence

loud music

television programs

having a plan for future

set specific time limit

don't turn away

Classified list of entries:

Why adult children return home:

out of money

couldn't afford high rent

no job

divorced or separated

How adult children may feel about it:

consider it a temporary situation

may feel bad about having to return

may feel need for security

Problems situation can create:

three people instead of two

eating habits

loud music

television programs

lack of privacy

disrupt living pattern

How to make situation work:

child needs to work (or go to school)

contribute to home expenses

take responsibility around the house

establish simple understandings

don't treat like children

set reasonable time limit (not permanent situation)

How parents should respond:

welcome child back

make them feel loved

don't make them feel guilty

don't reject them

help them out

enjoy their company

As I read over my brainstormed list, the entries fell nicely into five general categories. I have a lot of material for a paper, and a workable way of organizing it. My only concern is that my prewriting "outline" could hinder the creative drafting process.

I think I would use my classified material as a general guideline, remaining receptive to other ideas that came as I wrote. Making the list and classifying entries seemed a little too easy. This topic may have some subtlties and depth that I didn't plumb in my prewriting but which I might uncover while writing about it. It would also be smart to write this paper after my daughter has lived with us for some time.

Journal Entry 16

Relate how your brainstorming and classifying went. How did you classify the entries? What did you add or delete while you classified? Compare brainstorming/classifying to free writing and listing ideas. How would you rate each for helping you prepare to write?

Mapping

A prewriting technique for generating a lot of material for an essay is called mapping or "clustering." With this diagramming technique, you usually move from general to specific thoughts in a manner that produces main ideas, supporting points, examples for those points, details for those examples, and so on in increasingly specific terms.

The mapping diagram of Figure 3-2 (Topic: Maria's personality) clarifies the technique. The four main points are numbered.

Figure 3-2

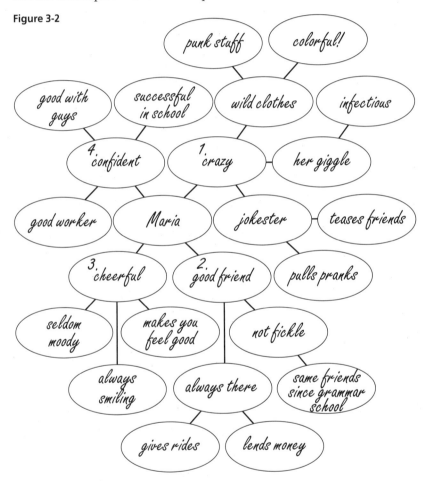

The results of mapping sometimes come closest to the traditional outline some writers use. The mapping diagram on Maria's personality could be outlined like this:

A. Crazy

    1. wild clothes (punk stuff, colorful)

2. her giggle (infectious)

3. jokester (teases, pull pranks)

B. Good friend

1. not fickle (same friends)

2. always there (lends money, gives rides)

C. Cheerful

1. seldom moody

2. always smiling

3. makes you feel good

D. Confident

1. successful in school

2. good with guys

3. good worker

However, mapping does not have to be followed rigidly in an essay. You can also use the diagram to generate some ideas that will help you get started on a paper. How you use mapping diagrams depends on whether you prefer highly organized writing plans or general guidelines. Writers have success with both approaches, and what you do depends on what works for you.

PREWRITING ASSIGNMENT 5

Do a mapping diagram on the following topic: "Why I Would Recommend _____" (a particular restaurant, college, instructor, car, apartment complex, vacation spot, sporting activity, summer job, hair salon, supermarket, clothing store, laundromat). Try to come up with at least three or four main points you can work with.

AUTHOR'S MAPPING DIAGRAM

Topic: I'd recommend swimming as a sporting activity. (Figure 3-3)

Journal Entry 17

Relate your process for constructing the mapping diagram for a particular topic. How did you go about it? How do you think you would use the mapping material in an essay? Compared to the other prewriting techniques you've tried, how do you rate mapping as a means of preparing to write?

Asking Questions

Another useful prewriting activity is to ask questions related to your essay topic. Asking and answering questions can help you generate ideas for an essay and analyze your topic from different perspectives.

Although your questions would differ depending on the topic, most could be posed from the journalistic angles of who, what, where, when, why, and how. For example, I might ask the following questions if I were writing on the topic "Growing Up, I Was a Difficult Child for My Parents."

1. *When were you so difficult?* From about ten years old through high school.

Figure 3-3

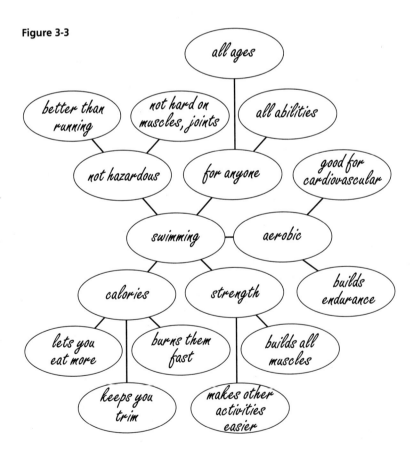

2. *Why were you so difficult?* I was caught up in my own world. I wanted to do what I wanted to do and had little concern for others. I didn't want to be bothered with family or responsibilities around the home. I also wanted to do things my way and wouldn't take advice. I had a bad temper and a mouth to match. I could be very cruel.

3. *How did you get this way?* I was spoiled from always being a good athlete. I never did anything but play sports, and I was gone from the house from morning until evening. I was very successful in school sports and it went to my head. I never felt I had to do anything but play, and I didn't learn to take other responsibilities. I also had a mean streak and temper that I can't really explain. I don't know where it came from.

4. *What are some examples of your behavior?* Instead of mowing the lawn on Saturday, I'd stay in bed until after noon so that my dad would eventually go out and do it. I'd fight against having to go to visit relatives with the family. I'd sit in front of the TV watching sports for hours and not talk to anyone. I'd talk back, saying terrible things to my mother. I didn't like to have my parents around when I was playing sports and I often wouldn't let them come to my games. I'd argue about anything, always taking a side my parents wouldn't like just to be ornery. I hated to pick up my clothes, take out the garbage, do yard work, take baths, go to church, go anywhere with my parents, do dishes, or get up early. I was in trouble regularly for not doing these kinds of things.

5. *How did this affect your family?* I didn't pay much attention. I really didn't care at the time. I'm sure I was a constant source of displeasure for them, and I would guess they didn't like me much of the time.

6. *How did your parents react?* I think they were amazingly tolerant of me. I'm sure they talked long into the night about their son many times, but they didn't lay a heavy guilt trip on me. I argued a lot with my mother, but she was still a good mother, better than I deserved. I think they gave in a lot, letting me slide around the house and do basically what I wanted. I don't think they (especially my dad) wanted to fight me all the time.

7. *How did this affect you?* It didn't for a long time, because I didn't worry about what my parents thought of me. They kept it to themselves most of the time, and I didn't really reflect much on what a pain I was until after I was married and had started a family. Later,

I began to realize what I had been like compared to my own children.

Answering those questions helped me reflect on my childhood relationship with my parents rather thoroughly. I realized in answering the questions that it's not a topic I would want to write on.

PREWRITING ASSIGNMENT 6
Come up with appropriate who, what, when, where, how, and why questions for an essay topic that involves your family (or some members, or a particular member). Then write answers to your questions to generate ideas for a possible essay on the topic.

Journal Entry 18
Relate your question-asking experience. How did you come up with questions, and how well did they work for your topic? How would your answers help you prepare to write an essay on the topic? What, if anything, did you learn through the process?

Thinking

Of course, all of the prewriting activities you've done require a lot of thinking about a topic. However, each requires a particular approach. A final prewriting activity is more open-ended: mentally mulling over a topic until you feel ready to write about it.

While thinking about your topic, you are preparing to write with the help of whatever ideas come to you. You may come up with a good approach to your topic, a good way to open, some ideas you want to include, a rough way to organize your thoughts, something you want to accomplish with your readers, or some examples you want to use. Rather than decide beforehand what you want to accomplish by thinking over the topic, see what you come up with first.

PREWRITING ASSIGNMENT 7
Come up with a topic for an essay that involves one of the following: your home, your neighborhood, your town (or a neighboring one), your county (or general area), your state, or your country. Once you have a topic, spend twenty to thirty minutes thinking about it in preparation for writing an essay. You will be recording your thoughts in the next journal entry.

AUTHOR'S PREWRITING THOUGHTS

There are lots of topics I'm considering. I wouldn't mind writing about my neighborhood, the town I live in, the neighboring large city, the general Valley area, or the state of California. However, I think I'll write about the town I live in, Reedley, because I've lived here over twenty years. Now I'm going to think about my topic for a while in preparation for writing.

After thinking about Reedley for about twenty minutes, I know I can write about the town. The one thing that kept coming to mind was my ambivalent feelings toward it: I like it but don't feel connected to it. I think I could leave tomorrow and wouldn't miss a thing about it. This attitude, which would be my general approach, came to me early in my thinking. It is this ambivalence toward the town I've lived in for twenty-three years that I would explore in the essay.

I started thinking about why I felt that way. I think I know some of the reasons, which I'll write about. Then I started thinking more generally about how other people might feel about Reedley. Through my pre-writing thought, I came up with a topic (my home town), a basic approach (my ambivalent feelings towards Reedley), some possible reasons for it, and a desire to analyze people's sense of community, including my own.

Journal Entry 19

Relate what came out of your prewriting thoughts. What did you think about that could help prepare you to write an essay on the topic? How did your thinking process unfold (what came to mind first, next, and so on)? How useful was your prewriting thought in helping you prepare to write? How would you compare it to other prewriting activities?

CHAPTER WRITING ASSIGNMENT

Select one of the topics from your prewriting activities. (If you're tired of those topics, come up with a new one.) Then use one or more of the prewriting activities to generate ideas. Before writing your first draft, consider the following.

1. What tentative approach (thesis) do you want to take toward your topic?
2. What audience do you want to write for?

3. What do you want to accomplish in the essay (purpose)? How do you want your audience to respond?

AUTHOR'S TOPIC

Of all the essay topics I used for the prewriting work, I think I'll write about the town I live in, Reedley. The topic is on my mind, because it's the last topic I worked with, and it interests me. Most of you are attached in some way to a particular town, so you may be interested in the topic, and my essay may cause you to think about your own feelings toward your community.

My approach, as I mentioned earlier, is to analyze my ambivalent feelings toward the town I live in. My college readers are my primary audience. I'm not sure yet what I want to accomplish with the essay. I hope that will become clearer as I write.

STUDENT WRITER'S RESPONSE

Sylvia

I don't watch much television because I'm usually too busy either studying or doing better things. But there's this one program called Aeon Flux on MTV that really fascinates me. It's an animated show that is really unique. I haven't seen anything like it on TV, and I'd like to write about it.

My approach seems pretty clear: This show is unique—the most clever animated show that I've seen on TV. I guess my generation grew up on Saturday-morning cartoons, and MTV's provided us with a cartoon for college-age people.

I'd write this for my classmates with the purpose of getting them interested in the show. I think if they watched it they'd find it fascinating.

AUTHOR'S FIRST DRAFT

Living in Reedley

When asked how I like living in the town of Reedley, I always say it's

a nice place~~, and mean it.~~ Situated in the agriculturally rich central

San Joaquin Valley and a half hour from the Sierra Nevada mountains, it has about 15,000 residents, a pleasant downtown area, a nice river running along its western border, and its own college, where I work.

At the same time, while I've lived in Reedley over twenty years, I still don't feel particularly connected to the town, and if I moved tomorrow I don't think I'd really miss it. I've never really considered *don't consider* myself a "Reedleyite" and don't identify with the town, or anything about it. *or* While I can honestly tell people it's a nice place to live, I don't feel a part of it.

wordy— *revise* It is this ambivalent attitude toward Reedley that I've carried since I came here. I grew up in the neighboring town of Sanger fifteen miles away, and all I remember about Reedley was we beat them regularly in sports when I was in high school. My first twenty years, *seldom* I never set foot in Reedley, except for sporting contests, and I couldn't have told you how to get there from Sanger. When I came to Reedley to live, Sanger was still home to me in the Valley, and I had little regard for my new community.

Beyond that, I'd heard a lot about how the "Mennonites" controlled the town. They were an established and well-to-do group *awkward* of German stock people with midwestern roots who practiced the *redundant* Mennonite religious faith. Their religion didn't bother me, but the thought of their dominating the town, or any other group for that matter, didn't seem right. When I first taught at the high school, I was warned that teachers shouldn't be seen having a beer in a Reedley bar. That Mennonite influence, I suspected.

Whether or not the Mennonite folks had undue influence in the town, I can't really say, because I didn't have much to do with Reedley or its politics. I did enjoy attending my children's activities as *meanders— rewrite* they went through the schools, and I taught a lot of the town's kids to swim when I was the local swimming coach, but other than that, I established few ties with the community.

Going over to, *to* teach at (the college) further removed me from the community. That may sound strange, but it turned out that about 90% of the teachers at the college didn't live in Reedley. Instead, they opted to live forty minutes away in Fresno, a city of over *residents* 500,000 population. Most of my friends lived in Fresno and had no attachment to Reedley, and over the years my social life revolved *reword— smooth out* around these people, *The* and the forty-minute drive to Fresno became a *, and while* regular occurrence, I lived in Reedley, but often ate out, went to movies, shopped, and socialized in Fresno.

Things didn't change much over the years. I never joined any social or service clubs in town. I admired the 1988 renovation of the

detail not needed here—delete downtown area, when they planted trees and flowers along the main street, added benches, and spruced up the facades of many of the buildings; however, I still didn't shop much there. When I attended the annual Reedley Rotary auction and dinner on free tickets, *from* my neighbor, ~~would give me,~~ I knew very few people and felt more like an outsider than a community member. And when my kids finally graduated from high school, I lost my one remaining connection to town through ~~involvement with~~ the school system.

revise— wordy! I don't know whether my lack of involvement or feeling toward what has been my hometown for twenty-three years is unusual or not. Perhaps more people than I realize live in places that they don't feel attached to. I've considered my attitude ~~rather~~ different mainly because my ~~own~~ father was so involved in his community, ~~of Sanger when he worked there.~~ He was in the Kiwanis club, ate breakfast and hobnobbed with the downtown folks every weekday, was active in the Methodist church, *announced* ~~was the announcer~~ at the annual Christmas Day Parade, and seemed to know everyone in town.

This may sound cynical, but I know *much* ~~a lot~~ of my father's involvement stemmed from his job as superintendent of schools. He needed the support of the community to pass bond elections and do his job effectively, so he got involved. When I see the people who serve on

city council or volunteer committees or who are active in service

clubs, ~~most~~ *many* of them, ~~it seems,~~ have a stake in the community ~~because of their professions~~: downtown businessmen, doctors and dentists, realtors, bankers, restaurant owners. Visibility in community

wordy—revise affairs helps their image and their businesses, and they do a lot of "networking" through their community contacts.

reword—stuffy sounding Having said that, I know it's only partly true, a somewhat defensive reaction of mine based on a residue of guilt I harbor for not being involved. I know there are also ~~numerous~~ *many* people who serve the community for selfless reasons. They simply want to help make

Reedley a better place for people to live, and they feel they owe the

wordy community something by residing in it. These people I respect, but

I've never identified with them.

Perhaps as with most relationships in life, you get out of a community what you put into it. Since I've never put anything into Reedley, I don't feel a part of it or anything positive that happens here.

Reedley has worked hard to keep its downtown viable, ~~it has~~ *maintain* a decent school system, and ~~it's~~ *provide* a safe place *for families* to live~~, and raise a family.~~ While

wordy I've played no role in any of that, I have taken advantage of the

better word? positives. I've also taken them for granted.

combine into
one sentence ⎰ I'm not a big joiner, and I don't think I ever will be. I don't think
I'll ever join Rotary or run for the school board or the city council.

But there are a couple things I could do, perhaps the least anyone

should do for his or her community. First, I could patronize the

downtown businesses more, putting some of my own money back

into the community. Second, my wife and I could eat out more in

Reedley rather than going to Fresno all the time. ~~Reedley has some~~

~~nice restaurants, and they need the support of locals.~~ Third, I could

take an active role in the police department's "Neighborhood Watch"

crime prevention program. If other residents are helping to keep our

streets safe, I should do my share.

better   <u>Analyzing</u> my relationship with the community, I've taken
word?

stilted   its <u>positive aspects</u> for granted without making a contribution

reword   myself, aside from helping to educate <u>a number</u> of its residents.

It's not too late to start doing the things I've mentioned, and it

wouldn't be that difficult. I'm never going to make "citizen of the

year," and I'll probably never feel that close to Reedley, but at least

Perhaps
I can start doing a few things that will help the community. ~~I guess~~

that's the best way to feel a part of it, and if I'd taken that atti-

tude twenty years ago, I might feel ~~much~~ different about Reedley

today.

**First Draft-
Reflections**

The first draft developed as I had planned during prewriting: to present and analyze my attitude towards Reedley. I didn't know how I was going to conclude the paper, but as I wrote, I started thinking more about making a contribution to the community. It wouldn't be a big deal, but it would be something. So that's how I ended the essay, and I hope that I follow through with what I wrote.

This wasn't an exciting essay to write, mainly because I'm not excited about where I live. Still, it was useful for me because it helped me understand my feelings and gave me some ideas on improving the situation. I'm not sure how interesting it's going to be for anyone to read.

I decided I didn't want a "preachy" ending for my readers about getting involved in their communities since I am the last person to be making that suggestion. Rather, I tried to express my feelings honestly so that readers might think about their own communities. I wanted readers to take what they could from the essay to apply to their own experience.

Journal Entry 20

Relate your own first-draft experience: how the writing went, how you used your prewriting plans, and how you feel about the draft.

Revisions

On reading my first draft, I was reasonably satisfied with its content and organization. I'd included most of what I wanted to say, and the paragraphing and order of ideas made sense. I couldn't think of anything better to do with the conclusion, so I left it basically the same. I'm still not sure how much readers will get from the essay, but I can't think of other revisions that would help. I think I've written the truth, and I'll leave it at that. (My final draft is at the end of the chapter.)

As always, most of my first-draft sentences were rather "flabby," and I made numerous wording revisions. As examples, I've paired up a number of first- and second-draft sentences so you can see the changes I made, and then added an explanation for each revision.

1. When asked how I like living in the town of Reedley, I always say it's a nice place, and mean it. (Readers will know Reedley is a town, and "mean it" adds nothing.)

Revised: When asked how I like living in Reedley, I always say its a nice place.

2. I've never really considered myself a 'Reedleyite" and don't identify with the town or anything about it. ("Really" adds nothing; "the town or anything about it" is redundant.)

Revised: I've never considered myself a Reedleyite and don't identify with anything about the town.

3. It is this ambivalent attitude toward Reedley that I've carried since I came here. (The construction "it is . . . that" is unnecessary.)

Revised: I've carried this ambivalent attitude toward Reedley since I came here.

4. They were an established and well-to-do group of German stock people with midwestern roots who practiced the Mennonite religious faith. ("German stock people" is awkward; "religious faith" sounds redundant.. . . .

Revised: They were an established, well-to-do group of German descendants with midwestern roots who practiced the Mennonite faith.

5. I did enjoy attending my children's activities as they went through the schools, and I taught a lot of the town's kids to swim when I was the local swimming coach, but other than that, I established few ties with the community. (A wordy, wandering sentence. Needs serious revision.)

Revised: Other then attending my children's school activities and coaching the local swim team for a few years, I established few community ties.

6. The forty-minute drive to Fresno became a regular occurrence. I lived in Reedley but often ate out, went to movies, shopped, and socialized in Fresno. (First sentence is boring and too general; it needs to be active. I can also combine the sentences.)

Revised: I drove to Fresno once or twice a week and, while I lived in Reedley, I often ate out, went to movies, shopped, and socialized in Fresno.

7. I admired the 1988 renovation of the downtown area, when they planted trees and flowers along the main street, added benches, and spruced up the facades of many of the buildings; however, I still didn't shop much there. (More detail than needed to make the point; my not shopping downtown is the main thing.)

Revised: I admired the 1988 downtown renovation when they planted trees and spruced up the buildings; however, I still didn't shop there much.

8. Having said that, I know it's only partly true, a somewhat defensive reaction of mine based on a residue of guilt I harbor for not being involved. (Wordy and stuffy sounding, especially that "residue of guilt I harbor." "It's" has nothing clear to refer to.)

Revised: However, I know that theory is not completely accurate, and it's part of my defense for not getting involved.

REVISION ASSIGNMENT 1

With a classmate, evaluate the following student first draft by applying the following revision guidelines.

1. What do you like about the essay (find interesting, informative, or thought provoking)? Cite specific examples.

2. What questions would you like the essay to answer (things that could be answered with an example, an explanation, or a detail or two)? Give specific examples.

3. What, if anything, do you not understand or find confusing in the essay? Cite examples.

4. Does the essay wander off topic distractingly at any point? Cite specific examples.

5. How well is the essay organized and paragraphed? Would you recommend any organizational or paragraphing revisions to make the essay clearer or more effective?

6. Find examples of sentences that need revising because of wordiness, awkwardness, or lack of clarity. How might you revise these sentences?

7. What approach is the writer taking towards her subject? How effectively does she present it, and why?

8. How effective are the opening and conclusion of the essay? How did you respond to each? Why?

9. What audience do you think the essay is intended for? What is the writer trying to accomplish, and how well does she do it?

10. What other revision suggestions would you offer the writer to make the essay clearer, more interesting, or more focused?

11. Are there some errors that you would point out to the writer?

STUDENT FIRST DRAFT

Then and Now

The town of Calabasas was a very secluded place with only two new houses that had beautiful surroundings in the front and back yards. A view of green meadows, oak trees, horses, and wild flowers.

When the Bell family first moved to Calabasas, California there were only two brand new houses next to each other on a huge lot. Behind our new house there was a beautiful view of a green meadow with a running creek down the middle of the meadow. In this meadow there is a huge, beautiful oak tree and along the highway is a white wooden fence. In front of the house, across the road is another vacant lot with lots of wild flowers growing all over and with a old red barn on one side. Directly across the road from our driveway on the same vacant lot is a small coral of Arbrain horses running free on their part of the land.

As years passed by the land started to develop. The lovely surrounds were now replaced with tract homes and neighbors.

After thirteen years, our little neighborhood in Calabasas has changed dramatically. Within the first five years, the green meadow with the running creek and the white wooden fence has been torn down. Now the Bell family has a lovely view of ten houses crammed closely together, but the builders couldn't take the oak they built around it. Years later, the oak tree eventually died and was taken out. After the first two years the Arbraian horses were taken away and there went up another house. We still had half of the vacant lot left. All the kids in the neighborhood made forts and bike trails in that part of the lot. But in time they sold the lot and new nine houses were built. Now that there are all new houses in the neighborhood the first two original houses do not look that new anymore, even though they are only thirteen years old.

Even though the Bell family has lost there beautiful views from there backyard and front yard. Their house and property has gone up in value. Also they gained several new neighbors.

REVISION ASSIGNMENT 2

Read your first draft, using the revision guidelines to aid your evaluation. When you have some general ideas for revision, exchange drafts with a classmate and get a second opinion. Then write your second draft, including all revisions you have noted to improve it.

Journal Entry 21

Relate the types of revisions you made in your draft. How do you feel your second draft compares to the first, and why?

Editing

The final step in readying your essay for readers is to proofread it for errors. Errors in a final draft may prejudice readers against the essay in general. Sometimes when I read an error-riddled paper, I find myself focusing more on the problems than on the writer's ideas. It's almost impossible to judge an essay's content fairly when errors get in the way.

EDITING ASSIGNMENT 1

Before editing your own essay, pair up with a classmate and proofread the following student draft for errors in punctuation, grammar, and spelling, correcting those you find.

STUDENT FIRST DRAFT

Being Different

Most of my childhood I was criticized for being different. The reason I was different from the rest of the children was because of my religion, I was a Jehovah Witness.

At school, I wasnt able to particepate in any holiday or patriotic activities. Because my religion forbid it. While the other children were doing their Christmas or Halloween cut-outs or coloring I was in the school office doing an assignment. In the morning when the class would say the pledge of allegance to the flag I always stood outside.

Jehovah Witnesses believed that celebrating holidays was pagan behavior. However because I was young I didnt understand why I had to be different. The only attention I got from other kids was when they made fun of me and the only ones who I could hang around were rejects like myself. Grade school was not a happy time for me.

Once I got to high school my family, and me stopped attending the Jehovah Witness church. My attitude began to change a lot, and I become more independent. Now I was able to talk to a whole new group of people without getting put down, it felt great.

When Christmas and all the other holidays came around it felt wierd to me. At Christmas I was finally able to give, and except presents. At Halloween I could dress up in a costume and go to parties like everyone else. But the day that I enjoy the most was my birthday. I had never had a birthday party until I was fifteen years old.

Some of my friends still teases me to this day, about my childhood as a Jehovah Witness. They ask me, What happened to that quiet and shy Teresa that we went to elementary school with? I just tell them to shut up. That Teresa no longer exists.

It's been four years now that my family and me celebrated holidays, and we love it. We look forward to them all the time, probably a lot more than most people do. I still dont understand what Jehovah

Witnesses saw wrong with celebrating such events, they are wonderful times for families to be together.

EDITING ASSIGNMENT 2

Proofread your latest draft for errors, and get a classmate's opinion if you feel the need. Refer to the editing guidelines (Chapter 9) if you need some help with a particular error problem. Then write the final error-free draft of your essay.

Journal Entry 22

What kinds of errors did you find in your latest draft, and why did you think you made them? How might you work toward eliminating such errors in future writing?

AUTHOR'S FINAL DRAFT

Living in Reedley

When asked how I like living in Reedley, I always say it's a nice place. Situated in the agriculturally rich San Joaquin Valley a half hour from the Sierra Nevada mountains, Reedley has about 15,000 residents, a pleasant downtown area, a lovely river along its western border, and its own college.

At the same time, while I've lived in Reedley over twenty years, I still don't feel connected to the town, and if I moved tomorrow I don't think I'd miss it. I've never considered myself a "Reedleyite" and don't identify with anything about the town. While I can honestly tell people it's a nice place to live, I don't feel a part of it.

I've carried this ambivalent attitude toward Reedley since I came here. I grew up in the neighboring town of Sanger, and all I knew about Reedley was that we beat them regularly in sports. My first twenty years, I seldom set foot in Reedley, and I couldn't have told you how to get there from Sanger. When I came to Reedley to live, Sanger was still home to me, and I had little regard for my new community.

Beyond that, I'd heard a lot about how the Mennonites ran the town. They were an established, well-to-do group of German descendants with midwestern roots who practiced the Mennonite faith. Their religion didn't bother me, but their dominating the town (or any group, for that matter) didn't seem right. When I first taught at the high school, I was warned that teachers shouldn't be seen drinking in local bars. That Mennonite influence, I assumed.

Whether the Mennonites had undue influence in town, I can't really say, because I had little to do with Reedley or its politics. Other than attending my children's school activities and coaching the local swim team for a few years, I established few community ties.

Going over to the college to teach further removed me from the community. That may sound strange, but it turned out that about 90 percent of the college teachers didn't live in Reedley. Instead, they chose to live forty minutes away in Fresno, a city with 500,000 residents. Most of my college friends had no attachment to Reedley, and over the years my social life revolved around these people. I drove to Fresno once or twice a week and, while I lived in Reedley, I often ate out, went to movies, shopped and socialized in Fresno.

Things didn't change over the years. I never joined any social or service clubs in town. I admired the 1988 downtown renovation, when they planted trees and spruced up the buildings; however, I still didn't shop there much. When I attended the annual Reedley Rotary auction on free tickets from my neighbor, I knew very few people and felt more like an outsider than a community member. And when my kids graduated from high school, I lost my one remaining connection to town through the school system.

I don't know whether my attitude toward Reedley is unusual or not. Perhaps more people than I realize live in places they don't feel attached to. I've considered my attitude different mainly because my father was so involved in his community. He was in the Kiwanis Club, ate breakfast and hobnobbed with folks downtown every weekday, was active in the Methodist church, announced the annual Christmas Day Parade, and seemed to know everyone in town.

This may sound cynical, but I know much of my father's involvement stemmed from his job as superintendent of schools. He needed the community's support to pass bond elections and do his job effectively, so he got involved. When I see the people who serve on city council or volunteer committees, or who are active in service clubs, many of them have a business stake in the community: downtown businessmen, doctors and dentists, realtors, bankers, restaurant owners. Community visibility helps their image and their businesses, and they "network" through community contacts.

However, I know that self-interest is not the only reason for community involvement, and that I use it as an excuse for not getting involved. There are also people who serve the community selflessly, wanting to help make Reedley a better place to live, and feeling they owe something to their community. These people I respect, but I've never identified with them.

Perhaps, as with most relationships, you get out of a community what you put into it. Since I've put nothing into Reedley, I don't feel a part of it or anything positive that happens here. Reedley has worked hard to keep its downtown viable, maintain a decent school system, and provided a safe place for families to live. While I'm responsible for none of that, I have taken advantage of all of it. I've also taken such things for granted.

Knowing myself as I do, I doubt that I will ever join Rotary or run for the school board or the city council. But there are things I could do—perhaps the least anyone should do for his or her community. First, I could patronize the downtown businesses, putting some of my money back into the community. Second, I could be active in the police department's Neighborhood Watch crime prevention program. If other residents are helping to keep our streets safe, I should do my share.

Looking at my relationship with the community, I've taken Reedley's good points for granted without contributing myself, aside from teaching at the college. It's never too late to start doing the things I've mentioned, and it wouldn't be that hard. I'll never make "citizen of the year," but at least I can do a few things to help the community. Perhaps that's the best way to feel a part of it, and if I'd taken that attitude twenty years ago, I might feel different toward Reedley today.

Chapter Four

Considering Your Audience

With every sentence I write in this book, I have my readers somewhere in mind. I try to envision how individual student reading the text might respond. After twenty years of teaching, I know my reading audience fairly well.

This does not mean that you are carbon copies. I know that you are male and female; of all ages and ethnic backgrounds; single, married, and divorced; many working full- or part-time; some with majors, some undecided; some certain about your future, others not sure what you'll be doing next semester. When I write, I try to keep your diversity in mind, but I also write to your similarities, as well as to what you and I have in common.

First, I know most of you want to do well in your writing course, whether for the grade, the units, the requirement, or the personal satisfaction. You also strive to write things that are worth reading. While you may not greatly enjoy writing, once you have written something you value, you are interested in how readers will respond. Most of you also want to get along with your classmates, and enjoy being in classes where you get to know them better.

As to what we have common, first we are all writers. In that respect we share a lot: the struggle to find things to write about and get our ideas on paper, the need to revise our drafts to improve them, and the desire for positive feedback from our readers. Since we share a common lot as writers, I show you my drafts and talk about my writing process. I also share your doubts about whether some things I write are worth reading or whether I have anything of interest to say on a particular topic.

Beyond that, we share the writing world of the classroom, the occasional boredom of writing or reading those papers that don't interest us, the pleasure of writing about something that we care about, and the satisfaction of seeing other people enjoying our writing.

I also share with some of you the tendency to put off writing until a deadline approaches, and the preference for writing something new over revising a draft, which I sometimes put off for days. Finally, as writers, we are trying to please others: you, to get a grade; I, to get my manuscripts published.

ABOUT THE AUDIENCE

Having thought and written about you, my reader, let me tell you how these considerations affected my writing.

1. Throughout the book, I write to you as one writer to another, both of us becoming better as we work together through this text.

2. I write to you as a friend (I am a friend to most of my students) and I communicate with you friend-to-friend about your writing. I see you as a person in many ways like myself, and I try to communicate on that level.

3. I never "write down" to students. I know what I know, and you know what you know, and I learn as much from students like yourself as you do from me. Of course, I should know more about writing than you do, but that doesn't make me better or smarter. You will know more about *your* job than I do.

4. I keep your diversity as a group in mind to make sure I don't write papers or provide examples of interest to only a few: men, 19-year olds, Californians, full-time students, city dwellers, or older returning students. Because you won't all have the same interest in a topic, I try to provide a range of topics and examples in the text, some of which I hope will appeal to each of you.

5. I keep in mind that writing courses may not be your favorite, and that a writing text may be the last book you want to open. Knowing this, I try to keep my tone conversational, my approach fairly personal, and my suggestions practical, so that you won't mind reading and working through the book.

6. I try to avoid wordiness. I'm probably more interested in writing than you are, and I can drone on and on about it. However, as a student I preferred textbooks that got to the point and presented information clearly and concisely. So I try to keep the reading segments brief and focus on what's most important—your writing.

7. I try to avoid composition jargon and to define terms that I do use. Composition teachers talk about making meaning, writer/reader response, writer- and reader-based prose, recursiveness in writing, protocols, metacognition, modeling, reflexive writing, and other things that mean nothing to most people. When some of that jargon creeps into my prose, I either explain it or replace it with more familiar terms.

General Guidelines

Now that you know my audience considerations for student readers, here are some general guidelines for your reading audiences.

1. What do you know about your readers? What are their ages, ethnic backgrounds, genders, and education levels, and how might these factors influence the way you write?

2. How much do your readers know about the topic? Do they know relatively little, or perhaps as much or more than you?

3. How do your readers feel about the topic: indifferent? interested? supportive or opposed to your viewpoint? How will their attitude affect the way you write?

4. Why are you writing to this particular audience? How do you want them to respond, and how can you best accomplish this purpose?

5. What specific things should you keep mind about this particular audience as you write?

 **AUDIENCE ASSIGNMENT 1**

Assume you are going to write short essays on one of the following topics to the two different audiences presented. Based on the topic you choose, analyze each audience and write a paragraph on what you would keep in mind while writing to them. Apply the five audience guidelines to aid your analysis.

Next, write a short essay (a couple hundred words) on the topic for *one* of the audiences. I'll do the same assignment for a different topic and different audiences so I won't use up one of the choices.

1. Write an essay opposing the proposed 20 percent tuition increase at your college for next school year. The current tuition is $700 a semester. Your two reading audiences: the Board of Trustees who proposed the increase, and students of the college, who will read your essay in the school paper.

2. Write an essay supporting the college's installing condom machines in the men's and women's restrooms. Your two reading audiences: the student council, who must approve the measure, and one of the local church councils, whose members have publicly opposed the issue.

3. Write an essay opposing the proposal to sell beer in the campus pizza parlor. Your two reading audiences: the teachers of the college, and the intra-fraternity council, whose members have made the proposal.

4. Write an essay supporting a proposal that the college library be opened on weekends, 9 to 5 on Saturdays, and Sunday afternoons. It is currently open only Monday through Friday. Your two reading audiences: the librarians, and the college business manager, who is leading the opposition for financial reasons.

5. Write an essay supporting the building of a swimming pool on your college campus, which currently doesn't have one. Your reading audiences: drama students on campus, who instead want the money spent on renovations to their theater arts building, and students from the elementary schools in town.

For my topic, I am going to write an essay in support of building a football stadium on our campus. (Our team plays at a local high school stadium.) Like you, I am writing a "canned" essay because, first, this isn't currently an issue at my college and, second, I don't have a strong opinion one way or the other. My two audiences: the academic faculty, who opposed a stadium about ten years ago, and the student body.

Faculty audience considerations: I know a lot of faculty who've been around for a while have opposed the stadium for years, but I don't know how new faculty feel. They probably don't know much about the issue and need a little background. Our academic faculty aren't crazy about athletics on campus, and I know they see a stadium as a waste of money and a symbol of overemphasis on sports. I can't expect some kind of miraculous turnaround in their attitude, but maybe I could at least neutralize them so they wouldn't unite to take a strong stand against a stadium. I'm not sure yet on what basis I can get them to look more favorably on a stadium; that will be my challenge. I'll write the essay in a tone sympathetic to their feelings. They are my colleagues, and I want them to understand I am not the enemy on this issue.

Student-body audience considerations: As for the student body, I know this will be a generally supportive group, and I can come up with a number of good "self-interest" reasons for their supporting a stadium that I couldn't use successfully with the faculty. I know there are some who share faculty concerns about the expense and overemphasis on sports, and others just attend school at night and aren't involved in campus life; I'll have to address both groups. My tone for this essay will be enthusiastic, and my purpose will be to get the active support of a majority of students for building the stadium.

To complete the assignment, I've decided to address the faculty, because that is the bigger challenge for this topic. I know what I'd write to students, but writing for faculty on this issue will be an adventure. I have to keep in mind that this is a short essay assignment and limit myself to a few hundred words.

AUTHOR'S FIRST DRAFT—TO THE ACADEMIC FACULTY

As you probably know, our college football team plays its games at the high school because we don't have a stadium. About ten years ago a proposal for an on-campus stadium came up, and many of you were adamant in your opposition. At that time, I myself didn't line up with the stadium advocates.

Since then I've attended a few games at the high school, and the atmosphere is not great. It's not a particularly nice facility, and there's no collegiate atmosphere. Football players have written papers about not liking to play there, and the location and facility don't attract many student spectators. I know how the coaches feel, and I'm not sure I'd be enthusiastic either about teaching my college classes at the high school.

If you're not a supporter of the football program these points may not interest you, so let me make a couple that might. The coaches are our teaching colleagues. They put in the same hours we do and are just as dedicated to their jobs. Not having a stadium on campus hurts their recruiting and program effectiveness, and they are evaluated publicly every Saturday by whether they win or lose. How would any of us hold up under that kind of weekly scrutiny? I admire their dedication, as I do yours, and I'm not comfortable coming out strongly against something they need to do their job the best they can: an on-campus stadium.

We're too small a faculty to pull apart on such issues. When we split on this issue, we also split our students, and those ninety football players are also my writing students and your sociology and psychology students.

Is the stadium issue so crucial to us that we publicly attack what is important to our coaching colleagues? And what happens when some of us push for a new theater arts building in a few years? We're going to need total faculty support, including the cooperation of our coaching colleagues. Why should they support us if we publicly undermine their program?

I'm not suggesting we carry banners for the new stadium. I am suggesting that we not mobilize efforts against it, as occurred ten years ago. Politically, let's give the coaches their day—so that one day soon they can help us have ours. Let's pull together as teachers.

When I wrote the draft, I really wasn't sure where it was heading but, as often happens, ideas came to me as a product of writing—ideas I may not have come up with otherwise.

Six things came to me at different times. First, I wanted my readers to look at the coaches as their dedicated colleagues. Second, I wanted them to see how splitting a small faculty on an issue of importance was counterproductive. Third, I wanted them to see the football players as their students, people they care about.

Fourth, I thought some would appreciate the politics of needing faculty support for the theater arts building, which we couldn't get if we torpedoed the stadium plans. Fifth, I didn't necessarily want to talk them out of their position, which they could hold privately without mounting public opposition. Finally, I found myself naturally using the pronoun *we*, aligning myself with teaching colleagues whom I identify with. There was no attempt to be clever; I felt no need to separate myself from them. Rereading the essay, I think *we* works better than *you* would.

Journal Entry 22

Write about your own draft: why you picked the topic how your audience influenced it, what you wanted to accomplish with your readers, and what you did in the draft to be successful.

AUDIENCE ASSIGNMENT 2

Here is a second audience-related activity to do before writing your next essay. Taking into consideration the different audiences presented, write a paragraph on the kinds of changes—in content, approach, presentation, expectations—you would make in a speech to each audience on the following topic.

Topic: What We Can Do to Improve Our Environment

Let's assume you've researched the subject and know a lot about the environment and how we can improve it. You will speak to the following audiences:

1. a class of second-grade students
2. a class of high-school seniors
3. a group of working mothers
4. a group of transients at a local rescue mission

Audience as Tyrant

Now that you are focused intently on your reading audience, you may have little else in mind when writing your next paper. When I've stressed comma usage in classes, commas sprout up all over students' papers, often where they aren't needed. To balance your concern for audience, let me add the following.

1. Don't be so concerned about audience that you worry over every word you write. Sometimes writers become so obsessed with what their readers might think that they write out of fear. If you find that audience concerns are making it more difficult for you to write, you are worrying too much.

2. Don't change what you believe to please your audience. There is a difference between bending your beliefs and presenting them in ways that may appeal to readers. If you find yourself writing things you don't really believe, your audience is controlling your writing instead of you.

3. While audience consideration is important, the most important concern is what you have to say. If you think more about your readers than your message, you may end up writing little of interest to anyone. Content is the heart of your writing. The role of audience consideration is to help you package that content most effectively.

4. No audience is homogeneous. No matter how specific an audience you are writing for, there are going to be differences among people: in their personalities, intelligence, interest in your topic, beliefs, sense of humor, experiences, emotional make-up, and resistance to change. There is seldom a common audience response to a writing, unless your audience is one person. Realizing that, for any essay you write, expect varied responses from readers based on their individuality.

CHAPTER WRITING ASSIGNMENT

For this chapter's essay, select any topic, with one consideration: include a comparison in your essay. The reason for the comparison is to give you a different writing experience from earlier chapters. Emphasizing comparison requires certain writing skills and considerations that will help you grow as a writer.

Along with selecting your topic, decide on the approach you want to take (thesis), the audience you want to write for, and your purpose for writing. Before writing the first draft, do one or more prewriting activities to generate ideas and discover a good approach to your topic.

All of your prewriting considerations—audience, topic approach, purpose—may not be apparent at first; at least they aren't always with me. Sometimes I have to get into the writing before deciding who would be the best reading audience or what in particular I want to accomplish. Other times I know where I'm heading and who my audience is from the start. However, it isn't always possible, or even desirable, to have everything planned out before writing.

The most enjoyable part of writing this book occurs for me now: going through the writing process along with you, from topic selection to final draft. I'm glad we are choosing our own topics. I feel more enthusiastic about writing this essay than the one for the audience-consideration activity. It wasn't much fun writing on a "canned" topic in which I had no real interest. Selecting my own topic, I choose from a world of possibilities, a liberating way to begin.

AUTHOR'S PREWRITING THOUGHTS

I'm going to stop at this point, eat lunch, relax a while, and do some casual thinking about using a comparison as part of the essay.

After a couple hours, I've thought about and discarded a lot of topics. I'm a basketball fan, and I could write an essay comparing the talents of two basketball stars, or on why men's basketball is much more popular than women's, or on the differing styles of East and West Coast teams. However, I can hear a lot of you yawning already.

Then I thought about comparing cars, like the Honda Accord and Toyota Camry, but decided that didn't interest me enough. Next I thought about comparing teaching jobs at different levels—elementary, high school, and college—because I've taught at all of them, but why should I prejudice future teachers against or in favor of a particular level? I thought about weather because it's hot and the compressor on our air conditioner went out yesterday, and on how the heat on the West Coast compared to the Deep South (places I've spent some time). But I'd be lucky to get a hundred words out of that topic.

Then I thought about comparing marrying young and having children to marrying later and having children. I figured, because the majority of you aren't married yet, this would be a topic that might interest you, and those of you who are married might compare my viewpoint to your own.

I went as far as to begin my first draft, but as I wrote I realized there are big differences between twenty-five years ago, when I married, and today. In the sixties, we could rent a house for $90 a month, and most wives didn't work. Today's economic reality is so different that what I know about getting married in the late sixties may not be relevant today. I gave up on the topic.

However, from starting that draft I got another idea: Why not compare the situation of students coming out of college in my day to students graduating today? That's something I think about quite a bit, and something readers might be interested in. I'll get into the draft to see where it heads and whether I can make it relevant for you.

STUDENT WRITERS' RESPONSES

Gwen

Well, recently I got a new boyfriend. We've been together now for a few weeks, and he's great. I can't help comparing him to my old boyfriend whom I broke up with about a year ago. What a difference.

I wouldn't mind writing a paper comparing these two guys and our relationships, as long as neither of them ever read the paper. Well, I guess I wouldn't mind my current boyfriend reading it, but not my ex!

After breaking up with my old boyfriend, I had decided that boys were the pits. The situation had gotten bad. But now with my new boyfriend, I see that the right person makes all the difference. So I've got a tentative approach to my paper. Something like "Don't stay in a bad relationship, because there is someone out there you can be happy with."

I feel like writing to the girls in my class because it seems that girls worry more about relationships working and have more problems with crummy guys than vice versa. I'd certainly feel more comfortable writing to girls, and I really don't have any advice for guys. So I think I've got my audience. I'll get started and see if I can really write about this. If it seems too personal or like I'm just dumping all over my ex, maybe I'll try something else.

Harry

Man, I miss my hometown of Washington, D.C. Here I am stuck out in a small town in the middle of California going to school and it's so boring. I came out to play basketball and I was thinking, "California, that's great. L.A., Disneyland, movie stars, beaches." But I'm stuck in a little country town nowhere near the city or the beach. What a shock.

I think I'll compare living in a big city, like D.C., to living in a small town, like where I am now. The small town isn't going to come out too well in the comparison, but I'll just give my opinion and be honest.

I'll bet most of the people in my writing class are small towners, so they may not like my paper, but maybe I can open their eyes to what it's like to live in a city. It may make them want to do some traveling or consider living elsewhere someday. I'll write to them. My approach will definitely favor big city living, and I'll also try to bring out what's good about a small town, but it's definitely going to come out second.

Frank

I love country music. I mean real country music like Willie Nelson, Johnny Cash, and Waylon Jennings sing. And younger singers like Randy Travis and Hank Williams Jr. are carrying on the tradition. But I don't care for the "crossover" singers who make country popular with bigger audiences, like Kenny Rogers did in the late seventies and Billy Ray Cyrus and Garth Brooks are doing now.

I'm going to compare real country music to what I call "country pop," and along with the music I'll compare the singers and the audiences who are into each. To me country pop isn't real country music, people who sing it aren't real country singers, and people who like it aren't real country music fans. That's my approach, and I'll share it with anyone who thinks he or she is a country music fan. I'll probably get some country pop people mad, but that's fine. They need some musical education.

Journal Entry 23

Relate your process for deciding on a topic: what possibilities did you consider before deciding on one topic? How did you work in a comparison? Then, relate your prewriting activity and how it helped you prepare to write.

AUTHOR'S FIRST DRAFT

Changing Times

Times have sure changed, and I'm not sure it's for the better. When

I think about what it would be like to start out as a young person in the world today, I get a little scared, and I ~~hold~~ *feel* the same ~~fear~~ *way* for my

grown children, ~~who are about to embark.~~ The world ~~is not getting to~~ *has not become*

be an easier place to live, and I'm not sure ~~how well my generation~~ *I've*

~~has~~ prepared ~~our~~ *my* children ~~to cope.~~ *for that*⊙

When I went to college, it was four years and out with a degree

that would get you a job. Coming out of college, I had four different

high-school teaching jobs to choose among, and I wasn't anything

special. Most of my friends got jobs in other fields with similar ease.

different point— *new paragraph to* *develop it* (I was married while in college, but when I got the job, my wife didn't

have to work because our rent was only $90 a month, less than

10 percent of my monthly income.

We had our son Tim in our second year of marriage and our

daughter Lori in our fourth. Before Lori came along we had already

bought a nice home for $25,000. I had gotten my Master's degree

through summer school and night classes, and had moved from

teaching at the high school to the local college. Now our house pay-

ments were up to $200 a month, but my income had more than dou-

bled in four years, so I was still paying less than 10 percent of

my income on house payments. ~~Twenty years later, with my in-~~

delete— *irrelevant* ~~come nearly tripling, my payments are less than 5 percent of my~~

~~income.~~

We certainly didn't live like kings and queens over the years, but we were comfortable and our children never wanted for anything. By choice, my wife stayed home until the children were through high school, and then she went back and finished college, ~~and~~ eventually *getting* ~~got~~ a teaching job. While helping to put our children through college was the biggest financial drain we'd faced, we managed (and are still managing) all right ~~and they are getting close to the end.~~ In a nutshell, life has been good, and there haven't been any great hardships. ~~Pretty smooth sailing.~~

wordy— revise

It's a different world ~~out there~~ today. First, for the professions my children are interested in, as well as a majority of others, a four-year degree means little. Graduate school is often a necessity rather than an option, and we're talking three to five more years. By and large, young adults are getting out into the "real world" later and later.

And once they're out there, what do they find? No guaranteed jobs, that's for sure. In my profession in California, we have about 50,000 part-time teachers, all armed with MA's and PhD's, trying to find full-time jobs. Most of them never will, and at some point will have to look elsewhere for employment. Similar situations are occurring in other professions; there are many more college graduates than there are jobs to fill, especially in hard economic times. I compare these situations to the five good jobs I could choose among my first year out of school, and the ease with which I moved into a college position.

insert 2 paragraphs from further on ⟶

Staying longer in school and finding full-time employment harder, young adults aren't marrying as early as in my day. I don't see this as bad, only different. While my wife and I were married at twenty-one, I don't see our children marrying before twenty-six or twenty-seven, after graduate school and employment. Maybe later marriages will have a positive impact on divorce

same paragraph

statistics.

Marrying later, young adults will also have their children later, which again may be a positive thing. I know I was still as much kid

new paragraph

as parent my first few years of marriage. But economics as they are, most young wives have to work these days rather than stay home the first years with their children. That I feel is a sad situation. While I fully support a woman's desire to work, I am saddened by an America where a woman has no choice but to work for the family to make ends meet. And to what degree do children of working mothers suffer by their not being around from 9 to 5 during the children's formative years? I think on how much my children would have missed had my wife not been home for them every day. My daughter probably won't have that choice.

I don't have to tell you about housing. Nowhere has the Ameri-[f]can dream become more nightmarish than in housing costs. While[f]10 percent of my salary went to monthly house payments twenty years ago, over 30 percent of my salary would go to payments if I were to buy a comparable house today. And I live in a relatively low-property-value area of California. If I lived in Southern California or the Bay Area, I would have a very difficult time buying a house at all.

move paragraphs back to follow jobs paragraph

What of my children and other young adults? They have that same thirst for home ownership that my generation did, and they'll eventually end up getting their houses. In return, wives will be signing thirty-year work commitments along with those thirty-year mortgages, children will become long-term wards of day-care centers, and the family castle will take a sizeable chunk of the monthly income forever, not to mention the high rate of repossessions on less fortunate home buyers.

conclusion begins

Have I in any way prepared my children for the nineties and beyond? I always felt as long as I provided them a college education, everything would be fine. Now I'm not so sure. They are certainly looking to the future optimistically, and why not? Life has been relatively smooth for them since day one, and I wanted it no other way. But what happens when they can't get a job, not just this year but the next one, or when they can't afford a house close to as nice as the one they lived in for eighteen years? What happens if my daughter wants to stay home with her newborn for at least a couple years but can't afford to quit her job or take a leave? These are tough situations that my wife and I and many of our generation never had to face, and it saddens me that my children and other young adults will more than likely have to.

consider deleting some of paragraph— longish

Perhaps I worry too much about what's in store for my children. I just see potential serious obstacles ahead in their lives that I never faced, and I'm not sure they have the toughness to deal with them. If they do, I know I didn't help put it there. But I can take blame, along with my generation, for putting up those obstacles. It was our greediness that touched off the wild property speculation of the eighties that created the soaring housing costs, and it is our reluctance to give up jobs, even after thirty or thirty-five years, that lengthens the unemployment lines for college graduates. Not to mention, of course, the environment we are leaving to them and the knowledge that marriage is something that usually ends in divorce.

They are the children of so many broken homes, a legacy that they will sadly pass on to their children.

off topic— stay with one generation

And if college education is expensive today, what will it cost my children's children to go to college twenty years from now? If college costs and housing costs continue to escalate, how will any parent be able afford to $40,000 or $50,000 a year for their child's college expenses? Then there's the skyrocketing medical costs to consider, and on and on. While my grandparents had it better than theirs, my parents better than my grandparents, and my wife and I better than our parents, I don't see that pattern continuing for my children. I'm afraid their generation will be the first to face the unravelling of the American dream.

There are things my generation can still do to help, such as push for affordable housing, national health care, and retirement incentive plans that will help create jobs for college graduates. However, with housing and medical expenses, the genie has been out of the bottle so long that I doubt we can squeeze him back in. I do see parents who are able helping their children out long after college graduation, particularly with things like housing down payments, car purchases (yet another inflated expense relative to the sixties and seventies), and educational expenses for their children's children.

I don't see that as a particularly good situation either for the parents or for their adult children, but I feel my generation has to take some responsibility for the economic situation we helped to create.

Where's the silver lining in all of this? I wish I knew. I could tell my children that owning their own home and having a nice car and a swimming pool really has little to do with happiness, but hearing this from a person who has the home, car, and pool, why should they listen? I'm not even sure I believe it myself, having bought into the American dream long ago. But rather than bring them down with my worrying, I try to feed off of their optimism, their sense that everything will work out fine in their lives. And maybe it will. I hate to end

divide last paragraph here

with my father's old bromide that "things always work out for the best," but I can think of nothing better to say. Maybe they do work out for the best, because we all have the capacity to make the best of

Consider audience change—more adult reading audience

what we have. And perhaps my children will find happiness and success in their lives well beyond what I ever found. Their economic reality is grounded in the nineties, while I'm still longing for the 10-cent double-scooped ice cream cone of my youth. Maybe I'm really the one with the coping problem

FIRST-DRAFT REFLECTIONS

In the first draft, I found myself writing down everything that came to mind about problems my children's generation may face in the future.

I let it all pour out. I'm not sure the paper didn't wander off track or whether it has a clear focus. It may also have some organizational problems. And I got so depressed writing it that I wonder if I wouldn't be depressing many of my readers about their future. Is that what I want to accomplish? I'm going to read the entire paper before doing any revising to see what the overall picture looks like.

Journal Entry 24

Reflect on your own first draft—how the drafting process went and how you feel about the draft.

REVISIONS

As I reread the draft, my suspicions proved right. While the first part of the comparison is not bad, I ramble on about my children's life. I get into things I didn't bring up in the first part of the comparison, and some of my paragraphs don't know when to end. I'm sure with some things I brought up, readers would ask "What's the point?" In my ending paragraphs I'm reaching out and trying to make sense of what's happening today, but it reads as if I'm thinking out loud on paper. The ending needs a lot of tightening and focusing to be effective. I've got some work to do.

After two hours' work on the draft, I'm much more satisfied. I must admit, however, that you are no longer the primary reading audience. As I revised, I realized that I was really talking to my own generation rather than today's college students. People my age are the ones who share my anxieties, and they are the ones with whom I feel like communicating on this subject.

While I want you to read and evaluate the essay from your perspective, those of you younger than thirty might have your parents read it too. As you can see, I don't always know the most appropriate audience until I write something, or I may think an essay will be best for one audience and it turns out I'm really writing for another. You may have the same experience.

Revision Summary

I made more revisions in this paper than in earlier essays. First, the comparison added a new dimension to content and organization. Second, because I wasn't sure of my audience in the first draft, I wasn't sure what I wanted to accomplish, especially with the ending. Here is a summary of my revisions.

1. As always, I found ways to improve the wording of almost every sentence. As an example, let me put the first paragraph of each draft side by side so that you can see the changes I made. Compare each of the sentences and evaluate how each second draft sentence is improved over the first draft.

   First Draft:

   Times have sure changed, and I'm not sure it's for the better. When I think about what it would be like to start out as a young person in the world today, I get a little scared, and I hold the same fear for my grown children, who are about to embark. The world is not getting to be an easier place to live, and I'm not sure how well my generation has prepared our children to cope.

   Second Draft:

   Times have changed, and I'm not sure for the better. When I think what it would be like starting out as a young adult in today's world, I get a little scared, and I feel the same for my grown children. The world has not become an easier place to live, and I'm not sure I've prepared my children for that.

2. I made a lot of paragraphing changes, mainly because the second half of my comparison was poorly organized. First, I split the second paragraph of the first draft into two paragraphs because it was talking about two different things. Next, in the second half of the comparison, I noticed I had mixed negative and positive features in a confusing way. I also hadn't followed the content order that I used in the first part of the comparison, which might add to a reader's confusion.

   To take care of the problems, I moved the two paragraphs on the housing dilemma so they followed the paragraph on the bleak job market. Then I followed them with the paragraph on the third negative feature: how the economy was hurting the family unit. I concluded by moving and combining the only two positive paragraphs—both on the effects of young adults marrying later—to the end of the comparison. I feel the middle part of the paper is greatly improved.

   In my lengthy conclusion, which follows the paragraph on the positive results of young adults marrying later, I noticed that I'd written some very long paragraphs. In the second draft, I divided three of the longest paragraphs in half, creating six paragraphs.

3. I deleted some material from the first draft for several reasons. First, I had gone on too long about comparing the percentage of my salary that went toward mortgage payments, so I deleted the last sentence in paragraph 3. Near the end of the draft, I had gone off on the escalating costs of college education for my children's children, and on rereading, I realized that didn't belong in the conclusion because it was a point of comparison. I decided to delete it since it was not a problem that young adults faced in their near future, and the essay was plenty long already.

4. I focused the conclusion on the adult audience I had decided to write for. Once I settled on this audience, I emphasized the responsibility my generation shared for the problems our children were facing, and the things we should be doing to help. I added the point that, if our children have to struggle longer and harder than we did, we should share in their struggle.

5. I retained the last paragraph, but split it in two, because it says something about me and my perspective: I'm a worrier, and I've always tried to make everything "right" for my kids. My wife says I worry too much and try to control things I can't, so I decided on a somewhat positive conclusion: that my children may find more happiness and success than I, that they are better prepared than I would be to face the challenges of the nineties, and that perhaps I'm the one who needs to learn to cope. I feel okay about the last paragraph.

REVISION ASSIGNMENT 1

Before revising your own draft, read the following student first draft and, with a classmate, discuss and evaluate it using the following revision guidelines.

1. What do you like about the draft (find interesting, thought-provoking, amusing, informative, realistic)? Give specific examples.

2. How well did the comparison in the essay work for you? Did the comparison cover what you considered important aspects of the subjects being compared? What did you learn from the comparison? What might make it more effective?

3. How well is the essay organized? Are the points of comparison presented in a clear way? Does the organization confuse you in any places? What might give the essay a better organization?

4. What is accomplished in the opening, and how effective is it? How might the opening be improved?

5. How did you respond to the conclusion? What is the point of the ending, and how effective is it? Does it tie in well with the rest of the essay?

6. What questions do you have that you wish the essay would have answered? Give specifics on where an example, detail, or explanation would have helped.

7. What do you find confusing or difficult to understand in the essay? Give specific examples.

8. Does the essay seem to wander off topic anyplace? Give specific examples.

9. Identify sentences where wording could be improved to make them clearer, smoother, or less wordy, and consider specific ways to revise them.

10. How effectively is the essay paragraphed? Are different points (ideas, steps, incidents) presented in different paragraphs? Are there overly long paragraphs that need dividing or very short paragraphs that need combining or developing?

11. What is the writer's approach to his topic—the main point he is making? How clearly is this point made and supported?

12. What reading audience do you think the writer had in mind? What was his purpose in writing to them? How well do you think he accomplished his purpose? Why?

STUDENT WRITER DRAFT

Los Angeles vs. Reedley

Growing up in Los Angeles would be culture shock to most people here in Reedley; I know, I grew up there. This paper compares and contrasts the differences of an L.A. childhood versus that of a child in Reedley or any other small town.

When I first came to Reedley, I was shocked! People move so slow here. I grew up in Santa Ana; just a hop skip and a jump from Newport Beach. Things there were exciting every single day. Fast-paced living is the norm there, and frankly, what I'm used to. You can imagine the contrast, when I moved to this community to play basketball. My aunt and uncle have spent their entire lives here, and I don't think they knew what to expect when I moved in with them.

I was used to a dangerous lifestyle. It seemed as if there was always a gang to watch out for, or gunshots going off—something was always happening; plus everybody and their mom was hooked on some sort of narcotic. The whole environment engulfs you whether you like it or not. You quickly become just a face in the crowd. Your close friends become islands in huge oceans of people. I managed to become quite lonely in crowds of millions.

From what I've seen in Reedley, the kids here take a totally different perspective on life. They are so laid back, that they lack identity. I guess that's because of the smaller population. People here are content with being mediocre. They need to challenge themselves to become stronger people.

As for the environment here, the kids don't know what they have. Sure it's a bit on the dull side, but this place make you feel solid and secure. If I didn't have so many roots left at home, I might just consider finding a girl from this area and settling down. In my opinion, this is the best place to grow up; away from danger, and away from loneliness.

REVISION ASSIGNMENT 2

Read your own draft and note the kinds of revisions you want to make. Then exchange drafts with a classmate to get a second opinion. Finally, write the second draft of your essay, including all changes you feel will improve its focus, interest, development, organization, wording, or audience effectiveness.

Journal Entry 25

Relate the specific kinds of revisions you made in your second draft and why you made them. In what ways do you feel your draft has improved? Are you satisfied with your second draft, or do feel that your essay still needs more work? You may want to revise the draft further after taking a break from it.

EDITING

I'm at the point where I correct most of my errors during the drafting process, and you may be too. There's nothing wrong with correcting errors while revising your draft for other reasons.

By now you should have a good idea of the kinds of errors you tend to make, and you should concentrate on spotting and correcting those errors as you proofread your draft. You also know whether it helps to have someone else proofread your draft. While you don't want to rely on your classmates or instructor to edit your paper, you may still need help locating those errors you have trouble identifying.

EDITING ASSIGNMENT 1
Before editing your paper, proofread the following student draft and correct any punctuation, spelling, or grammatical errors that you find.

STUDENT WRITER DRAFT

Clothes and People

In my opinion, clothes can sometimes tell a lot about a persons attitude that day or every day. Clothes can also tell you who or what people like and how they spend their past time. Take for instance, people who wear very slinky clothes may just be wanting attention, but most likely they are trying to attract the opposite sex, either trying to experience as many people as possible or just trying to find the right one. This can also be said about people who wear tight clothes, but tight clothed people may have alterior motives like making themselves appear thinner or just showing off how thin they are. Another reason for wearing tight clothes may be to show off how big they are in the chest. Usually people who wear very little clothes such as bikinis or bathing suits are trying to get sun tans or showing off their tans.

People who wear plain clothes or baggy clothes are often not trying to appeal to the opposite sex, such as married people or people who have been going together for a long time. Plain and baggy clothed people may also have other things on their minds, such as school or work. Plain and baggy clothed people are often some of the nicer people in life.

Loud and rad colored clothes, or dark, dingy, and drab clothes can make a very big statements about a person. Loud and rad colors can mean a loud, roudy person or just someone looking to be noticed. This can also mean that this person has a sense of humor, or is very outgoing. Dark and drab clothes usually black or brown mean that a person is going through a phase of heavy metal, very hard rock or some sort of satanic thing. Most of the time people grow out of it. Dark clothes can also be a sign of rebeling by doing something they know their parents will disapprove of.

There is one thing out of all of the fashion statements thats a fact, clothes can't really tell you whats in a persons heart.

EDITING ASSIGNMENT 2

Now proofread your own essay for errors, and get a second opinion if you feel the need. Then write your error-free final draft.

Journal Entry 26

Relate your error-correction process. At what points in the writing process do you concern yourself with errors? Do you make corrections whenever you find them or just at the end of the process? Are you able to find and correct most of your own errors, or do you still need some help?

What, if any, error tendencies do you still have to watch out for? What are you doing to eliminate those types of errors from your writing?

AUTHOR'S FINAL DRAFT

Changing Times

Times have changed, and I'm not sure for the better. When I think what it would be like starting out as a young adult in today's world I get a little scared, and I feel the same for my grown children. The world has not become an easier place to live, and I'm not sure I've prepared my children for that.

When I went to college in the sixties, it was four years and out with a degree and a job practically guaranteed. After graduation, I had four high-school teaching jobs to choose among, and I was no one special. Most of my friends got jobs in other fields with similar ease. We had no doubt that we'd find employment.

I got married my junior year of college, when I was twenty-one. Within a year our first child came, and my wife stayed home with our son Tim. With my working part-time and going to school, we were able to make ends meet, thanks to an $85-a-month apartment rental.

In our fourth year our daughter Lori was born. By then we had already bought a nice home for $25,000, I had gotten my Master's degree attending summer school and night classes, and had moved from the high school to a teaching job at the local college. Our house payments were $200 a month, but with my college teaching income, we were paying less than 10 percent of my monthly salary on house payments.

Over the years we certainly didn't live like kings and queens, but we were very comfortable and our children wanted for nothing. By choice, my wife stayed home with the children until they were through high school, and we never needed her salary. Then she went back and finished college and eventually got a teaching job. While putting our children through college hasn't been easy, we have managed fine, and they will soon graduate. In a nutshell, life has been good, and we have suffered no great hardships. Pretty smooth sailing.

It's a different world out there today. First, for the professions my children are interested in, a four-year degree means little. Today graduate school is more often a necessity than an option, so we're talking another two to five years. By and large, young adults going to college are getting out into the "real world" later and later.

Once they're out there, what do they find? In many cases, a bleak employment outlook. In my profession in California, we have about 40,000 part-time teachers, all armed with MA's and PhD's, hopeful of getting full-time jobs. Most of them never will, and at some point will have to change career plans. Similar situations are occurring in other professions: there are many more college graduates available than there are jobs to fill. Comparing this situation to twenty years ago when four good jobs awaited my choosing, I find something seems terribly wrong.

What about the housing market young adults are facing? Nowhere has the American dream become more nightmarish. While 10 percent of my salary went to monthly house payments twenty years ago, nearly a third would go to payments if I were to buy a comparable house today. And I live in a relatively low-property-value area of California. If I lived in Southern California or the Bay Area, I would have difficulty buying a house at all.

Of course, my children and their generation want their own homes like ours did, and many of them who find jobs will eventually buy houses. But here's the bleak trade-off: wives committing themselves to working full-time for thirty years to help pay the $1500-a-month mortgage payments; children becoming long-term wards of day-care centers and babysitters; and the family castle gobbling up so much income that there is little left for saving, for an educational trust fund, or for even the simpler pleasures. Of course, this is not to mention the high rate of home repossessions on the less fortunate souls who can't keep up the grinding payments.

Today's economics make family life more difficult for young adults. Most young wives have no choice but to work rather than stay home with their children. That is a sad situation. While I support a woman's choice to work, it doesn't seem right that most women will no longer have the option to be "housewives" during their children's early years. Not only does this put a greater work burden on women, but the children of a working mother may also suffer by her not being around from 9 to 5 year after year. I think of how much my children would have missed had their mother not been home for them, and I feel bad that my daughter probably won't have that choice.

There may be a couple positive results from the changing times. Staying longer in school and finding employment harder, young adults aren't marrying as early as in my day. While my wife and I married at twenty-one and many of our classmates married even earlier, I don't see our children marrying before their middle or later twenties. Perhaps with the added maturity and experience they will bring to marriages, the divorce rate will decline, and fewer children will suffer the consequences of broken homes. Marrying later, young adults will also have their children later, often waiting until their early thirties. At twenty-one, I was still almost as much kid as parent when we started our family, and I know I would have been a better father had we waited a few years.

Have I prepared my children for the nineties and beyond? I always felt as long as I provided them a college education, everything would be fine. Now I'm not so sure. They are looking optimistically towards their futures, and why not? Life has been relatively smooth for them since day one, and they don't expect that to change.

But what happens when they can't get a full-time job, this year or next, or when they can't afford a house that even compares to the one they grew up in? What happens when my daughter wants to stay home with her newborn for a couple years but can't afford to quit her job or take a leave? These are difficult situations that my wife and I and many of our generation never faced, and it doesn't seem fair that my children and other young adults more than likely will.

Perhaps I worry too much about what's in store for my children. I see those obstacles ahead of them, and I'm not sure they have the toughness to deal with them. If they do, I know I didn't help put it there. I can, however, take the blame, along with my generation, for creating those obstacles.

It was our greediness that touched off the wild property speculation of the eighties that started housing prices soaring. It is our reluctance to give up jobs, even after thirty or thirty-five years, that keeps many college graduates waiting in line. Of course, our legacy also includes the sickly environment, the devastating divorce rate, and the multi-billion-dollar deficit we will eventually leave to them. And, like it or not, the medical miracles that will keep my generation alive into our nineties will help push medical premiums to even higher levels for our children.

When it comes to their standard of living, my grandparents had it better than theirs, my parents better than my grandparents, and my wife and I better than our parents. However, I don't see that pattern continuing for my children. I'm afraid that for their generation the American dream will begin to unravel.

What can my generation do to help our children? We can push for affordable housing for first-time buyers, for national health care, and for retirement incentive plans for older workers, which will help create jobs for college graduates. Since most of us aren't strapped by oppressive mortgage payments, we can help our children with home down-payments, car financing, and educational expenses for their children's children. I'm not sure helping our children over a lifetime is the best answer for us or for them, but I feel my generation has to take some responsibility for the economic situation we helped create. Why should our children have to struggle longer and harder than we did? And if they do, shouldn't we share in that struggle?

I see no real silver lining in my children's future. I could tell them that owning their own home and having a nice car and swimming pool has little to do with happiness or personal success, but hearing this from a person with the home, car, and pool, why should they listen? I'm not even sure I believe it myself, having bought into the American dream long ago.

However, rather than bring them down with my worrying, I try to feed off of their optimism, their sense that everything will work out fine for them. And maybe it will. My father's old bromide that "things always work out for the best" seemed too trite to take seriously. But perhaps he's right, at least to the extent that we all have the capacity to make the best out of what life brings us. Perhaps my children will find happiness and success well beyond what I ever found. To their advantage, they are grounded in the reality of the nineties, so they accept $150,000 houses and double-income families as the norm. I, on the other hand, am still longing for the 10-cent ice cream cone of my youth. Maybe my kids will teach me how to cope.

Chapter Five

Organizing and Paragraphing

Organizing and paragraphing your writing are related concerns. Both help to present your thoughts in a clear, sensible way that readers can easily follow and understand. Your organization and paragraphing help readers see the relationships among ideas and the relative importance you place on them.

Effective organization and paragraphing don't come from easy-to-follow formulas, although they are sometimes taught that way. From my writing experience, the content of an essay determines its organization and paragraphing rather than the other way around. If you try to stuff content into a preconceived structural framework, your essay may seem stiff and contrived.

That does not mean that writing organization and paragraphing don't follow some general principles. However, those principles reflect how real writers write rather than how anyone *should* write. In other words, the writing preceded the principles.

This chapter presents some guidelines for organization and paragraphing that work for writers in a general way. I seldom think about organizing or paragraphing my essays while I am writing, but I discovered on analysis that my writing conforms largely to these guidelines.

ORGANIZING GUIDELINES

The following suggestions for organizing an essay are informal guidelines rather than hard and fast rules. In most cases, the general organization of an essay will evolve naturally as you express your thoughts to your readers. As you develop a conscious sense of organization, it helps you discover when something is out of place within your overall scheme.

1. Most essays have some type of opening. An opening often introduces the topic and reveals the writer's viewpoint or the general direction of the essay. Effective openings answer the first question of most readers: What's this essay about? An opening may be a single paragraph or two or three paragraphs.

2. Most essays have some type of ending that leaves readers with a sense of conclusion. Essays end in a variety of ways, depending on the writer's intentions. Like openings, they may be a number of paragraphs, a single paragraph, or even a single sentence.

3. Most essays have a "middle" section: a group of paragraphs that develop the essay's topic in some manner. The middle section may provide supporting points for the idea that a woman would make

a better president than a man; specific steps explaining how to study successfully for a biology lab test; a particular experience the writer had while registering for classes; a number of causes for the rise in SAT scores in the 1980s; or a number of effects that a proposed bill to double state college tuition would have on students. The middle section is the heart of the essay, where readers find out what the writer has to say.

4. Different types of essays are organized in different ways. Here are some common examples:

   a. Narrative essay. Most narrative, or personal experience, essays are organized *chronologically* (following the order of events in which the experience occurs). This helps readers to follow the experience as they would a story.

   b. Thesis/support essay. In essays where a writer presents a thesis—"TV commercials for tennis shoes have a harmful effect on children"—and supports it, the supporting points are often presented in some order: from most important to least important; from least important to most important; beginning and ending with two most important points; and so on. The purpose of organizing your points is to emphasize the key ones and show their relative importance.

   c. Comparison essay. In essays that center on a comparison—"Is Gore a more effective vice president than Quayle?"—there are different ways to organize: covering each subject (Gore, Quayle) separately on a variety of points; comparing the subjects one point at a time; or presenting first the advantages and then the disadvantages of each subject. There is no one best way to organize a comparison essay. The important thing is for readers to follow some organizational pattern that presents the comparison clearly.

   d. Cause/effect essay. In an essay where the causes and effects of a situation are examined—"Many children live in one-parent households"—the causes (high divorce rate, teen pregnancies) are usually presented before the effects (increased poverty, few male role models). As with most organizational schemes, the order of presentation is practical. Since causes precede effects in life, readers would be comfortable with the same order in essays.

   e. Problem/solution essay. In an essay where a problem is examined and solution(s) presented—"Depletion of the ozone layer"—the following organization is typical: Present the problem, its causes, its effects, and its possible solutions. Sometimes the cause/effect order is reversed, particularly if the writer wants to stress the bad effects early to get the readers' attention. Again, the order of presentation is logical: We need to know the problem and its causes before evaluating the suggested solutions.

 **ORGANIZATION ASSIGNMENT 1**

Pick two of the following topics for essays and think about how you might organize your content. In order to practice organizing two different types of essays, don't do both 1 and 4, 2 and 5, or 3 and 6. I'll do the same thing for two different topics.

Select two essay topics:

1. The problem of violence on television
2. Community colleges and four-year colleges
3. My viewpoint on beer's being sold on college campuses
4. America's air pollution problem
5. Comparing couples' living together vs. getting married
6. My viewpoint on rap music

AUTHOR'S ORGANIZATIONAL PLANS

Topic One: The Problem of Pesticide Contamination

In the agricultural area where I live, we have a problem with pesticides getting into the underground water and contaminating water supplies. After giving the topic some thought, if I were to write an essay on pesticide contamination I'd follow this general organization.

1. Present the problem of pesticide contamination. Convince readers that it is serious enough for them to be concerned.

2. Provide some background information on the problem: How did we get where we are today?

3. Discuss the causes of contamination: the pesticide spraying practices that are responsible for well contamination, and the particular pesticide compounds that are doing the damage.

4. Discuss the effects of water contamination on people, animals, and plant life.

5. Suggest possible solutions to the problem that address the causes presented in 3.

6. Conclude with what readers can do to help solve the problem: whom they might write to, organizations they might join, who or what they should vote for, and personal practices they might change.

Topic Two: Private vs. State Four-Year Colleges

I'm not sure I'd write an essay comparing private and state-run colleges, but if I did, it could include these areas of comparison: financial aspects, quality of education, reputation, and size. This is how I might organize the essay.

1. Present the topic—the option of attending a private or state-run college—to readers who are making college plans.

2. Compare the two subjects in each of the four areas: financial, quality, reputation, and size. For example, if private colleges were A, and state-run colleges B, and if financial concerns, quality, reputation, and size were 1, 2, 3, and 4, the organization would look like this:

$$A/1 \quad A/2 \quad A/3 \quad A/4$$
$$B/1 \quad B/2 \quad B/3 \quad B/4$$

I think this is the best organization to show readers the differences and similarities between the two subjects on each point. If I covered the subjects separately (the first half of the essay on private schools and the second on state schools) the comparisons wouldn't be as clear.

3. I'd probably conclude with a summary of the distinctive points between the two systems, and emphasize that the readers' choice depends on personal preferences and finances.

STUDENT WRITERS' RESPONSES

Margaret

If I were to write an essay on living in the dorms, it would be pretty negative. My tentative organization would be something like this.

1. Give some background on how I came to live in the dorms.

2. Write about the things that I haven't liked about living in the dorms. I think I'd start with the biggest problem, my ex-roommate, and end with another big problem, the lonely weekends. I'd put two or three other negatives in the middle.

3. I think I'd save the good about the dorms for near the end, like one rather short paragraph. I don't have a lot to say here, but I want to be fair.

4. I'd conclude with a little advice for readers on living in the dorms, or at least some things to consider before making a decision.

Pablo

This isn't a real big problem, but since I'm sitting in my classroom freezing at 8 in the morning, I feel like writing about the heater problem. Here is how I think I would organize a little essay.

1. I'd dramatize the opening a little—like walking into the classroom from the freezing outdoors only to find it like a refrigerator, or other times walking in and being blown away by the hot air. One extreme or the other!

2. Next I'd lay out the problem with the heater—either working to overkill or not working at all. The custodian repairs it, it works for a couple days, then we're back to freezing or burning up.

3. Third, I'd tell how the bad conditions affect me and other students in the class. It really messes up the class for us.

4. Fourth, I'd lay out how to solve the problem (that would be simple enough, I would think). That would be my ending.

Le

Some time I will write about being reunited with my sister in the United States. This is how I might organize my paper.

1. To begin, tell a little about the Viet Cong attack on Viet Nam and the Communist takeover.

2. Next, explain what happened to my family, and how my sister escaped to the United States with an aunt and uncle.

3. Write about life in Viet Nam after the takeover for me and what was left of my family.

4. Write about how I missed my sister and how we stayed in touch as much as we could for six years.

5. Write about how, after Mother died, I decided to come to the United States and be reunited with my sister.

6. Conclude with something about what my life is like now in the United States living with my sister, aunt, and uncle.

ORGANIZATION ASSIGNMENT 2

Write a short first draft (200 words or so) on one of your essay choices, following your organizational guidelines. As you write, feel free to change your organization if a better pattern emerges through the writing process. The purpose of writing the draft is to evaluate the effectiveness of its organization and see what, if any, changes you might make in a second draft.

I'm going to write on the pesticide contamination topic because its organization is less straightforward than my comparison topic. I won't be able to get into depth with a 200-word essay, so I'll keep it general and simple, because I'm writing this to evaluate my organization. A final essay on the topic would be much longer.

AUTHOR'S FIRST DRAFT

Pesticide Contamination

Once the San Joaquin Valley was known for its pure drinking water. Today it's becoming better known for its contaminated water, the result of pesticide poisoning. If something isn't done about the problem, Valley residents won't have enough drinkable water to survive.

The problem is an insidious one. During the last century, pesticide residues from agricultural spraying have slowly filtered through the soil and found their way into underground springs. Since these poisonous compounds can remain toxic for over fifty years, today water officials are finding wells contaminated from pesticides of the sixties and seventies. Continuing to add pesticides to the soil adds to the seriousness and longevity of the problem.

Pesticide contamination can cause cancer, according to health experts. Higher than normal incidences of cancer have been found in certain Valley farming communities, and contaminated water is viewed as the probable culprit. Since contaminated water looks, smells, and tastes normal, people don't know if they are drinking it unless their particular water source has been checked by the health department. More people are turning to bottled water all the time.

But bottled water isn't the answer. Cleaning up our ample natural water supply is. There must be an immediate ban on the use of all pesticides containing contaminating agents. No agricultural yield is worth the price of contaminating our water supply and causing cancer among our residents. Along with the ban, we must demand that all sources of Valley drinking water (and there are thousands of them) be checked by the health department for contamination. Every Valley resident should call his or her legislators and demand immediate legislation on these two matters. Our lives and our children's lives could be at stake.

I followed my basic organizational pattern, except for one part. As I wrote, I saw that two areas came together naturally: background and cause. Since the cause of contamination originated in the background information, I tied the two together.

Other than that change, each part seemed to follow naturally from the previous one, and I don't think I'd change the organization. I would have to add a lot of information and do some research to write a good essay.

Journal Entry 27

Describe the basic organizational plan for your essay and how closely you stayed with it. How do you feel about the organization of your first draft? What, if any, organizational changes might you make in a second draft? What other things would you need to do to write an effective essay on the topic?

PARAGRAPHING GUIDELINES

Paragraphing guidelines are as practical as organizing plans in presenting your thoughts clearly. If a paragraph runs too long, you may lose your readers' interest. If you string short paragraphs together, your readers may have trouble following your thoughts. If you change subjects frequently in a paragraph, you may confuse your readers.

I never plan out a paragraph before writing it or intentionally write a particular type of paragraph—one beginning with a topic sentence, or another centered on an incident. Like most writers, my paragraphs develop naturally from my thoughts. I do sometimes run on too long, so I go back and divide a paragraph where I've started a new idea or example. Usually when I've said what I want about a particular point (like my paragraphing process in this paragraph), I move to a new paragraph.

The following guidelines are based on the paragraphing practices of many writers.

1. In general, most paragraphs develop a single thought: an idea, supporting point, incident, description, step, or example. If you'll look back at my rough draft on pesticide contamination, you'll see examples of that type of paragraph.

2. Sometimes the main point of a paragraph is expressed in a *topic sentence*, which often begins the paragraph. For examples, look at the second and third paragraphs of my pesticide contamination draft. Other times, while the subject of the paragraph is clear, there is no topic sentence. For example, look at my last complete paragraph preceding this list of guidelines.

3. All sentences in a paragraph relate in some way to its topic. For example, look at paragraph 3 in the pesticide contamination draft. Each sentence relates to the topic sentence in a distinct way.

4. Begin a new paragraph when you finish one point and start another. Often you can sense that a particular sentence brings the paragraph to a good conclusion; other times you reach a point where you have no more to say about the topic.

5. If a paragraph is running on too long (half a typewritten page or more), reread it to see where you might divide it. Find a place near the middle where you shift gears by starting a different example, a new detail, another supporting point, or a different perspective. Usually you can find a place to divide the paragraph effectively.

6. If you tend to string short paragraphs together, one of two things is happening: you are continuing on the same subject in succeeding paragraphs, or you are not developing your ideas fully. In the first situation, which is most common, just combine two or three related paragraphs into one. In the second situation, either develop your points thoroughly through examples, details, and more explanation, or delete a paragraph where you have little to say.

7. Do your paragraphing revisions after writing the first draft. It's difficult to see how paragraphs fit together until you've seen the whole essay. Then you can go back and notice how overly long paragraphs, strings of short paragraphs, or disorganized paragraphs stand out. Usually the paragraph revisions aren't that difficult: dividing a long paragraph, combining a pair of short paragraphs, or revising a paragraph that changes subjects or contains unrelated sentences.

PARAGRAPHING ASSIGNMENT 1

Using the guidelines just presented, read the following first draft and put the paragraph symbol (¶) before each sentence that could begin a new paragraph. Then discuss your paragraphing with a classmate.

AUTHOR'S UNREVISED DRAFT

Summer Rut

I do a lot of writing in the summer. That's when I usually put together my first drafts for prospective textbooks. My closest teaching friends marvel at my discipline, because they know I'm not a very disciplined person by nature, and they've never had the discipline to devout summers to writing. How do I do it, they ask? The answer is relatively simple. I don't have a lot of competing interests. I like to play golf, but it gets too hot where I live to golf in the summer. I like to go on vacations, but I can't afford to take more than a week or two during a summer. I enjoy reading and watching TV, but I'm not going to do either for sixteen hours a day. I also play the piano almost daily, but that takes a half hour at most. I also lift weights every other day, but that's another hour to hour-and-a-half. I've still got most of the day to fill. Many of my friends fill their summers with puttering around the house, something my wife wishes I'd do. They paint their houses, build coffee tables and cabinets, calk their showers, wash windows, refinish old furniture, putter for hours in the yard, backwash their swimming pools, and generally keep things ship-shape. None of that's for me. I have neither the interest nor the aptitude, so I pay people to paint my house and take care of the pool, and I do only the mandatory yard work. Other friends are still going to school in the summer, getting those units to move them across the salary schedule, but I'm long past that ordeal. Still others teach summer school for six to ten weeks or find other types of summer work, like being fruit inspectors, managing a packing shed, or selling tax shelters or life insurance. More teaching doesn't appeal to me in the summer, and there's no way I'm looking for other kinds of summer work. Which brings me back to my computer and my manuscript writing in the summer. By process of elimination, there's not a lot else for me to be doing. If I weren't writing, there's an excellent chance that I'd be taking long, long naps or lounging on a pool mattress all afternoon. That's where my weak work ethic comes in. I couldn't live with myself if I did nothing but vegetate all summer, and my wife wouldn't live with me. So I write, first because it's something that I can do, second because I get satisfaction out of it, third, because I've had a little success, and fourth, because I can put in four or five hours a day and consider myself productive. Then the napping, TV watching, piano banging, junk reading, and weightlifting are all justified. I write so I can do lazy or indulgent things and feel no guilt. But I don't let my friends in on this. If they want to see me as the model of dedication and discipline, slaving and sweating over my computer all summer long for the sake of my profession and my craft, that's okay with me. As the TV commercial says, "Image is everything!"

That was kind of fun to write, first because it's so true, and second, because I enjoy occasional "confessional" writing like this. It's sometimes easier to confide in strangers than friends. As to not paragraphing, that felt strange, and it made it more difficult for me to move from thought to thought.

Journal Entry 28

Relate how you decided where to end and begin paragraphs in the draft. What factors did you consider? Where did you have problems making a decision, and why?

PARAGRAPHING ASSIGNMENT 2

Write your own "confessional" draft, something about yourself that your classmates might be surprised to know, and don't put in paragraphs. (My "confessional" was the *real* reasons behind devoting summers to writing.) Pick a topic about which you can write 300–400 words.

When you finish your draft, read it and decide how to paragraph it. Put the paragraph symbol (¶) in front of sentences that would begin paragraphs, and then exchange drafts with a classmate and get a second opinion.

Journal Entry 29

Relate what it was like to write an essay without paragraphs. How did it feel, and how did it effect your writing, if at all? Then tell how you paragraphed the essay, and evaluate your decisions. Finally, look at individual paragraphs and describe their content (topic-sentence paragraph? topic paragraph without a topic sentence? example paragraph? something else?).

CHAPTER WRITING ASSIGNMENT

For your chapter writing assignment, pick any topic, following one guideline: make a problem (yours, someone else's, your family's, the school's, your community's) a feature of the essay. Before writing, do the following prewriting activities.

1. To generate ideas, use one or more of the prewriting techniques introduced in Chapter 3.

2. Consider a tentative approach to your topic (thesis), the audience for your essay, and what you would like to accomplish (purpose).

3. Consider an organizational plan for your essay, and follow it in a general way while writing your first draft.

AUTHOR'S PREWRITING THOUGHTS

I like to write about things that are on my mind or that I am currently dealing with, whether they be personal, professional, political, or financial. On the college front, there has been a legislative recommendation to increase tuition by 100 percent to help decrease California's multi-billion-dollar deficit. That's a big potential problem for students. California's huge deficit itself is a problem that no one has a solution for.

Closer to home, I've got a problem as union president in deciding the fate of 450 part-time instructors. We've filed with the state to include part-timers in our full-time bargaining unit, and the college is resisting the move. They're willing to give them a separate unit, but we'd probably have to go to court to win a single-unit ruling. Which way should we go?

These problems interest me but I'm not sure they would interest my readers, most of whom don't live in California. Then I started thinking on a personal note about a disagreement my wife and I had over a sabbatical leave plan that I'd come up with. The disagreement typifies a recurrent problem in our relationship: I prefer making quick decisions and acting on them, and my wife likes to take her time, weigh options, and not be rushed to act.

Our problem is one most readers could identify with in some way. If I were to write about it, I would go beyond the specific problem to discussing compromise and avoiding conflicts in relationships. I'm no expert on the subject, but I've learned a few things to pass on to readers, especially those like me who like to have their own way!

Two hours later, I've decided to write about the difference between how my wife and I make decisions. For me, it's worth thinking about. As for organization, I'll start with the problem and then get into its effects. Then I'll talk about how we're working on the problem, and finally generalize about dealing with such problems in a marriage or relationship. I'll get started with the first draft and see what happens.

STUDENT WRITERS' RESPONSES

Joseph

Three people and one car. Now that's a problem. There's my mom, my brother, and me. Until I can afford my own car, I share with them. It's a problem that bothers me enough to write about, and I'll bet it's a problem that some of my classmates could relate to.

As to an approach, I don't know. It's such a lousy situation that I don't know if we can work things out so everyone's happy. Right now I feel it's impossible for three people with different schedules to share one car. That's my tentative approach, but maybe I'll come up some possible solutions when I write that will change my attitude.

For organization, I'll start by explaining the situation and why we have to share one car. Then I'll get into all the problems it causes for all of us, but particularly I think for me in coming to college. Then I'll try to come up with some things we could do to share the car and make the situation work better. I don't know how I'll conclude. It depends whether I come up with any good solutions.

Monica

Sitting here in April in the Valley, there's only one problem that always seems to be with me: my allergies. Come spring, I'm pretty much a mess with watery eyes, sinus headaches, and constant cold-like symptoms.

I know there are a lot of allergy sufferers in the Valley, so I'd be writing mainly to them. But, on the other hand, they know what I'm going through, so I'm not sure what I'd accomplish. What about writing to all those lucky non-allergic people who have no idea what it's like to face another spring in the Valley? Maybe I should write to them and educate them a little so they'd show some sympathy or at least understanding.

As to an approach, it'd be something like "Not *everybody* in this Valley looks forward to our wonderful springtimes with the trees blossoming and a ton of pollen in the air." It might be one of those whiny papers that no one wants to read, but allergies are a good topic to whine about.

I think I'd organize my paper by starting off with sort of a light-hearted opening with all the glories of spring around and me sitting in the middle, one big mess. Then I'd get into what allergies are and how they affect us allergic people and how the Valley's springs bring out the worst in us. I'd have to watch my whining here.

Then I'd move into what can be done for allergies, which unfortunately is precious little in some cases given the wonders of medical science. And sometimes the cure is worse than the ailment, as I'll get into the series of powerful shots that the most seriously allergic people take. Finally, I think I'd call for a little understanding for us people who suffer from allergies. We don't go around blowing our noses and looking and feeling miserable because we enjoy it. It's not like we're trying to annoy the non-allergics. I'll ask for some sympathy, and whine until I get it!

Poy

I don't have a problem, it's my cat that's got a problem. She's an ancient old cat, but she just keeps on living. She's got arthritis, she's getting more and more finicky about what she'll eat, her bowels are weakening, and on and on. I guess her problem is also my problem since I am responsible for her. She's getting to be a pain, and she's pretty much in charge.

I'll first write about all my cat's problems, and then explain how her problems become my problems. There's no solution to the problem, until of course she goes to kitty heaven, so I'm going to write about it as the perplexing situation it is. Maybe my point is that there are some problems you just have to live with and make the best of—you're not going to escape them. Maybe in the conclusion I'll apply this bit of wisdom to other situations well beyond my poor old cat and me. I think I'd write this paper for just about anyone although some of those super cat lovers might take offense.

AUTHOR'S FIRST DRAFT

The Tortoise and the Hare

My wife and I have been married over twenty years, and two things are

pretty clear. First, we are two very different people. Second, after twenty years, ~~it's clear that~~ neither of us is going to change ~~who we are~~ very much.

Thank goodness for the things we ~~do~~ have in common, which have helped make up for the differences. We both enjoy sports, eating out, our children, vacations, and lazy weekends, and we take an interest in each other's professional lives. Our biggest difference, which permeates many areas of our lives, is that I'm a "fast" person *reword* and she's a "slow" person. Let me explain ~~what I mean.~~

Almost everything I do, I like to do fast: eat, work, think, write, drive, shop, plan, and make decisions. Because this is the way I've always operated, I can do a reasonably good job at whatever I'm doing, although I'm certainly no perfectionist. On the other hand, everything I do fast, my wife prefers to do slowly. This is her basic nature, and trying to speed her up just ~~makes her~~ frustrate*s* *her*.

Examples abound ~~in our lives.~~ I'll take a half hour to shop for clothes while my wife ~~will~~ take*s* all day. I'll know what I want in a restaurant after a quick look at the menu *while* ~~My~~ wife is often not ready to order when the waitress comes. I could make my side of the bed three times in the time it takes my wife to make her*s* ~~side~~ once. I may take a month to find a car I like or new linoleum for the kitchen while my wife would take a good year or more, checking out every auto dealer in the Valley and every pattern and color of linoleum ever made.

The latest example is a biggie. I've hit upon the idea of taking a year's sabbatical leave in Europe, where I would visit colleges in England, Germany, France, and Italy and learn about their writing programs. My wife and I could rent a home or apartment in or around Paris, a good central location, and have the travel experience of our lives. The college would pay 70 percent of my salary for the year and we'd rent out our home, so we could make it financially.

cliché—
reword

wordy—revise

While I knew my wife wouldn't jump up and down about the plan, being as slow and cautious as she is in warming up to new ideas, I was still frustrated by her response: "That would be a nice thing to think about in five or six years." Five or six years! She's talking to someone who could be packed tomorrow! Realistically, I had figured on applying two years from now and going in the third year, ~~which seemed~~ ample time to plan, to secure my wife an unpaid teaching leave, and to make sure ~~the kids~~ *our adult children* will be well situated. ~~(They'll be twenty-five and twenty-eight by then.)~~ Just another example of the tortoise and the hare looking at a ~~situation~~ *things* from ~~their very~~ different viewpoints.

I don't know how the sabbatical leave situation will work out, but

my guess is if it ~~works out at all,~~ *does,* we'll end up compromising somewhere between her five or six years and my two ~~or three years.~~ In
my younger years, ~~I'm sure~~ I would have spent hours and days trying to talk her into doing things my way, and I would have made ~~her~~ *us*
~~and myself~~ *both* miserable. Maybe I would have gotten my way, at my
wife's expense, or we'd end up compromising after ~~lots of~~ *much* needless
and hurtful battling. Seldom would I ever "lose" a battle, meaning
doing things strictly on her terms.

I can't say I'm a lot wiser than I used to be, but I have learned a
few things. First, neither ~~nor~~ *my* wife ~~and~~ *nor* I will change our basic nature,
or we would have by now. I may try to slow down in a few areas and
she may try to move a little faster, but that's for ~~the sake of~~ accommodation *'s sake.* Once I accepted ~~that we are~~ the way we are, I tried to view
potential problems ~~through that perspective.~~ *accordingly.*

Second, I realize that there is no "right" or "wrong" in ~~the way~~ *how*
we are. Just because I do things fast and she takes her time doesn't
make either of us smarter, better, or wiser ~~than the other.~~ That may
seem obvious to most people, but believe me, I haven't always felt
that way. Today I recognize that we're just different, ~~and we do~~ *each doing* what
works best and feels most comfortable to us.

So how can two people so different in nature survive so many *not needed* ——— years of marriage, Not always easily. ~~I'd be lying if I said it was.~~

However, it continues to get better because we've gotten smarter, or

wordy— learned from experience, in how to deal with our differences.

revise

First, we don't let our different natures work against us when

we ~~don't have to.~~ *can avoid it.* Since she likes to spend the day shopping and I

take a half hour, we seldom shop together. Since I eat faster than

she does, I'm up from the dinner table and reading the paper while

she continues to enjoy dinner ~~at her pace.~~ While we both work

around the house, we seldom work together ~~because of our different~~

~~paces and degrees of meticulousness.~~ She does her thing and I do

mine. In earlier years, I'd follow her around the stores, we'd sit down

and get up from ~~the~~ dinner ~~table~~ at the same time, and we'd try to

work together around the house. All of these things caused conflict,

and none of them were necessary. So we quit trying to be so

traditional.

There are also territories we've staked off. While big household

purchases are ~~primarily~~ her domain, I take the lead in planning va-

cations, buying cars, and buying for the yard. She can take as much

time as she wants selecting new linoleum or curtains or a bedroom

set. I'll come in ~~on the process~~ when she wants my advice, ~~here or~~

~~there,~~ but I'm not there at every step. On the other hand, I can do the vacation planning or car purchasing or flower buying at what-

ever speed I'm comfortable ~~with~~ because she gets no more involved

than I do with the household considerations. This way we can help

wordy—revise

each other make decisions without going through the entire proc-

esses together that accentuate our differences and cause conflicts.

revise—boring

Then there's the small stuff that we've learned to deal with. She

has worked on speeding up her restaurant ordering, and I've learned

to pace myself when eating out so that we finish close together. When

we do shop together, I~~'ve learned to~~ find soft chairs, ~~to~~ take along a

book, or ~~to~~ find the bookstore or cookie counter at the mall. When we

go to get-togethers with her side of the family, I~~'ve learned to~~ plan on

staying longer than I'd probably choose, and she's accepted not stay-

ing well into the a.m. We've grown more sensitive to the other per-

son's sense of time, ~~and~~ I've grown a little less urgent, and she a

add paragraph about
how we turn negatives   →
into positives

little more so.

Finally, ~~I think~~ the most important thing is that we've accepted

who the other person is. I no longer ask her why it takes her two

hours to do what I'd do in a half hour. She isn't surprised when I say

on the spur of the moment, "Honey, let's buzz to the coast for the

weekend." Usually, we don't end up going, and that no longer

surprises me either. Our expectations are more in line with ~~the~~

~~other person's~~ reality, and consequently there are fewer ~~sources of~~ conflict.

too general—change or delete

Being tolerant and trying to find compromises and make things work out is a good part of what relationships are all about. If one person wins, the other person loses, and in the end there are no winners. Accept people for who they are, set your expectations based on reality, distinguish the important from the unimportant, and set up your life patterns to avoid needless conflict. Of course, none of this is easy, and they are things you work on every day of your life.

I still don't know how we are going to resolve our differences of ~~opinion~~ over the sabbatical leave ~~situation.~~ All I know is that it will get resolved ~~some~~ *in a* way that we'll both accept, that neither of us will totally "get our way," and that no blood will be drawn ~~over it.~~ There were times not ~~too~~ long ago that I wouldn't have been *so* sure ~~of any of those things. You~~ just keep learning as ~~you~~ go, and if my situation is ~~in any way~~ typical, ~~I expect that~~ men usually have more to learn than women.

AUTHOR'S DRAFT RESPONSE

I followed my prewriting plan well in the first draft: present the problem, give lots of examples, tell how we're dealing with it, and then, in the conclusion, discuss general problem solving in relationships. The organization worked fine.

I'm not happy with the conclusion. I made it too general, listing suggestions that could come from a generic "how to fix your relationship" manual. I'm not sure readers would get anything out of the conclusion.

I think the examples in the draft are important. Without them, the essay would be pretty boring. I'll go over them carefully and see what I can improve. I also think I repeated myself a couple times, going over the same examples too much. I'll look at that.

My wording is particularly rough in this draft. I didn't like the way most of the sentences were sounding as I wrote. I've got some major sentence revision to do.

Finally, before beginning the second draft, I had my wife read the paper to make sure she didn't mind my writing about her. She didn't feel it was too personal to put in the book. She thought the draft presented an honest portrayal of the situation, which encouraged me to leave it in.

Journal Entry 30

Relate your feeling about your first draft: how the writing went, what you feel good about, and what you want to change in the next draft.

REVISIONS

I spent about two hours revising my first draft, and I'm satisfied with the results.

1. I revised almost every sentence, eliminating unnecessary words and phrases, rewording awkward sentences, and replacing questionable word choices with better ones. Over half my time was spent on wording revisions.

2. I added a paragraph because a new idea came to me: My wife and I take advantage of our different natures. This was a good addition because first, it was positive, and second, it offered an interesting idea: how you can turn a negative into a positive in a relationship. We've found one way that I felt was worth passing on.

3. I labored over the conclusion because I wasn't happy with the first draft. In the next-to-last paragraph, I had strung a few platitudes together, and they weren't effective. I got rid of what I didn't like and reshaped the rest in more personal terms: This is how my wife and I are dealing with a major difference, and if readers can get something out of it, great. I am happier with the next-to-last paragraph.

   I also moved the last two sentences of the first draft's next-to-last paragraph to open the final paragraph. They worked where they were, but they served as a better lead-in for the final paragraph.

I deliberated on keeping the final sentence about men, but I decided to keep it because I believe it's true. People may disagree, and that's fine. The final draft appears at the end of the chapter.

Journal Entry 31

Write your response to the "Tortoise and Hare" draft: what, if anything, you found interesting or thought-provoking; what you found boring or irrelevant; what you could relate to in some way; what questions the draft may have left unanswered for you; and what suggestions you'd make for improving the paper.

REVISION ASSIGNMENT 1

Before revising your own draft, read the following student draft. With a classmate, evaluate the draft using these revision guidelines.

1. What are the strengths of the essay? What did you find interesting, informative, or thought provoking? What did the writer do well?

2. What questions, if any, would you have liked the essay to answer? Find specific places where the addition of an example, explanation, or detail would have helped the reader.

3. Does the essay ever get off track? Does anything need deleting or revising that isn't really relevant to the topic?

4. How well is the essay organized? Are the different parts of the essay presented in a sensible, logical order? Would any paragraphs or parts of a paragraph be more effective in a different location in the essay?

5. How well is the essay paragraphed? Does the paragraphing help the reader move clearly from one point to the next? Does each paragraph center on one particular thing: a point, example, incident, description, explanation? Are there any distractingly long paragraphs that need dividing or strings of short paragraphs that need combining or developing? What, if any, paragraphing revisions might you recommend?

6. Find examples of first-draft sentences that are wordy, awkward, or confusing. How might they be revised to improve their clarity and smoothness?

7. How effective are the opening and conclusion of the essay? What is presented in each, and what effect do they have on the reader?

What suggestions, if any, would you make for improving the opening or conclusion?

8. What is the writer's approach to her topic, and how well does she develop and support it? What audience might she be addressing, and what do you think she wants to accomplish with the essay? How successful is she, and why?

STUDENT FIRST DRAFT

The Dream

Since the day that I turned twelve, my dream has always been to be a lawyer. A future plan that I never knew would change my life forever. That dream made lose out on so many things during my high school years and again during my adult years. It made me neglect my children and even drive my husband into the arms of another woman. Never satisfied, always striving to be the best, that's what that dream made me become. I gave up so much, in hopes of reaching my goal. I never went to a football game, a dance was out of the question for me, those things took too much time and would interfere with my plans. So, all I did was study and my grades were great, straight "A's," and "B's," I could not see a "C" that meant a failing grade for me. Through my high school years and toward the end of the last semester my grades were stupendous and I had letters coming in from all types of colleges and universities, inviting me to attend their college. I even had the army knocking at my door, with offers of great value, but my dream was to become a lawyer, and not to go off too far from home. I recall, my father, he was so proud of me. I lived to make him proud.

Then during my last semester in high school, my brother was killed in a tragic accident. He was only sixteen and we were awfully close. I could'nt sleep or concentrate and my grades came down to failing. I saw my dream just drift away and I called myself a failure.

I graduated anyway, but without honors, as I'd planned. I had lots of extra credits which made it possible for me. Then I went to work and met my husband and I became a wife. My first child came and then the other and by the time I realized I already had four children. Oh well, I thought. This is my life and I shall be content. We'll raise the kids and then maybe I can follow my dream again.

My husband disagreed, he wanted me at home. We fought and argued and then before I knew it, Susie, my baby, came into this world and as she was being born I knew my dreaming was dying forever.

Two years later, my husband left and into the arms of another woman he went. So, I started to work, day and night, trying to make ends meet. In a few years I was able to save some money and I bought a house and a new car. I took the kids to Disneyland for three days and when we got back I quit my night job. The kids were so excited to have me home again. I began to really know my kids and to love them even more.

Then in 1988 I quit my other job and got a better one that did'nt keep me out at night. Now my oldest daughter Cindy tells me how hard it was for them when I was gone working all the time. She's the one who convinced me to come back to college and pursue my dream again. So, here I am, starting where I left off and maybe I won't be a lawyer, but at least I'll be working for one.

I tell my children to follow their dreams, but don't miss out on the good things in life, the way I did.

REVISION ASSIGNMENT 2

Revise your first draft, using the revision suggestions as guidelines. If you'd like a second opinion, exchange drafts with a classmate and apply the suggestions to each other's papers. Then write the second draft of your essay, including all revisions that you feel will improve it.

Journal Entry 32

Relate the kinds of revisions you made for your second draft. Why did you make them, and how do you think they improved the essay? How do you feel about your latest draft? What changes, if any, might you still want to make?

EDITING

The last step in preparing a paper for readers is to proofread it for errors in spelling, punctuation, or grammar. If you correct most errors during the drafting process, the proofreading should be light work.

EDITING ASSIGNMENT 1

Proofread the following student draft and correct any errors in spelling, punctuation, or grammar. Then compare your corrections with a classmate's.

STUDENT FIRST DRAFT

Drop Out

During my schooling from elementary to my sophomore year of high school was very exciting, challenging, and quiet easy to accomplish. Throughout those years I participated in many sports activities, lunch activities, and class participation was also common with me. My grades were above average and the teachers seemed to enjoy my humorous attitude in their classroom. Wresting was my favorite sport and I was a major contributor to the varsity wrestling team in high school. But as a teenager a person makes a lot of careless mistakes that are regretful when later seen through the eyes as an adult.

The summer after my sophomore year I met a few different friends and began to party ; drinking beer and smoking was the way we partied all night long. We enjoyed the summer days and nights at the river and, as we used to say, getting loaded off of the beer! Unfortunately the summer and river water ended and high school began. So it was one or the other, and summer time fun was now to be just a past memory until next year.

As a result the following year, as a junior, my school work performance dropped as well as my attendance. The class participation turned into extra time to sleep with my head on the desk. The once 4.0 grade point average dropped to 1.5 and the the sport of wresting was not important to me anymore. We began to party on weekend and sometimes on weekdays till late at night. My home work was seldom handed in and occasionally not fully completed. I began to believe that it was in the best interest, to all that was involved, that cutting class was best for all of us to do. Cutting class became more and more common until it got to the point that I would miss school for weeks at a time.

One day a letter was sent in the mail saying that I was no longer enrolled in school due to my attendance. The summer life was now here to stay and I enjoyed every minute of it until reality struck me hard. It was time to get a job and pay my own way, the assumption my parents projected to me was if I was too mature to return to school I must be mature enough to pay my own dues.

This was completely wrong after a while when I realized a minimum wage occupation and long hard labor hours were not for me. The sad part about the whole situation was that I knew I could do better and how can my eyes looking from out side and in were so blind to see the obvious. This is when I realized that I was wrong to leave school in the first place.

Straighting my life out was long and difficult but it was accomplishable with hard work and new parting morals, the sober kind. By paying all the bills I've accumulated as a hard working young adult and saving all the money that would have went to purchase beer and smokes I purchased a new car. Now I'm back in school and now work in a better job as a manager of a store. As a young adult you can say that I've seen the light and realize right from wrong and glad that the mistake was correctable.

EDITING ASSIGNMENT 2

Proofread your latest draft for errors you may have overlooked earlier. Make the necessary corrections, and then write the final draft of your essay. This is also the best time to review relevant sections and do exercises from Chapter 9, the editing chapter.

Journal Entry 33

Based on your latest draft, how much of a problem are errors in your writing? What improvement have you made during the course in identifying and eliminating mistakes? What error tendencies, if any, do you still need to work on, and what can you do to help yourself?

AUTHOR'S FINAL DRAFT

The Tortoise and the Hare

My wife and I have been married over twenty years, and two things are pretty clear. First, we are very different people. Second, after all these years, I don't see either of us changing very much.

Thank goodness for the things we have in common, which more than make up for the differences. We both enjoy our children, sports, eating out, vacations, and lazy weekends, and we are interested in each other's professional lives. Our one big difference, which creates its share of problems, is that I'm a "fast" person and she's a "slow" person. Let me explain what I mean.

Almost everything I do, I do fast: eat, work, think, write, drive, shop, plan, and make decisions. Because this is how I've always been, I do a decent job at most things, although I'm no perfectionist. On the other hand, while I do everything fast, my wife prefers to take her time. She is as slow as I am fast. Our basic natures couldn't be more different, and my speeding her up or her slowing me down only leads to frustration.

Examples abound. I take a half hour to shop for clothes while my wife will shop all day. Eating out, I'll know what I want after a quick look at the menu while my wife agonizes over what to order, often keeping the waitress waiting. I could make my side of the bed three times in the time that my wife makes her side once. I might take a month to find a car I like or new carpeting for the living room. My wife, on the other hand, could take a year or more, checking out every auto dealer in central California and every color of carpet ever made.

The latest example is a big one. One day I came up with the idea of taking a year's sabbatical leave in Europe, where I would visit colleges in England, Germany, France, and Italy and learn about their writing programs. My wife and I could rent a house in or around Paris, a good central location, and have the travel experience of our lives. Since the college would pay 60 percent of my salary and we'd rent out our home, we could make it financially.

While I knew my wife wouldn't be exuberant about the plan, given her cautious treatment of any "sudden" proposal, I was still frustrated by her response: "That would be a nice thing to think about in five or six years." Five or six years! She's talking to someone who could be packed tomorrow! Realistically, I had figured on applying two years from now and going in the third year, which left ample time to plan, secure an unpaid teaching leave for my wife, and make sure our adult children would be well situated. For my wife, two years of planning was rushing it dangerously. Just another example of the hare and the tortoise looking at a situation differently.

I don't know how the sabbatical leave situation will work out, but I suspect we'll reach a compromise. In my younger years, I would have spent days trying to talk my wife into doing things my way, and I would have made us both miserable. Maybe I would have gotten my way, at her expense, or we'd end up compromising after much needless and hurtful battling. I always hated to "lose" a battle, meaning doing things on her terms.

I'm not a lot wiser than I used to be, but I have learned a few things. First, I'll always do things fast by nature and my wife will do things slowly. There's no use trying to change each other. I may try to slow down occasionally and she may try to move a little faster, but only for accommodation's sake. Once I accepted the way we are, I tried view everything accordingly.

Second, I realized that there is no "right" or "wrong" in our approaches. Just because I do things fast and she takes her time doesn't make either of us smarter or better. That may seem obvious, but believe me, I haven't always felt that way. Now I recognize that we do what comes naturally for us, and there's no sense fighting it.

So how can two people so different in nature survive twenty years of marriage? Not always easily. However, the situation continues to get better because we've gotten smarter in dealing with our differences.

First, whenever possible, we don't let our different natures work against us. Since my wife likes to spend the day shopping and I take a half hour, we seldom shop together. Since I eat faster, at home I'm up from the table and reading the paper while she continues enjoying her dinner. While we both work around the house, we seldom work together because of our different paces. In earlier years, I'd trudge around the stores after her, we'd always sit down and get up from the dinner table together, and we tried to work around the house as a "team." All of these things caused conflict, and none was necessary. So we quit being so traditional.

There are also territories we've staked off. While household purchases are her domain, I take the lead in planning vacations and buying vehicles. She can take all the time she wants selecting new linoleum or curtains or a bedroom set. I'll give advice when asked, but I'm not there at every step. On the other hand, I do the vacation planning or car purchasing at my speed, and ask her advice when needed. This way we help each other make decisions without doing everything together, which lessens potential conflict.

Then there are the small things we've learned to deal with. At restaurants, she has worked on speeding up her ordering, and I've slowed my eating so that we finish about the same time. When we do shop together, I now find soft chairs, take along a book, or locate the bookstore or cookie counter at the mall. When we attend evening get-togethers with her side of the family, I've learned to stay longer than I'd choose, and she's accepted not staying well into the a.m. We've grown more sensitive to the other person's sense of time; I've become a little less urgent, and she a little more so.

The most important thing is we've accepted who the other person is. I no longer bristle when it takes my wife two hours to do something I'd do in a half hour. She isn't surprised when I say, on the spur of the moment, "Honey, let's go to the coast tomorrow." Often, we don't end up going, but that no longer bothers me greatly. Our expectations are based on how things are rather than how we'd like them to be, which makes life more pleasant.

Finally, when possible, we play to the strength of our differences. For example, when my wife is up to her ears in school work and needs quick ideas for a lesson plan, or a bulletin board changed in her classroom, she leans on her speedy husband. When I need something done that requires the attention to detail I don't have the patience for, like laying out a design for a manuscript section, I turn to my wife and give her all the time she needs. This way we learn to appreciate the differences that have sometimes caused us problems.

Learning to tolerate our differences and reduce the conflict they can create has been important to our relationship, and I suspect to most relationships. Differences between two people are seldom a matter of good or bad, right or wrong, smart or foolish, and viewing them that way will only cause grief. Gradually, my wife and I have come to accept each other's natures, set realistic expectations, distinguish the important from the trivial, and do things in ways that avoid needless conflict.

Of course, none of this is easy, and new situations arise regularly that test our resolve. For example, I still don't know what will happen with the sabbatical leave. These are uncharted waters. I do believe, however, that it will get settled in a way we'll both accept, that neither of us will completely get our way, and that no blood will be spilled. There were times that I wouldn't have been so sure. With relationships, you keep learning and adjusting as you go, and if my situation is typical, men often have the most learning and adjusting to do.

Chapter Six

Developing an Essay

When I write, I usually have plenty to say. Ideas come to me throughout the drafting process. Sometimes I end up with too much material and I have to decide what's worth keeping. However, other times I struggle to get my thoughts on paper, as do most writers.

When you have problems writing about a particular topic, you may be short on ideas. In that case, you might try a different topic. However, there are also ways to develop a paper so as to lengthen it and make it more interesting and informative. The methods of development presented in this chapter should help you get beyond certain "sticking points" in your writing.

Journal Entry 34

Relate in general how easy or difficult it is for you to write an essay. What do you do when the words come slowly? How do you keep going?

METHODS OF DEVELOPMENT

To research methods of development, I analyzed my own writing, student essays, and professional writing. In most instances, essay development is determined by the writer's topic and purpose. Writers don't decide in advance to use particular methods of development in an essay or to develop paragraphs in a variety of ways.

Experienced writers develop their writing in more ways than less-experienced ones, suggesting that the more you write, the more tools you acquire. However, any writer can become more effective in "fleshing out" an essay by being aware of different kinds of development.

What, Why, and How

Writers develop papers by unconsciously answering their readers' unvoiced questions. While I don't consciously answer questions as I write, my writing is actually a series of responses to one query after another throughout a paper.

For analysis, I wrote a series of short essays. These are the most common questions my writings answered.

1. *What* questions:

   What's your topic?
   What are some examples?
   What do you mean? (What does that mean?)

What happened? (What happened next?)

What is it? (What are they?)

What does it (he, she) look like?

What are the steps?

What are the reasons?

What's the problem?

What caused it?

What was the result?

What's the solution?

What did you learn?

What's your conclusion?

What's your point?

What about the future?

2. *Why* questions:

Why is that?

Why do you feel that way?

Why do you believe that?

Why not?

Why did it happen?

Why did it change?

3. *How* questions:

How did (would) you do it?

How did it happen?

How did it change?

How does it work?

How did it effect you?

How did you feel?

I wrote the following essay with questions inserted in parentheses to show how my writing answers a series of questions.

AUTHOR'S SAMPLE DRAFTS

Fence Extenders

(What's your topic?) A couple years ago I invented something and lost a lot of money. You'll read about it later in the chapter. After

that experience, I swore off inventions, having supposedly learned my lesson. However, lately I've gotten the bug again, and history may unfortunately be repeating itself.

(What do you mean?) I'm looking into manufacturing what I call a "fence extender." *(What is it?)* It would be a piece of wrought-iron fencing three feet tall that attaches to the top of any wooden fence that is located on an alley. It could be attractive and also raise the height of an average fence to about nine feet.

(What's the point?) Millions of homes are built on lots with alleys behind them. Burglars find hopping the back fence the easiest way to get onto a property undetected, and a number of "back alley" burglaries have occurred in my neighborhood in recent years. However, a nine-foot fence is not inviting to scale, and burglars would look for greener pastures. An entire block lined with these back alley security fences would be a deterrent to crime.

(What's the next step?) I've checked a number of fencing stores, and apparently there are no fence extenders on the market. I have seen wrought-iron security bars in store windows that could be modified for fence extenders. *(What are some modification examples?)* They'd have to be shortened a couple feet, holes would need to be drilled in the horizontal bars to attach to the wooden fence, and they'd have to be cut in five-foot lengths for easy transport and mounting.

(So what's the problem?) I'm still at the "wouldn't that be a good idea" stage, and I should probably stay there. Proceeding further requires a number of steps that take time and money, neither of which I can spare. *(What are the steps?)* First, I'd need to find a wrought-iron manufacturing company to design a prototype fence extender for me. *(Why is that?)* Until I actually put one up, I don't know how it would look or whether a wooden fence would hold the extra weight. That initial prototype could cost a couple thousand dollars.

(What's the next step?) Next, I'd need to know the manufacturing cost of mass producing the fence extenders to see if they'd be affordable for homeowners. I'd have to compare prices at a number of companies, probably starting in the Los Angeles area. *(What's the next step?)* Then I'd have to do some test marketing to see if homeowners would even be interested. *(How would you do that?)* I'd need a brochure showing some attractive professional photographs of the fence extender on my own fence, which means marketing and design expenses.

(What's the next step?) Beyond that, assuming good news at each step, I'd still have to figure out transporting and storage expenses for the fencing, and the best method of selling them.

(What are some examples?) I could try door-to-door sales with reps, placing the product in lumber or fencing stores, or perhaps working mail order through do-it-yourself catalogs. Finally, I'd have to get an honest estimate of my initial investment. *(How would you do that?)* I'd sum the costs of buying the prototype, the marketing expenses, the costs for the first manufacturing run, and so on. We are talking many thousands of dollars.

(What's your conclusion?) My fence extender idea will probably not go much further. *(Why not?)* My previous experience tells me that putting anything new on the market is a long shot; that if fencing is the product, leave it to the pros; and that I've got to spend too much money with no guarantee of making any. My wife says to let it go. My kids say, let it go. My common sense says, let it go. So I guess I will. Maybe.

DEVELOPMENT ASSIGNMENT 1

For each of the next statements, come up with what, why, and how questions that would help you develop a paragraph. A number of options could work, depending on how you want to develop the topic. Then, write two paragraphs beginning with two of the lead sentences. I'll do the same.

1. The _____ (s) on campus is/are _____ .

2. _____ is easy to play.

3. _____ has a _____ sense of humor.

4. Taking notes in class is _____ .

5. The _____ in the _____ is starting to leak.

6. The _____ thing about summer is _____ .

7. _____ is my _____ relative.

8. I can't believe that I _____ .

Author's sample responses:

3. Steve Martin has a unique sense of humor. (What do you mean? What are some examples?)

5. The washing machine in the garage is starting to leak. (What's the problem? What's the solution?)

7. Uncle Hal is my strangest relative. (What do you mean? What are some examples?)

8. I can't believe that I'm rewriting half of this chapter. (Why is that?) (What are some examples?)

Paragraphs:

Uncle Hal was my strangest relative. He was a wild-looking old man with buggy, bloodshot eyes, an unruly shock of white hair, and a sly, crooked grin. When I visited his house as a kid, he'd get this menacing look and say, "Don't go behind the house. I've got an alligator back there," or "There's a crazy man prowling around the house who cuts off boys' ears." After he scared the daylights out of me, he'd whoop and holler and slap his bony thigh. "I got you good," he'd chortle. He loved scaring his nephews. That's all I remember him doing.

I can't believe I'm rewriting half of this chapter. When I reviewed the manuscript one last time before mailing it to the copyeditor, I made simple wording revisions in most chapters. Then when I got to this chapter, I wasn't happy. I'd written a lot on development, but I didn't see how you were going to apply it to your writing. I decided to scrap the first ten pages and start over, which is unusual this late in the process. I started writing essays and analyzing my paragraph development, and the question and response patterns emerged that I am now using. This was my most difficult chapter to write.

Here are more of my sample drafts with questions in parentheses that are answered by the writing.

Traveling Through China

(Opening paragraphs of a draft)

(What's the topic?) Last summer my wife and I spent three weeks traveling through China with a group of twenty-five Americans. Since my return, I've been asked countless times "What's China like," and my answers never satisfy me. *(Why not?)* The truth is, I

don't *know* what China's like. A three-week, 2500-mile trip across the country doesn't qualify me as an expert. What I brought back from China were a number of impressions rather than a clearly formed viewpoint.

(What's one impression?) China seems a country in perpetual motion. *(What are some examples?)* From dawn until late at night bikers glide through the streets, miraculously dodging a decrepit parade of old government trucks, sardine-can taxis, and overcrowded buses. In and off the streets people are selling wares, buying vegetables, fixing bicycles, hanging out clothes, sweeping tiny rooms, cooking in pots, digging trenches, carrying baskets on poles, and busying their hands in a hundred ways.

(What's another impression?) Driving through the streets, you glimpse swatches of color everywhere. *(What are some examples?)* A busload of yellow-capped, red-scarfed students; flower wreaths adorning a newly opened business; bikers in hooded rain ponchos of red, purple, and yellow; brightly colored laundry hanging from apartment ledges; maple-lined streets; and young women awash in colors, disdaining the government-imposed drabness of the past.

(What's another impression?) China is a country under repair. *(What do you mean?)* Brick and concrete rubble line the sides of streets like the remains of a bombing or earthquake. *(Why is that?)* Old edifices are being torn down to widen roads or build new apartments or commercial buildings. Given the age of its cities and the slow pace of building in China, where shovels are more common than power trenchers, it will be under construction for decades.

House Painting

(first few paragraphs and conclusion)

(What's the topic?) When my son suggested last summer that we paint the outside of the house ourselves rather than hire painters, I liked the idea. We could save a couple thousand dollars and knock out the job in two days. Little did I know what we were getting into.

(What happened?) First, I discovered that you don't just start painting your house. You have to prepare it for painting. *(What does that require?)* On the advice of a friend, we rented a power water sprayer to hose down the house, knocking off all the dirt and loose paint. Then we went back and scraped and sanded the wood trim where it was too rough to paint. Then we cleaned up the debris that had fallen the ground. End of day one.

(Then what happened?) Next, we had to take care of everything we didn't want to get paint on. That meant trimming the backs of shrubs and bushes that were touching the house, unscrewing light fixtures and taping off wires, and masking and newspapering all of the windows and sliding glass doors. End of day two, and not a drop of paint on the house yet.

(What happened next?) Finally, on day three we started painting. *(How did you do it?)* We hooked up the power spray gun rented from a paint store, but nothing came out of the nozzle. Two hours later, after numerous calls to the store and a visit from an experienced friend, we got the thing working and started covering the northside wall. Then another problem. *(What now?)* We had planned to cover the house in a single coat but, since we were painting white over brown, we needed two coats to cover the darker paint. *(What were the effects?)* Thus we used twice as much paint as anticipated, and the spraying took twice as long. I ended up taking three hour-long trips to the store for more paint. End of day three, with the trim and eaves yet to paint—by brush.

(skipped several paragraphs to conclusion)

(What did you learn?) House painting is a big job. *(Why is that?)* You need to plan at least a week of work to do the preparation, spraying, and time-consuming trim. You also need all the essential equipment, like a spray rig, different-sized brushes, sturdy ladders, thinner, drop cloths, and lots of rags. Make sure you order enough paint, especially if you need to do two coats like we did.

(What else?) If you're not an experienced painter, start on the least visible side to practice, and count on messing up a few times. Have a wet rag beside you to wipe off your mistakes before they dry. Be patient, don't try to go too fast, be careful on the ladders, and take breaks when you get weary. If you know in advance the size of the task and what it entails, you should be fine. You'll eventually end up with a good-looking house, save a lot of money, and take pride in doing it yourself.

College Football Playoffs

(first draft)

(What's your topic?) College football needs a playoff system to determine the true national champion. *(Why is that?)* The present bowl

system doesn't establish a clear-cut champion, and often three or four teams can lay claim to being the best. The only fair way to settle the matter is a playoff system where the last team left standing is the undisputed national champion.

(How does the present system work?) Today there are about twenty-five bowl games to which the "winningest" Division I teams are invited. Each team plays in one postseason bowl, and that's it. Often the two top-ranked teams in the polls are pitted against each other in one of the more prestigious bowls. and the "mythical" national champion is crowned. *(So what's the problem?)* But other top teams, some of which may be undefeated, win their bowl games and say rightfully, "How can anyone say that Podunk College is the national champion when *we* have a better record and they've never played us?" The season usually ends in dispute.

(How would the playoffs work?) Football playoffs would work just as they do in college baseball and basketball: The top-ranked teams would play each other in a single-elimination format until the two undefeated playoff teams squared off in the national championship game. *(How many teams would compete?)* To keep the season from dragging on too long, only the top eight ranked teams would compete, and three weeks later two teams would be playing for the national championship.

(What about the bowls?) In order not to disrupt the popular bowl-game tradition, all the bowls would still be played, but on New Year's Day the four most prestigious bowl games (say, the Orange, Cotton, Sugar, and Rose Bowls) would feature the first round of the national playoffs. This could make the bowls more exciting and popular than ever, and just as many teams would compete in the post-season.

(Why hasn't it happened?) Although opinion polls show most Americans favoring college football playoffs, the American Football Coaches Association is still split on the issue. *(Why is that?)* Since the majority of college teams would never play for the national championship, their coaches favor the present bowl situation. They don't seem to understand that the bowl games and the playoffs can work together, as they would under my proposal. However, each year more coaches lean toward a post-season playoff format, so it seems just a matter of time before it happens.

(What's your conclusion?) Until that occurs, a Brigham Young University can go undefeated and be declared national champion without playing one top-ten team (1986), a great Florida State team can stub

its toe once early in the season and never get a shot at the national title (1991), or a deserving team like West Virginia can go undefeated and not be invited to the "championship" bowl (1993). *(How would that change?)* With a playoff, Brigham Young would have to prove its mettle against the best, and Florida State and West Virginia would have the chance to show what they could do.

(More conclusion) College basketball playoffs are among the most exciting events in sports, and no one questions whether the eventual winner deserves the national championship. *(What's your point?)* A college football playoff could be equally exciting and we could, once and for all, delete the "mythical" qualifier in front of the title national champion: one winner, fair and square, decided on the field rather than by a poll.

DEVELOPMENT ASSIGNMENT 2

As an experiment in essay development, write an essay that is a series of responses to questions. Pick your own topic.

Insert your questions in parentheses within the essay, answering each question as it comes to you. Refer regularly to the list of how, what, and why questions to determine which questions would best be answered at what points in the essay. To start the essay, answer the question "What's your topic?" and go from there. I'll do the same.

Single Mothers

(What's the topic?) When students in one of my classes were asked to write about a close friend or relative, four single women wrote about their young son or daughter. As it turned out, six of the ten women in the class, all in their late teens or early twenties, were single mothers. I was surprised, and a little troubled. I don't see single motherhood as a positive trend.

The single mothers in my classes have a lot in common. *(What are some examples?)* In most cases, the fathers of the children are out of the picture: they contribute no child support and have little if any contact with their child. Most of the mothers share the raising of their children with their own mothers and fathers, with whom they usually live. Grandmothers are often involved as well.

(What are other examples?) Most of the women come from low-income families and are struggling to get by. They dream of a better life for their children, and are in school to make that dream a reality. None of them seems to regret having had children or being tied down at an early age. Their children are the brightest spot in their lives.

I admire these young women for being in college. *(Why is that?)* Most of them are juggling motherhood, working, and going to school, and their days are long. Many are the first in their family to go to college. Unfortunately, too many of them never finished high school because of teenage pregnancies, and they will struggle long and hard in college to obtain the required skills for a decent job.

I also regret the ease with which they seem to accept their situations. *(What do you mean?)* For them, it seems natural to be young and unmarried and a mother. They accept the absent father's irresponsibility as the norm. *(What's the effect?)* Sadly, they will likely raise their children without fathers, and their children may someday perpetuate the cycle.

(What's your conclusion?) Most of the women are really good people, and I don't judge them. Their self-esteem and peer status are tied to early motherhood; they are not only unashamed of being unwed mothers, they are proud of it. I have much contempt, however, for the young men who are the absent fathers. What could be more irresponsible than fathering a child and walking away, and how can they get away with it?

(More conclusion) When I read these women's papers, I feel their pride and love for their children. They are trying hard to be good mothers, and their children are lucky for that. *(What about the fu-*ture?)* I can only hope that these young women will buck the odds, complete college, and find good jobs, breaking the cycle of poverty that seems most responsible for their situations. And I hope they can instill in their sons the responsibility and pride in family that their absent father's lacked.

Journal Entry 35

Relate your experience writing paragraphs by generating and answering questions. How easily did questions come to you? What kinds of questions did you ask and answer? How might you use the questioning method in your regular writing process?

CHAPTER WRITING ASSIGNMENT

For this chapter's main essay, write about any topic of interest with which you've had some personal experience—doing, observing, or reading about. Once you select a topic, think about the following.

1. What do you want to do with your topic? What approach might you take?

2. Who might be interested in reading your essay? Whom will you write for?

3. What do you want to accomplish (what is your purpose in writing to this particular audience)?

Before writing, do some type of prewriting activity—brainstorming, making a list, free writing, clustering, asking questions—to help you generate some ideas (and perhaps find an approach) for your essay. When writing your draft, consider the what, why, how questions if you get stuck (or as a general means of developing your paper).

AUTHOR'S PREWRITING THOUGHTS

There are a lot of things I'm interested in and have some experience with: playing golf, composing songs on the piano, watching sports live and on TV, going to movies, eating out, reading mystery novels, going on vacations, being a parent, weightlifting, inventing, and writing. I could enjoy writing about most of these things, but I'm not sure you would enjoy reading about them.

I don't want to write about typical "guy" things that wouldn't interest many women readers, and I don't want to write about something that might interest me but bore most of you. I've written enough about writing, so that's out. I've enjoyed some nice vacations, but they aren't the type that most college students could afford or that I could have afforded as a student, so why write about them?

There's also no point in my writing about some great local restaurant because you'll probably never eat there. I could write about serious problems at our college or in my state, but such topics may hold little interest for students who live far away.

I'm thinking about writing about my piano composing or my one inventing experience. Which would be more interesting for readers? Which could they get something out of? I'm leaning toward the inventing experience because there's a story in it that might interest you, and the experience is in the past, so I can reflect on it. With the composing, I think the process of creating melodies is more interesting to me than to you, and I don't even know if they're any good. With my invention, I think I can answer that question.

A couple hours have passed, and I've decided to write about the invention. I've got plenty to say about it, so I won't have trouble getting started. My audience, of course, will be you—my student readers. My basic approach is to reveal the errors in what I did and apply them to situations in which my readers may find themselves. Maybe you can learn from my mistakes.

STUDENT WRITERS' RESPONSES

Derrick

Let's see, what have I experienced, observed, or read that I could write about? Some of the things I know a lot about I'm not too proud of, and I wouldn't write about them. There are other things I've gone through, like my folks' divorce, that I don't want to write about. I can't think of anything special that I might know more about than the next person. I just don't know.

After giving this more thought, I decided that the only thing I have some inside knowledge about is what it's like being in a gang. I was in one from the time I was twelve until I was about seventeen. You read and hear so much about gangs from people who don't know anything about them. I could set a few things straight from my experience.

I would write this to anyone who was interested in knowing more about gangs and what they're all about. I'd write this mainly for people my age since I'd feel most comfortable with them reading it. I wouldn't write it for young people because I'm not into giving advice to kids about gangs. They'll learn like I did, and no one could have told me any different.

I'm not sure what my approach will be. Gangs aren't all bad as most people think, but they aren't all good either. I know that gangs fill needs for a lot of city kids, and unless the situation changes in the cities, gangs will always be around. That could be a possible approach. I'll do some free writing before I start my first draft and see what comes out of it.

Lourdes

I guess the one thing that I know a lot about is waitressing. I've been a waitress on and off for a number of years, and I know all the tricks, like how to work customers for the best tips, how to carry lots of plates to cut down on trips to the kitchen, how to keep orders straight, how to handle rude customers, and how to deal with lousy bosses. I think I could write a book.

Waitressing isn't a bad way to make money if you can get enough hours and know the best places to work. Wow. Rereading that sentence I think I just came up with my thesis for the paper. That's the way I feel about waitressing. But then again, if you don't know the tricks of waitressing, it's not such a good job. So I need to change my approach some, maybe more of an "If you know the basic tricks of waitressing, it can be a well-paying and enjoyable job." I don't like the word "tricks" though. I'll come up with a better one.

AUTHOR'S FIRST DRAFT

Yard Tongs

Whenever I go out to the garage and see 800 pairs of Yard Tongs staring at me, I'm reminded of the biggest commercial fiasco of my life. ~~Sure,~~ I'd lost time and money on other ~~projects,~~ *failed ventures,* like the old apartments I'd bought and sold for a loss, and the "how to get published" book that cost more to advertise than ~~it brought~~ *I recovered* in profits. *However,* ~~but~~ I really topped myself when I became an inventor.

Maybe most people at one time or another have thought about inventing something, but I'm one of those people who, once I get an idea, I carry it to its ultimate conclusion. One time while I was out in the yard ~~scooping~~ *picking* up some bush trimmings with my hands, I thought "Gee, if there were a tool that could scoop things up like my hands do, only with a lot larger scoops than my hands, it could be useful for yard cleanup." I figured the idea was so simple that there was

wordy—rewrite

probably a tool like that on the market already, so I went to a number of hardware stores and found nothing. I came away excited, and determined to ~~invent~~ *introduce* that *wonderful new* yar'd tool ~~that everyone would find as useful as I imagined it.~~ *to thousands of grateful workers.*

Then followed two years of experimenting with different tool designs and materials in search of that perfectly functioning prototype. *define* — I gave up at one time because the various plastic scoops I tried out didn't do the job well. Then the idea struck me of scoops made from *"scoop" overused* metal tines shaped similarly to pitchfork scoops that would scoop under the pile of brush or leaves or trimmings and compress them together as the scoops closed together. I had such a prototype made, *tighten* — with scissoring handles that separated and closed the scoops around their loads. I tried it out at home, and it worked quite well. I finally had what I wanted.

I showed the prototype to a few friends and relatives, and most of them thought it was a good idea. That was all I needed to crank into high gear. I scoured the state for a wire welding company that could make the tool in volume at a reasonable price, and finally came to terms with one in the Los Angeles area. I had them make a thousand for me, a very modest first run based on what I imagined the future to be: Yard Tongs, the name I christened the tool with, selling at Sears, K-Mart, True Value, Ace, and independent hardware stores across the country.

Never one to think small, I wrote letters and sent videos ~~I had made~~ of the tool in action to the lawn and garden buyers for all of the big national chains. At the same time, I sent similar materials to a dozen national catalogue companies that specialized in yard tools.

Contemplating an ever-widening market for Yard Tongs (before I had even sold one), I put "help wanted" ads in all of the major city newspapers across the country to attract tools salesmen to sell my tool directly to school districts, golf courses, and city parks and rec-reation departments. And to cover my invention, of course, I began the legal process of applying for a patent so that no one could "steal" my idea.

As I started hearing from people, I was ~~surprised that~~ there wasn't a lot of interest shown in my invention. Most of the national chains and the catalogue companies said they weren't interested, ~~in~~ *not needed* ~~a nice way of course,~~ and a couple expressed what I considered at least mild interest. Well, those companies I pursued with a vengeance, and after a lot of phone calls and persistance, I was off to Chicago to meet with the national buyers for Ace and True Value, the largest hardware chains in the country.

My trip to Chicago was my first real eye-opener. First, I discovered that the buyers have hundred of people coming to them a month with new products, most of which they aren't interested in carrying in their stores, and don't have room for even if they were. Second, I discovered that the buyers are interested in "lines" of tools, not single items. A common question I was asked was "What else do you have?" Well, of course, I had nothing, and they proceeded to tell me how tough it was to get a single item going; they were interested in dealing with the big manufacturing companies such as True Temper that sold complete lines of yard tools. I was the smallest of fish in a very large pond.

I came home depressed but not devastated. The big companies had left me with a little hope: "Show us a sales record and we'll talk to you again" (a nice way to send folks packing). Well, I was still confident that the public would love my invention as much as I did, so I got a few units of Yard Tongs placed on a consignment basis in over fifty stores throughout the central California valley. I had posters made to put in the stores, ran ads in several papers, and even got some free publicity on a "unique new invention" from newspaper articles and a television news feature.

The results of my efforts were sporadic sales over a period of four months. Only one store sold out and was restocked a couple times. The rest sold two or three of the original five I placed. Clearly,

unnecessary I hadn't gotten the results I needed to interest the big chains, and it wasn't a lot of fun going back to these stores after four months and collecting the ones that hadn't sold.

So here I sit with 800 out of my original thousand Yard Tongs crowding our cars out of the garage. My national network of sales-men never materialized. Once those ~~that~~ *who* inquired learned more of the product and the "commission" nature of the job, they weren't inter-ested. From my own inquiries, I realized that the school/golfcourse/city parks market wasn't really there. They've got big machines that do everything my little tool does, and on a much larger scale.

wordy—revise And the news from the patent office wasn't good: other tools had been invented over the years similar enough to mine that they wouldn't grant an outright patent without further evidence of differ-ences, and it would cost me another $2000 in legal fees to reapply. Forget it.

I've flat run out of ideas on where to go from here. Frankly, I'm think I'm whipped. There were so many things I should have done differently before pouring some $20,000 down the drain in manufacturing, advertising, and legal fees. As usual, I've learned the hard way, but at my age you'd think I'd have found a better way to learn. Since I don't seem to learn well from my past experiences, maybe you can.

First, if you're an amateur playing among professionals, you're probably in trouble. There are individuals and companies who invent products for a livelihood who have a lifetime of experience and savvy over me. I was playing a game without first learning the rules or checking out the competition. If I had, I would have realized I was in over my head, just ~~like~~ *as* a ~~successful~~ tool inventor would probably be in writing a textbook.

Second, don't expect others to ever see your creation the way you do. I *knew* that my Yard Tongs was one of the greatest lawn and garden inventions in history. All anyone had to do was see it to agree. In thinking that, I was a majority of one. Along the same lines, don't base business decisions on what a few friends and family members tell you. No one wanted to hurt my feelings when assessing the invention, and everyone was as naive as I was about ~~the~~ *its* chances for ~~it~~ doing well. I should have sought out ~~the~~ experts and listened to their advice.

emphasize

Third, research, research, research, before spending any money on a project. I spent over $15,000 on my invention before I had any concrete indication that the public would buy it or that any stores would be interested in carrying it. I could have done a lot more investigation and consultation with real experts in the trade before ordering that first batch of 1000. And the more I hear about how large companies pay people to do nothing else but find ways around legal patents on successful products, I would guess that, had I gotten a patent, it wouldn't have been worth more than the paper it was written on.

rewrite— wordy and boring

Having said all that, I'd still never discourage anyone from dreaming and pursuing those dreams. I had some great fun working out my invention and trying to market it. It was very exciting at times, and I don't regret putting in the time. I certainly learned a lot. However, I was also stupid in getting way ahead of myself and letting my emotions overwhelm my reason. I was determined I was going to succeed, and I blocked out anything negative I heard or saw. I spent money I should have never spent without having a very good idea that I could recoup it in sales, and I'm stuck with a garage full of Yard Tongs that I'm not sure what to do with. If you've got any ideas, let me know.

add how to do things the smart way—contrast wiser plan to mine

Journal Entry 36

Relate the kind of prewriting activity you used, and how it helped you with your first draft. Next, tell how, if at all, you used the what, why, and how questions during your drafting and with what results.

REVISIONS

One thing that surprised me when I printed my first draft was its length. When I was on the computer I didn't realize how long the essay was. Reading the first draft, I looked for things to cut without hurting the overall effect, and frankly, I didn't find much. I think that, for this particular topic, I wrote the appropriate length essay to say what I wanted. I hope that my readers aren't put off by its length and will find it interesting enough to plow through.

Most of my revisions were sentence rewordings, with a few content additions I thought of as I revised. I'll take you through the first two paragraphs to show how and why I made certain revisions.

Paragraph 1: I liked the first sentence, because it is so true, so I left it as it was. In the next sentence, I deleted "Sure" because it implied an assumption the reader wouldn't make, and I changed "projects" to *failed ventures* because "projects" wasn't the right word and the word *failed* tied former ventures to the current one. I also changed "brought in" to the more accurate *recovered*, meaning "retrieving money spent." Finally, I ended the sentence after "profits" because it was already plenty long, and began a new final sentence. I changed "but" to *however* to begin the sentence, because *however* separates the final sentence more clearly from the previous one, which was my intention.

Paragraph 2: My first sentence was wordy and a bit awkward, so I revised it considerably. In the second part of the sentence, I changed "I'm one of the those people who, once I get an idea, I carry it to its ultimate conclusion" to "I'm a person who often acts on his ideas, for better or worse." I got rid of the wordiness and awkwardness in the first part, and changed "carry it to its ultimate conclusion" to *acts*, because you *act* on an idea rather than "carry it." I added *for better or worse* to show that I don't always use good judgment.

In the next sentence, I changed "time" to *summer* for specificity and changed "scooping up" to *picking up* because I overuse "scoop" in the paragraph. Then I got rid of the quotation, changing it from a thought (which I could express in a quote) to a visual image because, as I remembered, I had envisioned something in my mind.

After making minor revisions in the next sentence, I added the sentence "Rather than take that as a sign that there probably was no need for such a tool, I got excited," because this was the first of many signs that I ignored or misinterpreted in order to keep me going. For the last sentence, I changed "determined to invent that yard tool that everyone would find as useful as I imagined it" to "determined to introduce a wonderful new cleanup tool to thousands of grateful yard workers," a phrase which is less wordy, more specific, and more accurate than my first one.

Throughout the essay I made similar types of revisions, which took a couple of hours. I also defined words like *prototype* and *consignment* that some readers may find unfamiliar, and I combined two rather short paragraphs about getting the word out nationally on my product.

Finally, in the last paragraph, where I wrote that I wouldn't discourage people from pursuing their dreams, I qualified that by saying there are smart ways to do it and also foolish ways, as mine had been. I hoped my readers would be smarter. I added those thoughts because, otherwise, it seemed my positive advice to readers in the end may have contradicted the negative things I wrote about my own experience. I wanted to clarify that the problem wasn't trying to market my invention as much as it was how I went about it.

CONCLUDING THE ESSAY

Once again, I spent more time on both writing and revising my concluding paragraphs than on other parts of the paper. There are a couple reasons for that. The main one is that, until the conclusion, I am simply telling the story of how I invented and tried to market my tool. I am reporting things that happened and adding my thoughts and feelings, which for me is one of the easier types of writing.

In the conclusion, I shift from reporting to reflecting on what happened to me, attempting to analyze the experience and then articulate what I have learned. This is a different kind of writing, requiring more contemplation than retelling does.

A second reason the ending took more time is that everything I wrote in the essay leads to the conclusion. The ending is where I had to put everything into perspective for my readers and leave them with something worth thinking about. The more I think about my writing, the more I understand the value I place on the conclusion, because for me it is frequently the most important and difficult part of the essay.

A final difficulty I have with conclusions is how much to say. Sometimes I'll read an essay that doesn't need a reflective or summarizing conclusion because the rest of the essay speaks for itself. For example, a writer who told about flipping his motorcycle at 100 miles per hour, breaking twenty bones, and being hospitalized for two years doesn't have to conclude by warning us not to ride motorcycles at dangerously high speeds. We get the point—painfully.

I did feel that my latest essay needed a strong conclusion because I wanted what I had learned from my experience to apply to readers' exexperiences beyond inventions, which would interest only a few. In addition, I think a longer essay like mine needs a longer conclusion for balance, so readers won't come to an abrupt stop for which they aren't ready. But every essay is different, and my next conclusion might be far briefer.

My final draft is at the end of the chapter.

Journal Entry 37

Since you are my reading audience, please respond to the "Yard Tongs" essay: what you liked or found interesting, what if anything you could relate to your life, and what may have gotten out of it, what you found uninteresting or unnecessary, and what suggestions you'd make for improving it.

REVISION ASSIGNMENT 1

Before revising your own first draft, read the following student draft and, with a classmate, respond to these revision questions.

1. What did you like (find interesting, thought-provoking, informative) about the draft? What would you tell the writer that she did well? Give specific examples.

2. What questions do you have that the draft left unanswered? What would you like to know more about that the writer could probably have provided you?

3. What paragraphs, if any, could use further development, and why? Give specific examples, and suggest the type of development that might be effective.

4. What do you not understand, or find confusing, in the essay? Give specific examples.

5. How well is the essay paragraphed (helping readers move clearly from point to point, step to step, or incident to incident)? What, if any, paragraphing revisions might you recommend?

6. Does the draft stray off topic in any places? What would you suggest the writer do?

7. Find examples of first-draft sentences whose wording and/or structure could be improved. How might you revise them?

8. How did the opening and the conclusion affect you? How might either be improved?

9. What do you think the writer was trying to accomplish in the draft? How effectively did she do it? Whom do you think would be the best reading audience for this essay? Why?

STUDENT WRITER DRAFT

Where I Grew Up

I was born in Los Angeles and moved up to Dunlap, California, when I was two years old. My parents wanted my brother and me to grow up in better surroundings than L.A., so they moved us up to the mountains. Moving up to the mountains was a very good place for a child to grow up.

There are very nice surroundings; the air is clean and the water is pure. There are lots of trees for shade, and pastures for kids to play in. It is very peaceful in the mountains; there is not a lot of traffic or people. There are a lot of places for kids to run around and play.

Where we live there is a school near by. My brother and I could ride our bikes to school and play there on the weekends. Dunlap is a very small town and there are not a lot of troublemakers to bother the children. I always had a lot of nice friends to play with.

Dunlap is a very good place for a child to grow up, there are not a lot of problems with kids and drugs or alcohol, like there would be in a big city. Where we live there is a hang-gliding park next door. I spent fun times there at the park during the summer time. The park included a little store, mobile home parking and camping, a baseball field, and a pond. There are lots of good things for children to do and stay out of trouble at the same time. We could play baseball whenever we wanted to go fishing in the pond. The pond use to be real clean and we could swim in it under supervision, but now there are a lot of weeds and it is not safe.

I would say that Dunlap or anywhere in the mountains is a good, safe place for children to grow up. Now that I am older it is boring up there and it is so far away from the city, but I still feel that I got a safer childhood than most of my city friends.

REVISION ASSIGNMENT 2

Now reread your own draft, applying the revision questions and noting the kinds of changes you want to make. If any parts of the draft seem short on development, consider what, why, or how questions that might help you add some good material. Before revising your draft, exchange drafts with a classmate and get a second opinion. Then write the second draft of your essay, making all revisions that will improve it for readers.

EDITING

The final step in the writing process is to proofread your latest draft for errors. If you have been correcting errors throughout the drafting process, you may find little or nothing to correct. If you pay little attention to errors while you are drafting, you may find a number of mistakes in your draft. It doesn't matter what approach you take to error detection, so long as your final draft is relatively mistake-free.

EDITING ASSIGNMENT 1

Proofread the following student first draft for errors in punctuation, spelling, and grammar and make necessary corrections. Then compare your findings to a classmate's.

STUDENT WRITER DRAFT

8 Street 80's

In the neighborhood that I grew up in sometimes it was bad but most of the time it was good. I lived on the east side of the railroad tracks in Orange Cove.

In the summer time mostly every kid on the block owned a bike or skate board. We all would go riding around the block. It was our street in the day time, the only time we would go home was to eat and sleep. My sister and I where not allowed out side of the gate after 8 o'clock in the night. We lived two blocks away from a school and by the school there were the ''Projects'' and it never failed five nights out of seven there was always a police car or some kind of trouble there, that's why we always went inside the gate before dark.

In our neighborhood there where Hispanic, caucasian, and some oriental. Our house was the second house next to the corner of 8 street. Mostly everyone that lived by our house either moved to Reedley or into the country, but their are still a lot of people living in 8 street that we used to play with in the summer. When we see them we laugh and remember of the days when we would ride and play not worrying about anything but having fun and our friendship. All of us kids grew up together and we all stayed friends. You still picture everyone riding around, getting dirty and having fun. Some of our friends are still in school others moved away or got married and yes some are even dead.

EDITING ASSIGNMENT 2

Proofread your own draft for errors, paying particular attention to the kinds of errors you tend to make in your writing. If you feel the need, exchange drafts with a classmate for a second proofreading.

Journal Entry 38

Evaluate your ability to write without errors. What problems, if any, do you still have, and how are you working on eliminating them? What progress do you feel you've made in understanding and lessening your error tendencies?

AUTHOR'S FINAL DRAFT

Yard Tongs

Whenever I go out to the garage and see 800 pairs of Yard Tongs staring at me, I'm reminded of the biggest commercial fiasco of my life. I'd lost time and money on other failed ventures, like the old apartments I bought and later sold for a loss, and the "how to get published" book I wrote that cost more to advertise than I recovered in profits. However, I really topped myself when I became an inventor.

A lot of people think about inventing something at one time or another, but I'm a person who often acts on his ideas, for better or worse. One summer when I was in the yard picking up some bush trimmings with my hands, I suddenly envisioned a tool that could scoop up yard debris like my hands, only on a much larger scale. The idea seemed so simple that I figured there was a similar tool in stores already, so I went to dozen local hardware stores and found nothing. Rather than take that as a sign that there probably was no need for such I tool, I got excited. I was determined to introduce a wonderful new cleanup tool to thousands of grateful yard workers.

Next followed two years of experimenting with tool designs and materials in search of that perfectly functioning model. At one point I gave up for a couple months because the various plastic scoops I tried didn't work that well. Then a new idea struck me: two scoops made from metal tines shaped like large pitchforks that would slide under a pile of brush or leaves and then close around the load. I had a prototype (model) made, with handles that acted scissor-fashion to separate and close the scoops. I tried it at home on a pile of leaves, and it worked much better than the plastic models. I finally had what I wanted.

When I got some positive comments from my family and a few close friends (although I'll admit my wife remained somewhat skeptical), that was all I needed to crank into high gear. I searched the state for a wire welding company to manufacture the tool at a reasonable price, and finally came to terms with a Los Angeles–based company. They made a thousand Yard Tongs for me, a modest number based on my future projection: Yard Tongs selling at Sears, K-Mart, True Value, Ace, and independent hardware stores across the country.

Never one to think small, I wrote letters and sent videos to all national chains that sell hardware. I also sent similar materials to a dozen national catalogue companies specializing in yard tools. Contemplating an ever-widening market for Yard Tongs (before I'd even sold one!), I placed "help wanted" ads in major city newspapers across the country for tools salesmen to sell my Yard Tongs directly to school districts, golf courses, and city parks and recreation departments. Finally, I hired an attorney to begin the process for attaining a patent on my precious invention.

As the national chains and catalogue companies began responding, I was surprised by their lack of enthusiasm for my invention. Most of them weren't interested in carrying it, and only a couple expressed even mild interest. I pounced on those companies immediately, and finally talked their lawn and garden buyers into meeting with me. So off I headed to Chicago to talk with folks at the Ace and True Value headquarters, the largest hardware chains in the country.

The trip was my first real eye opener. First, I discovered that the buyers see hundreds of people a month with new products, most of which they're neither interested in nor have room for in their stores. Second, I found that the buyers are most interested in "lines" of tools rather than single items. I was commonly asked, "What else do you have in your line?" Of course I had nothing, and they'd tell me how tough it was to deal in a single item. They do 90 percent of their business with big companies like Ames and True Temper that manufacture every yard tool imaginable. I was the most insigificant of fish in a very large pond.

I came home depressed but not devastated. Ace and True Value had left me with a little hope: "Show us a healthy sales record and we'll talk again" (a nice way to get people out the door). Still confident that the public would love my invention, I went about placing a few units of Yard Tongs on consignment (the store only buys what it sells) in over fifty stores throughout central California. I had posters made to put in the stores, ran ads in newspapers, and got some free publicity from newspaper articles and a television news spot featuring local inventors.

The results of my efforts were sporadic sales over the four-month consignment period. Only one store sold out and needed restocking a couple times. The rest sold two or three of the original five I placed. Clearly, I didn't get the results I expected or the sales volume needed to interest Ace or True Value. It wasn't great fun going back to these stores to collect the Yard Tongs that hadn't sold.

So here I sit, with 800 of the original 1000 Yard Tongs crowding our cars out of the garage. My national network of salemen never materialized. Many people inquired, but when they learned more about the product and the "commission" nature of the job, they weren't interested. From my own inquiries, I realized that the school/golfcourse/city parks market wasn't really there. They've got big machines that do everything my little tool does, but on a much larger scale. The news from the patent office wasn't good either: Yard Tongs wasn't different enough from other tools that had been invented to grant an outright patent. My idea wasn't so new; it just hadn't been marketed successfully by previous inventors. I could reapply with more evidence, but that would cost me another $2000 in legal fees. Forget it.

I've run out of ideas on where to go from here. I'm as close to whipped as I'll ever admit. If only I had done some things differently before pouring $20,000 down the drain in manufacturing, advertising, and legal fees. As usual, I've learned the hard way, but at my age you'd think I'd have found a better way. Since I don't seem to profit from my experiences, maybe you can.

First, if you're an amateur playing among professionals, you're probably in trouble. There are individuals and companies who invent products for a living who have the wealth of experience and savvy I didn't have. There are also big manufacturing companies with long lines of products that have a virtual stranglehold on the tool business. I was playing a game without first learning the rules or checking out the competition. If I had, I would have realized I was in over my head and should have stuck with something I know better, like writing textbooks.

Second, don't expect others to view your creation as you do. I knew that Yard Tongs was one of the greatest lawn-and-garden inventions in history. Anyone who used it would agree. In thinking that, I was a majority of one. Along the same lines, don't base important business decisions on what a few friends and family members tell you. No one wanted to hurt my feelings when evaluating my invention, and everyone was as naive as I was about its chances for doing well. In the beginning I should have sought out the experts and listened to their advice.

Third, research, research, research, before spending serious money on a venture. I spent over $15,000 on my invention before getting any clear indication that people would buy it or that stores would carry it. I should have done more market research and consulted with experts in the field before ordering that first batch of 1000 units. In addition, the more I hear about how large manufacturing companies pay people to find ways around legal patents, had I gotten a patent, it might not have been worth much even if the product had sold. One more area I didn't research well.

Having said all that, I'd never discourage anyone from pursuing his or her dreams. I had great fun working on my invention and trying to market it. It was very exciting until things began falling apart, and I don't regret the time I spent.

However, I *was* stupid in getting ahead of myself and letting my emotions overwhelm my reason. I was determined to succeed, so I blocked out anything negative. I spent money I should never have spent without having a good idea that I could recoup it, and I'm stuck with loans to pay off and a garageful of *Yard Tongs*. There are different ways to pursue dreams, and my way wasn't too smart. I hope yours will be.

By the way, if you're looking for a really good tool to clean up your yard, I've got something in my garage . . . .

Chapter Seven

Writing Beyond Experience

To this point, our writing has been grounded in personal experience. We've analyzed that experience, drawn conclusions from it, compared it to other experiences, and used it to support our viewpoints. Writing from experience is valuable for both writer and readers, but it has its limitations.

We also need to write effectively beyond experiences and observations. Without this ability, we couldn't comment on the break-up of the Soviet Union, the national deficit, the Los Angeles riots of 1992, private school vouchers, euthanasia, ozone-layer depletion, or sexual harassment. While we may draw on personal experience for some of those topics, we couldn't write from experience on all of them, or on many other important issues that haven't touch us personally.

While it is good to "write what you know about," we shouldn't limit our writing to personal experience. Since writing is a tool for learning, we should also write to discover things we don't know.

Writing from experience has another limitation: its inadequacy to support arguments. If a writer bases the belief that policemen are crooked on one cop who offered to fix a ticket, the writer may be generalizing from an exceptional situation. Most readers wouldn't accept one incident as adequate proof of the contention. However, if the writer includes similar experiences friends have had with other policemen, and documents examples of police corruption in other cities, readers will pay attention.

I find that the quality of essays often suffers when students write beyond their experience. Rather than learn about a topic for themselves, they substitute the "common wisdom" of the day on the death penalty, the deficit, abortion rights, or gun control, or they parrot their parents' beliefs.

We can all write worthwhile and interesting essays on topics beyond our experience. Often student writers don't get enough help in making the transition from experience-based to research-based essays. To rectify that, I am going to assign myself such an essay, analyze its demands on me, and then tell you what I learn.

INVESTIGATING A TOPIC

The topic I have chosen is the legalization of drugs, meaning marijuana, cocaine, heroin, and other currently illegal substances. I have no experience with such drugs, nor do my family, so I cannot based the paper on personal experience. However, I am interested in the topic, which is important for the investigative work I'll need to do.

Where do I start? First, I think the legalization of drugs is an interesting proposition. I'm going to list the reasons I think so.

1. Legalizing drugs may eliminate most of the drug-related violence from illegal sales.

2. Legalizing drugs, thereby decriminalizing their use, may greatly relieve the overload in prisons and courtrooms. Police could concentrate their efforts on other crime.

3. Inner-city youths would no longer have drug dealers as role models.

4. The "war on drugs" doesn't seem to be working. We're wasting billions of dollars that could be spent on educating people about the evils of drugs.

5. Legalizing drugs wouldn't increase usage. People who want to use drugs today can get them easily.

Those ideas make drug legalization seem appealing. However, each of them is speculative. I don't know if anything would work as I envision it. I could include them in an essay about what may happen if drugs were legalized, but, without any evidence, readers shouldn't be impressed. Clearly, I need to do some investigation.

Of course, many people are against the legalization of drugs, and I need to consider their viewpoints. These are the main concerns I've heard.

1. Drug usage would increase tremendously if drugs were legalized. We'd become a nation of zombies.

2. The incidence of drug-addicted babies would become epidemic.

3. We'd be sending a morally corrupt message to youth.

4. We'd be accepting drug use as inevitable—giving up on the problem.

5. Legalizing drugs wouldn't stop the violence.

As with my own arguments, I know of no evidence supporting these opposing claims. I need to investigate such allegations and find out what else anti-legalization people contend.

How can I discover what may or may not be true, since drug legalization hasn't been tried in America? Here are some things I can do.

1. Find out what's happened in countries where drugs have been legalized. This is important, since these countries would have

evidence about the effects of drug legalization. My paper may be based on what I find out.

2. Investigate whether America's failed experience with alcohol prohibition may be similar to the current drug prohibition. It is a possible parallel, but I need to know more about the Prohibition era to make a case.

3. Find out how serious a problem drug-related crime is. I feel that it is very serious, but I will have no proof until I research the topic. I also want to research gang involvement in illegal drug trafficking.

4. Investigate whether the war on drugs is the failure I suspect. I have no evidence, and perhaps it's going better than I realize.

5. See what else my reading uncovers. There's much I don't know about the drug problem and the pros and cons of legalization.

While I lean towards supporting some form of drug legalization, I don't have the evidence to be sure. If in my investigation I find that the best arguments favor the current U.S. policy, I may change my mind. It would be foolish for me to take a hard position before learning more about drug problems.

PREWRITING CONSIDERATIONS

Based on my thoughts to this point, I suggest you take the following prewriting steps before investigating a particular topic.

1. Select a topic you are sincerely interested in, one for which people have differing viewpoints. Your interest in the topic will help you research with enthusiasm.

2. Write down what you think about the topic and the reasons for your opinion. Note what you need to check out during your research, the kinds of evidence you'll need for support.

3. Write down an opposing viewpoint you have heard and ideas that support it. Decide what you need to check on.

4. Make a list of other things you want to find out about the topic.

5. Determine how to proceed with your investigation. Where are you going to get your information?

CHAPTER WRITING ASSIGNMENT

Select a topic that interests you, that you know something about, that people have differing viewpoints on, and that a good deal has probably been written about. Take your time to consider a number of possibilities. You may want to ask your instructor whether a particular topic is readily "researchable." For prewriting work, follow the five steps just presented.

Journal Entry 39

How did you decide on a particular topic, and why did you choose it? What opinion do you have on the topic, and what could change that opinion as you do your research?

BEGINNING RESEARCH

To learn more about the legalization of drugs, I'm going to start reading. I'll begin in the library with the *Reader's Guide to Periodical Literature* to find articles written since the late 1980s. I want articles with differing viewpoints, so as to get a variety of perspectives. I hope to find articles about drug legalization in other countries and articles that compare our current drug laws to Prohibition. I'll also check *The New York Times Index* for relevant newspaper articles and the library's card catalog for recent books on the subject.

Three days have passed, and I've completed my first round of research on the legalization of drugs, primarily using periodical articles. I have more to do because I'm not satisfied with the breadth of information I've found.

Based on my research experience, here are some suggestions for you.

1. Begin in the library with the *Reader's Guide to Periodical Literature*. This is a great starting point for many topics. I was able to find over twenty articles, from 1988 through 1992, related to my topic. *The New York Times Index* also produced a few good articles, and I recommend using it or other major newspaper reference books available at your library.

2. Ask for help. Use your librarians as resource people. I was disappointed in the number of articles I was finding under "drugs" in the *Reader's Guide*, so the librarian suggested I check under "narcotics" or "legalization of drugs." Bullseye! I found a lot more articles.

3. Relevant articles may be under more than one topic heading in the *Reader's Guide* or the *Times Index*. As I said, I found articles under "drugs," "narcotics," "legalization of drugs," and "legalization of narcotics."

4. Find the most current articles available. Begin with the latest *Reader's Guide* or newspaper article reference and work backwards. The more you rely on recent material, the better.

   For example, in researching drug use, I realized that even in 1987 or 1988, the situation was different. In articles from those years, crack cocaine was just emerging and drug-related HIV infection wasn't a big problem. I won't use information that presents a false picture of today's drug situation.

5. Don't expect all periodicals to be in the library. Of the fifteen periodicals my articles came from, only ten were available in the college library. No library has every periodical listed in the *Reader's Guide*, so make a longer list of articles than you think you will use. You won't find some of them.

6. Duplicate articles from periodicals or microfilm. It will cost a few dimes, but it's important to take copies of the articles home, since you can't check them out.

7. Examine each article before duplicating it. I found some articles that weren't relevant to my topic, so I didn't copy them. You can't always tell by a title whether an article will be of use.

8. Expect surprises. The readings didn't match my expectations. Here are some examples:

   - Legalization of drugs was a hot issue in 1988. Since then, with the media emphasis on the war on drugs, little has been written about legalization. How shall I deal with an issue that is dormant?

   - Some big names, both liberals and conservatives, have lined up in favor of drug decriminalization, including mayors, judges, and former narcotics agents. I was surprised at the range of people, though the numbers were always small.

   - No country has legalized hard drugs. Only Holland has certain aspects of decriminalization in their laws. I was hoping to find more comparisons to use.

   - There are some options between legalization of drugs and American-style Prohibition. I hadn't considered options but now I will.

   - Predictions on the effects of drug legalization are speculative. Since only Holland has tried a limited form of decriminalization, there's little of substance to draw from. I was disappointed by the lack of evidence supporting positions on either side of the issue.

9. Plan on putting in some time. Identifying, tracking down, and duplicating relevant articles is not a quick process. It takes work and is not without frustrations. Plan on spending a day in the library locating sources and duplicating materials.

10. Read relevant articles at least twice, noting anything that may be of use for your paper. It's surprising how much more you understand and retain on a second reading.

11. As you read, consider your sources. Is the author an expert on the topic? Is the viewpoint colored by politics or self-interest? Does the magazine or newspaper have a reputation for credibility?

RESEARCH ASSIGNMENT

Complete your library research on your topic, making copies of relevant articles. Then read them carefully a couple times, noting anything you feel may be usable in a paper.

Journal Entry 40

Relate your research process: the steps you took, what you were able to find, what frustrations you had, and what you ended with. What did you learn that will help your research the next time?

PLANNING THE ESSAY

Now that I have done most of my research, I am going to make some general plans for the essay. I wasn't sure what I wanted to do until I investigated the topic. These are my initial plans.

1. I want to present a short history of the legalization movement of the late 1980s.

2. It's important to present Presidents Reagan and Bush's war on drugs, which quieted the legalization movement, and to reveal the "war's" results after years of implementation.

3. My tentative approach is that, after eight years of a failed war on drugs, it's time to look again at the option of legalization.

4. I don't think readers will be interested in legalization unless I convince them that the current approach is hurting more than helping. This will be a crucial part of the paper.

5. I still have ambivalent feelings about legalization, even after the reading I've done. I need to read more and develop stronger arguments before I write. I want to be more convinced before I try to convince readers. On the other hand, if more reading doesn't lead to better evidence, I might change my approach. This is not an easy issue.

6. You, my readers, are a good audience for this essay, since most of you are in the 18 to 30 age group that will determine the direction of our drug policy in the future.

PLANNING ASSIGNMENT

Based on your research, write an initial plan for your essay: what you want to include, what approach you may want to take (thesis), what you would like to accomplish, the general order for presenting your ideas, who your audience is, and what you need to do before beginning your first draft.

Convincing Your Readers

When writing an essay on a controversial topic, you need to convince readers that your viewpoint makes sense. Here are some points to consider.

1. Provide evidence to support your viewpoint. I can't just tell readers that Reagan and Bush's war on drugs has been a failure. I have to convince them by providing proof: showing that drug trafficking, drug availability, and drug use have not diminished over recent years, and revealing the amount of money and manpower that has been wasted in this failed effort.

2. Support every claim. Every time you make a statement that many readers won't automatically accept or believe, you need to support it.

I'll be making many such claims in my essay: that the war on drugs isn't working; that there is a lesson to be learned from our failed attempt to prohibit alcohol use; that much of the violent crime in America is attributable our drug policy; that the legalization of drugs will sharply reduce the amount of crime in America; that education, not punishment, is the way to reduce drug use; that addicts are not criminals any more than alcoholics are; that legalization will not increase the number of drug users in the country; in short, that it is time to take another look at the decriminalization of drugs.

I cannot make any of these statements without supporting facts and expect readers to accept it. I must provide proof that what I contend is true, or at least highly probable. Without proof, my statements are of little value.

3. Present opposing arguments and refute them. It is not enough to present my side of the issue. I also need to address the doubts that many readers have about drug legalization. I will refute the assumptions that legalization will result in increased drug use, and that we can win the war on drugs by spending more money, hiring more police officers, and building more jails. Many people believe these things, and I need to convince them otherwise. If I don't, they won't listen to my viewpoint.

4. Relate to readers. I want readers to know that I respect their viewpoints and understand their feelings. I won't alienate the people I am trying to convince by belittling them or their ideas. I want them to reconsider their thinking based on new information. I want them to know that we're in this drug mess together, and that we want the same things: safe streets and a drug-free country. We all want the same ends, but I want my readers to consider a different means.

SUPPORTIVE EVIDENCE ASSIGNMENT

1. Decide which of the following statements would require support for most readers to accept or believe it, and which probably wouldn't. For those that need support, decide what you might provide for evidence.

   a. Arsenio Hall is the best talk show host on television.

   b. The Chicago Bulls won back-to-back NBA championships, only the third team in the history of the NBA to do so.

   c. The AIDS epidemic is changing the sexual practices of many single Americans.

   d. Nothing in a man's experience can compare to a woman's giving birth.

   e. Long-haired cats shed a lot more fur in the summertime than short-haired cats.

   f. It is easier to revise papers on a word processor than on a typewriter.

   g. President Clinton's popularity rose dramatically in the months following approval of NAFTA.

   h. If you're moving from Florida to Minnesota, you'd better prepare for a lot colder weather.

i. Japan and Germany have better educational systems than the United States.

j. If we don't start "buying American," millions of jobs in the United States will be lost to foreign countries over the next ten years.

2. Assume you are going to take the following viewpoint on each of the subjects presented. List at least one *opposing argument* that you would include and refute in an essay. How might you refute the argument?

a. To combat violent crime, we need stronger gun-control laws in the United States.

b. No one has the right to take the life of an unborn child.

c. The high cost of tuition is robbing many young Americans of the opportunity for a college education.

d. Capitalism based on owners getting wealthy off the productivity of poorly paid workers is wrong.

e. The United States should send amateur athletes to the Olympics and leave the professionals at home.

f. Elementary school teachers are the most important members of their profession.

g. The legal drinking age should be lowered to eighteen.

First Draft

I am ready to start my first draft. I feel strongly enough about my approach to begin writing, and my research has provided me with the means to make my case. There comes a time in the research process where you want to start writing, and I'm there.

For my first draft, I am *not* going to provide all my research or cite all my sources. I want you to read the paper before and after, so that you can see where and how I use the research to advance my purpose.

AUTHOR'S FIRST DRAFT

Legalizing Drugs

America's "war on drugs" is now into its tenth year. So how goes the war? We have arrested and locked up hundreds of thousands of drug users and dealers, confiscated tons of illegal narcotics, and spent more money and manpower on fighting drugs than ever before. We must surely be winning this war.

However, studies reveal that the war on drugs has made no perceptible change in America's drug problem. Drugs are continuing to come into the country in record amounts, drug use throughout society has not decreased noticeably, and drug-related violence is higher than ever. How can an all-out assault on the problem produce such negligible results?

There are a number of possible reasons. First, drug addiction, like alcohol addiction, is a disease, not a crime. Locking up users rather than treating their addiction does not help. When they get out, they are still addicted and will turn again to crime to support their habit. Second, if people desire drugs, they are going to get them one way or another. Prohibition taught us that making alcohol consumption illegal and enforcing the law doesn't keep people from acquiring and drinking it. Why would drug users act any differently when it comes to getting heroine, cocaine, or crack? Obviously, they won't.

Third, the numbers of drug users hasn't dropped appreciably because you can't lock them all up. A small percentage of Americans who use illegal drugs are ever arrested, so the impact on the number of people taking drugs is small. Finally, many drug users are poor people in the cities, primarily minorities, who turn to drugs out of despair or hopelessness about their future. Since they have little to look forward to, they settle for the quick gratification of a crack or heroin high. Until the economic and unemployment problems of the inner cities are dealt with, drug use will probably remain high.

Perhaps the answer is to throw more money, policemen, and border patrol at the problem, and to build more prisons and increase sentences. The trouble is, that is exactly what we've done the past few years, and it hasn't helped. We already have a greater percentage of our population in prisons than any other country. Could building more prisons and incarcerating more people, primarily minorities, be the answer? How about giving more time to the "war?" Should we give it another five years and see where we are? The government gave Prohibition over ten years to work, and it never did. Why would it be different with drug prohibition?

Drug prohibition in the United States causes more problems than it solves. The high incidence of drug-related crimes, many of them violent, is related to the illegality of drugs. First, it creates an underworld of drug smugglers, dealers, and users who commit violent crimes against one another and against innocent bystanders. America is a frighteningly violent place to live, and drug-related crime is a major reason. Second, drug dealers use children as lookouts and provide inner-city youths with a prosperous role model: the neighborhood dealer. "Why work for minimum wage at McDonald's when you can make $500 a day dealing drugs?" asked an African American teenager in the acclaimed movie *Boyz 'n the 'Hood*. Drug prohibition creates youthful criminals and immoral role models for millions of children.

Finally, locking up droves of drug users puts a tremendous strain on our overburdened judicial and prison systems, and the war on drugs has diverted billions of dollars and tremendous manpower toward fighting a hopeless battle. In fact, some experts believe the emphasis on drug enforcement has been responsible for an increase in other types of crimes.

If the war on drugs is failing, and if the effects of drug prohibition are negative, what's an alternative? Picture, if you will, an America where drugs are decriminalized, where adults can legally use heroin or cocaine, and where drugs can be purchased at a pharmacy. What would be the results?

First, violent crime in America would decrease. Illegal drug trafficking would cease, drug suppliers and dealers would be out of business, and the price of drugs would drop, reducing the users' need to rob and burglarize. America would be a safe place to raise a family.

Next, the billions of dollars and thousands of police officers used to enforce drug prohibition could now be concentrated in other areas, reducing the crime rate further. With drug decriminalization, the prison population would drop, saving taxpayers money, and our clogged judicial system would be able to prosecute serious offenders more quickly.

The advantages go on and on: children no longer involved in drug dealing, no more inner-city gang involvement, no more drug-dealer role models, no more HIV-infected needles passed among heroin users, no more treating addicts as criminals, and no longer the attractive allure of illicit, forbidden drugs.

Let's end the war on drugs and launch a "war on ignorance." Using the money currently spent on drug prohibition, let's educate our youth on the evils of drugs. Cigarette smoking in the United States has dropped dramatically the past fifteen years as people have learned about its harmful effects. The same would be true for drug use if a massive educational program were implemented. Knowledge, not fear of punishment, is the key to solving our drug problem.

Detractors of legalization believe that it would lead to a huge increase in drug use, creating a nation of zombies. This scenario insults the American people, most of whom are intelligent and willful enough to disdain the pernicious pleasures of narcotics, legal or otherwise. And with our efforts redirected towards educating rather than punishing people, the net result of legalization plus education will be a significant reduction in drug use over time.

Legalizing drugs does not mean giving in to the problem—nor condoning drug use. Rather, we would eliminate the violent crime related to drug prohibition and concentrate our efforts on educating America to the horrors of narcotics. The government's "just say no" campaign and TV ads like "your brain on drugs" are pathetically inadequate in educating youth. Drug education should be a cornerstone of the health-education curriculum in every school in our country from first grade through high school. Our war on drugs would continue, but by using a more effective weapon: knowledge.

I would like to see the decriminalization of drugs in the United States within a year. However, I know that isn't going to happen. Too many people believe that legalization would mean giving in, and would result in increased drug use. No matter how strong a case is made for legalization, the issue is so emotionally charged that many people won't listen objectively.

Holland has taken a half-way step towards decriminalization that we could consider as an alternative to going straight to legalization. In Holland, while drug trafficking is illegal and offenders are prosecuted, since 1982 people aren't prosecuted for marijuana or "hard drug" use, or for possessing small amounts.

Holland's relaxed drug laws haven't led to an alarming increase in use, and while 90 percent of its drug addicts who seek help can get it, fewer than 10 percent of American addicts can get help. In addition, Amsterdam, with a population of 600,000, had twelve drug-related murders in 1988, while Washington, D.C., with a comparable population, had over 200 drug-related murders.

Holland's twelve-year drug decriminalization hasn't led to widespread abuse. However, it has reduced drug-related violence, recognized drug addiction as a disease rather than a crime, and remained tough on drug traffickers. This approach is working well in Holland, and worth considering as a model for the United States. Our failed war on drugs needs to take a new direction, and we don't need more arrests, more prisoners, more prisons, and more money and manpower spent in the same futile way. Decriminalizing drugs will make us a safer country and put the emphasis on educating our youth for a drug-free tomorrow.

DRAFTING ASSIGNMENT

Write the first draft of your essay based on your plan devised from the assignment on page 190. Don't be concerned with citing your research sources in the first draft.

Incorporating Research Material

Throughout my first draft, I made a number of factual claims that my research confirms. In my second draft, I will include the support for those claims and where I found it. Without that support, my paper would have little weight.

The following guidelines will help you incorporate research materials into your essay.

1. For each claim you make, support it with evidence from your research.

Claim: America's war on drugs has made no perceptible difference in the country's drug problems.

Research support: Baltimore mayor Schmoke's contention that the country is "awash in drugs" and that tougher enforcement, great interdiction efforts, and harsher rhetoric have done and will do absolutely no good. Schmoke's contention is corroborated by former justice Sweet and criminal justice professor Trebach.

Claim: Drug addiction is a disease, not a crime.

Research support: Respected opinion of the American Medical Association.

2. Provide the source for each piece of research material you use in the essay, including the author's name and the page number. You may do it any of these simple ways:

a. Introduce the author and put the page number in parentheses at the end of the research material: "According to Baltimore Mayor Kurt Schmoke, America's war on drugs has made little impact on the drug problem (22)."

b. Present research material, and put the author's last name and the page number in parentheses at the end: "America's war on drugs has made little impact on the drug problem (Schmoke, 22)."

c. Introduce the name of the article and the magazine, present research material, and put the author's last name and the page number in parentheses at the end: "The article 'A War for the Surgeon General' in *Nation* magazine concluded that America's war on drugs has made little impact on the drug problem (Schmoke, 22)."

3. Include a "works cited" page at the end of the essay, listing all research sources used in the essay. (See Works Cited at the end of my upcoming second draft.) Follow these guidelines.

    Works Cited
    For articles:
    Author's last name, first name. "Title of article." *Title of periodical or newspaper* volume, (date of publication): page number (s).

    For books:
    Author's last name, first name. *Title of book*. City, state of publication: Publishing company, year of copyright.

4. In your essay, *paraphrase* the majority of the research material: put the author's thoughts in your own words. Use direct quotations sparingly, mainly to capture a particularly well-worded or powerfully phrased sentence. (Note the use of paraphrasing and quoting in my second draft.)

5. Anything in your essay that does not include a source reference is assumed to be your own thoughts, a conclusion you've drawn, or a generally acceptable fact that readers wouldn't contest.

REVISIONS

Beyond my usual wording changes, my revision efforts went into adding supportive research material and providing source references. To show you how I incorporated the research material, I've highlighted in bold print examples of the information I included from the research in my second draft:

America's "war on drugs" has made no perceptible difference in America's drug problems. Drugs are continuing to come into the country in huge amounts, drug use has actually risen, and drug-related violence is extremely high. **Baltimore mayor Kurt Schmoke, a former state's attorney and highly visible drug prosecutor, said "The United States has become absolutely awash in illegal drugs," and "tougher laws, greater efforts at interdiction, and stronger rhetoric . . . have not and will not be able to stop the flow" (11). Former federal judge Robert Sweet attacked the war** on drugs as being "bankrupt" (Morganthau, 48); criminal-justice professor Arnold Trebach calls drug prohibition "a good idea that doesn't work" (42); and the European community, skeptical of George Bush's war on drugs, has looked at other options (Dickey, 37).

Third, the numbers of drug users hasn't dropped appreciably, because you simply can't lock them all up. **According to Schmoke, a relatively small percentage of the number of Americans who use illegal drugs are ever arrested, so the impact of arrests on the numbers of people taking drugs is very small (12).** In addition, even if we tried to lock up every drug user in the country, we couldn't build enough jails to put them in, and the cost to taxpayers would be extraordinary.

Even in a city that is supposedly a model for successful drug-enforcement practices, Tampa mayor Sandy Freedman admits, "Until there is adequate jail space, stronger sentencing guidelines, and greater commitment to drug education and rehabilitation, the country will be fighting a losing battle" (Methvin, 60). This is a telling statement, coming nearly ten years into the drug war from the mayor of a model war-on-drugs city. The war simply isn't working.

Drug prohibition in the United States causes more problems than it solves. A high number of violent crimes are drug-related. Prohibition creates an underworld of drug smugglers, drug dealers, and drug users who commit violent crimes against one another and against innocent bystanders. **According to Trebach, of the 367 murders committed in Washington, D.C., in 1989, over 200 of them were drug-related (43).**

In addition, a majority of drug addicts support their expensive habit by committing robberies and burglaries, often with violent results. **According to Eddie Engelsman, the Dutch "drug czar" in charge of Holland's drug policy, on average a drug addict will commit a crime every other day to support his habit (45).** America has become an increasingly violent place to live, and illegal drug activity is a major reason.

As you can see, I used the research material to provide evidence for the claim I made in each paragraph. The research material gives weight to the claims, and without it my paper would be weak.

AUTHOR'S SECOND DRAFT

(research material and references included)

Legalizing Drugs

America's "war on drugs" is a decade old. So how goes the war? We have arrested and locked up hundreds of thousands of drug users and dealers, confiscated thousands of tons of illegal narcotics, spent billions of dollars, and used vast human resources fighting the war. With all of that effort, we should have made a dramatic impact in the illegal drug business.

Unfortunately, America's war on drugs has made no perceptible difference in America's drug problems. Drugs are continuing to come into the country in great amounts, drug use has actually risen, and drug-related violence is high. Baltimore mayor Kurt Schmoke, a former state's attorney and drug prosecutor, said "The United States has become absolutely awash in illegal drugs," and "tougher laws, greater efforts at interdiction, and stronger rhetoric . . . have not and will not be able to stop the flow" (11). Former federal judge Robert Sweet attacked the war on drugs as being "bankrupt" (Morganthau, 48); criminal justice professor Arnold Trebach calls drug prohibition "a good idea that doesn't work" (42); and the European community, skeptical of George Bush's war on drugs, has looked at other options (Dickey, 37).

How can such a powerful assault on the drug problem produce negligible results? There are a number of reasons. First, according to the American Medical Association, drug addiction, like alcohol addiction, is a disease, not a crime (Schmoke, 11). Locking up drug users rather than treating their addiction does little good. Back on the street, they will still use drugs and turn to crime to support their habit.

Second, if people really want drugs, they are going to get them one way or another. A number of drug-enforcement experts, including Schmoke and Trebach, agreed that the era of alcohol prohibition taught us one thing: Declaring a substance illegal and enforcing the law doesn't keep people from acquiring it. Why would people act differently in obtaining heroine, cocaine, or crack than they did with alcohol? Obviously, they won't.

Third, the numbers of drug users hasn't dropped appreciably because you can't lock them all up. According to Schmoke, a relatively small percentage of Americans who use illegal drugs are ever arrested, so the impact on the numbers of people taking drugs is small (12). In addition, even if we tried to lock up every drug user in the country, we couldn't build enough prisons to house them, and the cost to taxpayers would be extraordinary.

Fourth, with the tremendous profits in illegal drug trafficking, there will always be people willing to risk bringing drugs into the country. For example, a kilo of heroine that costs an importer $10,000 could have a street value in the United States of $1 million (Schmoke, 13). Arrest ten big-time traffickers and there will be ten to replace them tomorrow. In addition, the number of tons of cocaine produced in a year in Latin America is five times greater than that needed to supply the U.S. market (Schmoke, 13). No matter how much cocaine we confiscate, there is more available to meet the demand.

Finally, according to Schmoke, many drug users are poor people in the cities, primarily African Americans and Hispanics, who turn to drugs out of despair or hopelessness about their future. With little to look forward to, they turn to the quick gratification of a crack or heroin high. Until the economic, unemployment, and educational problems of the inner cities are dealt with, widespread drug use will continue (11).

Even in Tampa, supposedly a model city for successful drug enforcement, Mayor Sandy Freedman admits "Until there is adequate jail space, stronger sentencing guidelines, and greater commitment to drug education and rehabilitation, the country will be fighting a losing battle" (Methvin, 60). This is a telling statement, coming ten years into the drug war from the mayor of a model "war on drugs" city. The war simply isn't working.

Perhaps the answer is to throw more money, police officers and border patrol at the problem, and to build more prisons and stiffen sentencing. The trouble is, that is exactly what we've done for the past ten years, and it hasn't helped. We already have a higher percentage of our population in prisons than any other country (Trebach, 41). Could building more prisons and incarcerating more people, primarily African Americans and Hispanics, be the answer? Should we perhaps give more time to the war—another five or ten years? We gave the "war on alcohol" over ten years to work during Prohibition, and the situation didn't improve. Why would the drug war be any different, given the failure of the first ten years? Enough is enough.

Drug prohibition creates more problems than it solves. A high percentage of violent crimes are drug-related. Prohibition creates an underworld of drug smugglers, dealers, and users who commit violent crimes against one another and against innocent bystanders. According to Trebach, of the 367 murders committed in Washington, D.C., in 1989, over 200 of them were drug related (43).

In addition, a majority of drug addicts support their habit by committing robberies and burglaries, often with violent results. According to Eddie Engelsman, the Dutch "drug czar" in charge of Holland's drug policy, on average a drug addict will commit a crime every other day to support his habit (45). America has become a frighteningly violent place to live, and illegal drugs are a major reason.

Second, the drug trade preys upon inner-city children by using them in the business and providing prosperous role models: local drug dealers. The acclaimed moved *Boyz 'n the 'Hood* raised the troubling question, "Why work for minimum wage at McDonald's when you can make $500 a day dealing drugs?" Drug prohibition has created child criminals and immoral role models.

Finally, locking up droves of drug users puts a tremendous strain on our overburdened judicial and prison systems, and the war on drugs has diverted billions of dollars and tremendous manpower toward a failing approach (Trebach, 42). In fact, according to economist Bruce Benson of Florida State University, the emphasis on drug enforcement has been responsible for an increase in other types of crimes that have been neglected (Koretz, 22).

If the war on drugs is failing, and if the effects of drug prohibition are negative, what's the alternative? Picture, if you will, an America where drugs are decriminalized, where adults can legally use heroin or cocaine, and where drugs can be purchased at a pharmacy. What would be the results?

First, violent crime in America would decrease. Illegal drug trafficking would cease, drug suppliers and dealers would be out of business, and the price of drugs would drop, reducing the users' need to steal. In the city of Amsterdam, where drug use has been decriminalized for ten years, there were thirteen drug-related murders in 1988, while in similar-sized Washington, D.C., there were 220 (Trebach, 43). By decriminalizing drugs, America would become a safer place to raise families and walk the streets.

Next, the billions of dollars and hundreds of thousands of police officers used to fight the war on drugs could be concentrated in other crime areas, leading to an even safer America. Our prison population, many of them drug offenders, would drop dramatically, saving taxpayers money and allowing our clogged judicial system to prosecute serious criminal offenders quickly.

The advantages go on and on: no more children involved in the drug business, no more inner-city gang involvement, no more drug-dealer role models, fewer HIV-infected needles passed among heroin users (Trebach, 43), no more treating addicts as criminals, and no more allure of the forbidden—illicit drugs (Dickey, 37).

Instead of a war on drugs, let's launch a "war on ignorance." Using the money currently spent on the failed war, let's educate our youth to the evils of narcotics. Cigarette smoking dropped dramatically in the United States as people were educated to its harmful effects. The same would occur for drug use through a massive educational program. Knowledge, not fear of punishment, will reduce America's drug problem.

Detractors to legalization believe that it would lead to a huge increase in drug use, creating a nation of zombies. This scenario insults the American people, most of whom are intelligent and strong enough to resist the pernicious pleasures of narcotics, legal or otherwise. With our efforts redirected toward educating rather than punishing people, the net result of legalization and education will be a significant reduction in drug use over a period of time.

Legalizing drugs does not mean giving in to the drug problem or condoning drug use. Rather, we would eliminate the problems related to drug trafficking that Prohibition has created, and concentrate our efforts on educating Americans to the horrors of drugs. The government's "just say no" campaign and TV ads like "your brain on drugs" are pathetically inadequate for educating youth. Drug education should be the cornerstone of the health-education curriculum in every school from first grade through high school. We would continue the war on drugs by using the most effective weapon: knowledge.

I would like drugs to be decriminalized immediately. However, I know that won't happen. Too many people believe that legalization means giving up—and subsequent increased drug use. No matter how strong the case for legalization, the issue is so emotionally charged that many people won't listen objectively.

Holland has taken a half-way step towards decriminalization that we should consider (Engelman, 44). In Holland, while drug trafficking is illegal and offenders are prosecuted, since 1982 people aren't punished for using marijuana or "hard drugs" or for possessing small amounts.

Holland's relaxed drug laws haven't led to increased use, and while approximately 70 percent of Holland's drug addicts who seek help can get it, less than 10 percent of American addicts can get help

(Engelman, 45). As mentioned earlier, while Amsterdam had thirteen drug-related murders in 1988, similar-sized Washington, D.C., had over 200.

Holland's ten-year-old drug decriminalization plan hasn't lead to greater drug use. However, it has reduced drug-related violence, recognized addicts as people in need rather than criminals, and remained tough on drug traffickers. This approach is working well in Holland, according to Engelman (46), and we should consider it as a model for the United States. Our failed war on drugs needs a new direction, and we don't need more arrests, more prisoners, more prisons, and more money and manpower used in the same futile way. It's time to re-examine our thinking on drug decriminalization and consider it as a feasible alternative.

Works Cited

Dickey, Christopher. "A Common Market for Crack?" *Newsweek* 18, September 1989: 37.

Engelsman, Eddie. "The Dutch Model." *New Perspective*, Summer 1989: 44–45.

Koretz, Gene. "How Cracking Down on Drugs Can Foster More Crime." *Business Week*, 2 December 1991: 22.

Morganthau, Tom. "Taking on the Legalizers." *Newsweek* 25, December 1989: 46–48.

Methvin, Eugene H. "Tampa's Winning War on Drugs." *Reader's Digest*, July 1991: 57–60.

Schmoke, Kurt. "A War for the Surgeon General." *New Perspective*, Summer 1989: 14–18.

Trebach, Arnold. "Why Not Decriminalize?" *New Perspective*, Summer 1989: 40–43.

REVISION ASSIGNMENT 1

Read the following student first draft and, with a classmate, evaluate the draft using these revision guidelines.

1. What is the topic of the essay, and what approach is the writer taking toward it? How clearly are these things revealed in the essay?

2. How does the writer develop and support her viewpoint in the essay? How strong are her supporting points?

3. What research evidence does the writer use to back each claim she makes? Is the research material used effectively, and is it clear where each piece of material came from?

4. Evaluate the writer's use of paraphrasing and quotations for presenting research material. Does the paraphrased material appear to be in the writers own words? Are quotations used sparingly and effectively? Is it clear when the writer is using research material and when she is presenting her own ideas or analyzing or summarizing research findings?

5. Where does the reader introduce and refute opposing viewpoints? How effectively is this done?

6. How well is the essay organized? Does each part follow logically from the previous one? Would any sentence, paragraph, or group of paragraphs be more effective in a different location?

7. Locate sentences whose wording could be improved through revision. How might you revise specific sentences?

8. How effectively is the essay paragraphed? Does the writer deal with a different point in each essay? Are there overly long paragraphs that bog the reader down or strings of short paragraphs that could annoy readers?

9. How does the essay conclude? What is the writer trying to accomplish in the ending, and how successful is she?

Liberal Television

Since the Federal Communications Commission has eliminated the regulations that protected children from today's advertisements in 1983 on national television, it has left our children with little protection from the large toy manufacturers in displaying anything they want to without restrictions (Duston). Their desire is to increase sales only to make a profit by using whatever tactics they may to cause children to imitate toys displayed on the television commercials. By this means, children are watching TV shows and witnessing the latest toys in the market today. Also this method is putting more of a strain upon the parents to purchase TV linked products. Besides the toys, anything that displays the toy's emblem on items like: lunch boxes and toothbrushes linked with popular television programs for children are meant to sell their products despite what parents try to set as limits for their children. Children are deprived of the natural play and development of imagination children need to possess for natural development. Children cannot fully distinguish between advertisements and programs; they are unable to understand the purpose of the advertisements. They are not able to make logical judgments about good and bad products necessarily, or how the reality of a toy matches up with what an ad or program says (Carlsson-Paige 38).

In fact, children cannot vote so the free speech doesn't apply for them as well as legislative and legal systems are quite different for them than adults (Carlsson-Paige, 38). The free speech of toy makers and TV programmers are protected under deregulation as children lose freedom of expression (Carlsson-Paige 39).

In a lower court ruling, Justices left intact a 24-hour ban on radio and television programming. The ban violated constitutional rights protecting the freedom of expression (Duston).

One supporter said that a lawsuit will most likely be filed immediately after the rule is published, either by the side who thinks it's too strict or the one who thinks it's too lenient (Duston).

However, not all television is negative, television programs also provide commercials and educational programs that provide much information about society. Children can learn general knowledge of people, places, and events and learn about the tasks of doctors and lawyers, police officers, and firefighters from television (Popenoe 144).

Television gives children a lot of information about real and the make-believe worlds of humans behaviors. But children can easily misunderstand what they see and hear. They are not mature enough to make clear judgements. For example, people—unlike cartoon characters—cannot be hit over the head, pushed over a cliff, and come back smiling (Popenoe 144).

Children model the behavior of the people around them. Social scientists have tried to find out whether children imitate the people they see on television or whether or not violent television programs produce violent behavior in children (Popenoe 144). In some respects, children's programs reinforce the values taught by other socializing agents. A television program may bring a geography lesson to life or interest a student in science (Popenoe 144).

More than 98 percent of Americans have at least one television set which is quite a concern to many people and social scientist in regards to what kind of effects it may have on children. The average American household has the set on for 6–7 hours daily with the average high school student to have spent 20,000 hours watching TV (Popenoe 143).

In place of television, teachers have asked parents to read to elementary children having difficulty in school. Children of usually minority groups who have language bearers and have who have parents that are not able to speak or read English well, as one parent's situation: "A teacher who told a mother that her son hadn't mastered the basics of reading and thus needed to repeat first grade. After mother asked to help, the teacher said that, "if the mother worked with the child on reading over the summer, he could repeat the reading test in the fall; if he passed, he would be promoted. Two weeks later, the mother told the teacher she had just enrolled in an adult literacy program in night school to learn to read so she could help her child" (Walde, 41).

Works Cited

Carlsson-Paige, Nancy, and Diane E. Levin, Why Children's Television Should Be Regulated, *Education Week*, September 1989, pp. 37–39.

Duston, Diane, "Indecent Broadcasts," *The Associated Press*, March 3, 1992.

Popenoe, David, *Sociology*, Englewood Cliffs, New Jersey, 1991, pp. 143–144.

Walde, Anne C., and Keith Baker, "When Parents Don't Care If Their Children Learn," *The Education Digest*, April 1991, 41–43.

REVISION ASSIGNMENT 2

Reread and evaluate your first draft with the help of the revision guidelines. Note the changes you want to make, including citing all of your sources. Then exchange papers with a classmate and get a second opinion. When you are ready, write the second draft of your essay.

Journal Entry 41

In what ways did your research paper differ from previous essays? What problems, if any, did you have that you hadn't experienced with earlier assignments? What were the hardest things to handle during the writing process? What did you learn to apply to future research essays?

I'd like to respond myself to the Journal questions. The research paper was much more time consuming than the earlier essays. The researching of reference sources, reading articles, and taking notes took many hours but was essential to writing a decent paper. The research formed the core of the essay, whereas my own ideas dominated earlier essays.

Incorporating research into the paper effectively, paraphrasing the authors' ideas, and including source references are additional considerations I didn't have with other papers. The investigative essay is very different from experience-based writing, and it requires a lot more work. I will prepare my students better for that reality when they write research papers, and will give them the time to do everything they need to be successful.

EDITING

The final step in preparing an essay for your audience is to proofread it for errors in spelling, punctuation, and grammar. Since your latest draft is one of your longer ones, proofread it two or three times, each time looking for a different kind of problem: spelling errors the first time, comma and period usage the second, and subject-verb agreement and pronoun usage the third.

EDITING ASSIGNMENT 1

With a classmate, analyze the use of quotation marks and commas to set off direct quotes in my second draft. Devise some basic rules for punctuating direct quotations in an essay.

EDITING ASSIGNMENT 2

Proofread the following student draft and correct any errors in punctuation, spelling, or grammar. Then share corrections with a classmate.

Children and Television

Many authorities believe that children watch to much television; but it is unclear how much real harm excessive TV watching can do to a child.

One of the most important tools for children's emotional and intellectual growth, healthy play brings together their personal needs, experiences, and understanding. Today, many children are losing control of their play. TV–based toys channel them away from the play they would naturally create. Their own ideas are lost as they imitate the scripts they see on TV. We need to ask ourselves about the long-term social costs of the erosion of play and the loss of imagination in childhood. (Paige and Levin, 37)

Simply advertising products to children on television is unethical to the point that they are ready victims to the desire of the manufactures to sell them more toys. Children cannot make logical judgements about products that are good and bad for them, and they can't understand why parents limit what they can't and can watch. As parents we should limit the time that our children watch TV. Parents need to have control over how much time and what children can watch. Told by a teacher to turn off the TV, one parent said, "Oh, my son would never let me do that!" (Walde and Baker, 41)

To learn, youngsters must be awake. Children as young as six often describe late-night programs to their teachers—and catch up on missed sleep in the classroom. Some parents allow their children to watch TV whenever they please—but do they really know what too much television can do to a child? Parents should take responsibility for their child's physical, emotional, and intellectual well-being. (Walde and Baker, 41)

The only way to protect children from commercial exploitation is to ask ourselves "When can children safely watch television without parents wondering if they are watching something inappropriate?" The FCC informally decided the hours between 8.P.M. and 6.A.M. was the time, under the theory that parents have more control over children's activities. "Millions of children are in the audience 24 hours a day." (Duston) How is it possible to designate a time of day for "indecent" broadcasts that can be hidden from children?

The Association of American Advertising Agencies (AAAA) is seriously considering a court challenge to a new law limiting the minutes of advertising on children's TV programs to twelve per hour on weekdays and ten and one half on weekends. "The time limit violates the free speech clause of the First Amendment." (*U.S. News*, 16). Clearly, children are more susceptible to advertising (*U.S. News*, 16).

Children cannot fully distinguish between advertisements and programs on TV. The only way to protect children from commercial exploitation is to enact bold legislation that will make the actions of manufactures more compatible with the best interests of the children. (Paige and Levin)

"Television viewing for children in now practically a full-time job, equal to the time spent in school." (Gortmaker, E34) More American children and youth are fat than ever before and Harvard researcher Gortmaker attributed the "fattening of America" to generation of couch potatoes who spend too much time in front of the TV screen. (Gortmaker, E34)

Work Cited

Carlson-Paige, Nancy and Diane E. Levin. "Why Children's TV Should Be Regulated." *Education Week*. September 89.

Duston Diane. "Indecent Broadcasts." *Associated Press*. 3 March 92.

"Kids and Courts." *U.S. News*. 21 January 91: 16.

McNulty, Jennifer. "Researchers Blame Excessive TV For Obesity In Kids." *Fresno Bee*. 9 October 88: E34.

Walde, Anne C and Keith Baker. "When Parents Don't Care." *Associated Press*. April 91.

EDITING ASSIGNMENT 3

Now proofread your latest draft for errors and make necessary corrections before writing your final draft.

Journal Entry 42

Relate how your error-correction process is going. Are you catching and correcting most mistakes as you work through the first two drafts? What kinds of errors are you finding in your final proofreading? If you still have problems with certain error tendencies, what can you do to reduce those tendencies in future writing?

Chapter Eight

Sentence Combining

In analyzing my sentences, I find that I use a variety of structures to express myself. In one of my latest essays, I used introductory prepositional, participial, and gerund phrases, simple sentences, compound sentences, complex sentences, compound/complex sentence combinations, relative clauses, appositives, and series of three or more subjects, verbs, objects, infinitives, or clauses in the same sentence.

While it's not important that you know the terminology for sentence structures, it does help if you can call upon a variety of structures to express yourself. If I were limited to using only half the structures I mentioned, it would have been more difficult for me to get my thoughts across.

Unfortunately, some writers have such limitations because they haven't been exposed to a range of sentence structures. They rely on a few simple structures they are comfortable with, and their writing is both predictable and limited (in what they can express). The good news is that anyone can increase his or her repertoire of sentence structures through *sentence-combining* activities. To make the best use of this chapter, do the sentence-combining activities throughout the semester (or quarter) and apply what you learn to your writing for the course.

WHAT IS SENTENCE COMBINING?

Sentence combining is a technique for varying sentence structures by combining relatively simple sentences to form more complex ones. Here are two simple examples.

Example

Let's go to the mall today. Let's go directly after work.

Combined:

Let's go to the mall today directly after work.

To combine these sentences, the repeated words were eliminated and the remainder of the second sentence was added to the first.

Example

Ralph mowed the lawn yesterday. He weeded the rose garden. He also trimmed the hedge.

Combined:

Yesterday Ralph mowed the lawn, weeded the rose garden, and trimmed the hedge.

To combine the sentences, the repeated words were eliminated and the three things Ralph did were joined with commas and *and*.

How to Combine Sentences

Sentences can be combined by doing any of the following things:

1. Deleting repeated words or phrases
2. Moving words or phrases from one sentence into another
3. Adding words to join sentences together
4. Moving words or phrases to new locations, and deleting words that, as a consequence, are no longer needed

During the sentence-combining activities in this unit, you will have many opportunities to use those sentence-combining strategies, and I will show you how and when to use them. You will also apply your own creative ideas for combining sentences within paragraphs.

WHY COMBINE SENTENCES?

The purpose of sentence-combining activities is to give you practice generating a variety of sentence structures, some of which you may never have used. As you learn to use these structures through sentence combining, you will gain confidence in using them for your own writing purposes, thus increasing your sentence variety and your ability to express yourself.

As you grow familiar with various structures, you will find opportunities to use them naturally in your writing with no need to force them. Studies show that many writers transfer their newly acquired structural skills to their writing with little conscious effort.

COMBINING ASSIGNMENT 1: WORDS IN A SERIES

Combine the following pairs or groups of sentences into single sentences in this manner:

1. Put similar words or phrases together in a series.

2. Join your words or phrases with commas and joining words like *and, but, or,* or *so.*

3. Delete unnecessary words.

Examples

Maria walked to the corner. She waited for the bus.

Combined:

Maria walked to the corner and waited for the bus. ("Walked" and "waited" joined by *and*, and "She" deleted.)

Ralph likes pizza. Simon likes pizza. Raphael likes pizza.

Combined:
Ralph, Simon, and Raphael like pizza. ("Ralph," "Simon," and "Raphael" joined by commas and *and*, and "like pizza" deleted in last two sentences.)

1. I'm going to college to get a degree. I'm going to meet new people. I'm going to get a well-paying job.

2. Muriel hates walking to work. She hates asking her friends for a ride. She hates taking a bus. She should buy her own car.

3. We need to buy bread at the market. We also need to get some cereal. We need to buy some vegetables. We also need some canned sodas.

4. I'm alarmed at how fast you spend money. I'm troubled by how you don't keep track of your checks. I'm frustrated by your always borrowing money from me. I'm going to have to tell your wife.

5. The check-out clerk at Stop 'n Go went to the Michael Jackson concert. The manager of the store also went. The box boy went with them. The bookkeeper was invited, but she didn't go.

6. The Bank of Tokyo was robbed. Taylor's Drugs was broken into. The window of Bob's Cycle Shop was smashed. This all happened on Saturday. It occurred in the town of Lompoc.

7. Frank was excited about getting a job interview with IBM. He was confident that he would interview well. He was also curious about who would interview him. He was annoyed at the 7:00 A.M. interview time.

8. Your hiking boots may be in the garage behind the washing machine. They may be in the attic. They may be in the pick-up truck behind the driver's side. You may have left them at the lake Saturday.

Free Combining Activity 1
In the free combining activities, combine sentences within the paragraphs provided in any manner you wish: delete words or phrases, add joining words, put similar words or phrases together, and change punctuation. However, do not alter the meaning of the paragraph or eliminate any content. Combine pairs or groups of sentences whose content is somehow related.

Example

The habit of compulsive editing doesn't only make writing hard. The habit of premature editing doesn't just make writing hard either. Such editing also makes writing dead. Your voice is damped out by all the interruptions. It's damped out by the changes. It's damped out by the hesitations between your consciousness and the page. In your natural way of producing words there is a voice. It is the main source of power in your writing. I don't know how it works. This voice is the force that will make a reader listen to you. It is the energy that drives the meaning through his thick skull.

COMBINING ASSIGNMENT 2: COMPOUND SENTENCES

One of the most common sentence structures is formed by combining complete sentences with the joining words (conjunctions) *and, but, so, yet, or,* and *for.* Combine each of the following pairs of sentences with the most appropriate of those words. Put a comma after the word before your joining word.

Example

I want to type at least five pages today. I have until noon to do it.

Combined:

I want to type at least five pages today, and I have until noon to do it.

1. In biology class, Malcolm has a difficult time understanding the photosynthesis process. He does the best he can.

2. This is the coolest summer we've had in southern Tennessee in ten years. I'm beginning to doubt the global warming theory.

3. Country music is become more popular across the country. I think this is because the music is moving closer to rock 'n roll.

4. Most college students watch little television. They are too busy or have better things to do.

5. The U.S. divorce rate is higher than ever. Americans continue to get married in record numbers.

6. Marian has never used a major credit card. She never plans to have one.

7. We could eat out tonight at the new Mexican restaurant. We could stay home and barbecue swordfish.

8. There is no way you can study for the composition assignment on Friday. Don't worry about it.

9. Most small investors are putting their money into mutual funds. They are currently the most secure investment.

10. You may want to take fifteen units both semesters. You may want to take eighteen units in the fall and drop to twelve units in the spring.

Free Combining Activity 2

Combine sentences in the following example however you want. Your goal is to create better sentences for readers, making them more interesting and more diverse.

Example

I'd really like to be a runner. I probably never will. I envy the men and women who run by my house every morning. I admire their discipline. I admire their bodies. I admire their courage. It may look easy, the way they glide by my window. I know it isn't. There are months of hard work and sacrifice behind those effortless-looking gaits. There may be years. All I see out my window are the results. They look good to me. Unfortunately, I don't think I have what it takes to get there. I'll probably just sit here and watch. I'll read my paper and have another sweet roll. Maybe I'll close the drapes.

COMBINING ASSIGNMENT 3: COMPLEX SENTENCES

Another useful sentence structure is the complex sentence, which involves the following joining words: *because, if, although, unless, since, until, while, as, when, after, before, whenever, where, wherever.* These words may either begin the sentence or go in the middle.

Combine the following pairs of sentences by using the most appropriate joining words. Use some of the words to begin sentences and others in the middle of the new sentences.

Examples

The ship must anchor in the harbor. The water is too shallow by the dock.

Combined:

The ship must anchor in the harbor because the water is too shallow by the dock.

The traffic is going to be bad on 405. Let's take Route I-5 instead.

Combined:

Since the traffic is going to be bad on 405, let's take Route I-5 instead.

1. The rain began to fall. The huge concert audience in Central Park didn't move.

2. You've been watching television all morning. I've done the dishes, mopped the kitchen floor, and folded a load of wash.

3. One of the three candidates gets 50 percent or more of the votes. Our next President will be decided by the House of Representatives.

4. This is a great time to start a trust fund for your children's college education. You haven't already done so.

5. The storm reached its full force along the coast. All of the beach-front residents had evacuated to higher ground.

6. Don't go to Las Vegas or Atlantic City to gamble. You can't afford to lose your money.

7. The price of an airplane ticket between Washington, D.C., and Philadelphia goes down, I'm going to drive back and forth to meetings.

8. Muriel is the shortest person in her sixth-grade class. She grew almost three inches during the year.

9. The bus of tourists pulled up to the stadium entrance. Vandals threw rocks at its windows.

10. The Torborg Museum is closed on Saturday. We'll just wait and go on Monday.

Free Combining Activity 3

Combine sentences in the following example in the most effective ways possible.

Example

The linoleum in our kitchen looks bad. It's difficult finding a new color and pattern we like. We've brought home over fifty different linoleum samples. None of them has been what we wanted. The biggest problem is matching up the linoleum with our new kitchen wallpaper. It has different shades of blue and tan. They have been hard to match. We are sick of the old linoleum. We've just got to keep looking. I hope we'll find something before July. Over forty relatives will be at our house. They are coming for a Fourth of July get-together.

COMBINING ASSIGNMENT 4: RELATIVE CLAUSES

Another type of complex sentence contains relative clauses—groups of words beginning with *who, whom, which,* and *that.*

Examples

The man who robbed the C Street liquor store used to be my neighbor.

Sally Struthers, who played Gloria on the old "Archie Bunker Show," devotes much of her time to working on behalf of needy children around the world.

I prefer doing my grocery shopping at Town and Country Market, which is located across town from where I live.

Combine the following pairs of sentences by forming a relative clause from one of the sentences, using *who, whom, which,* or *that* to begin the clause. Place the clause after the word to which it refers.

1. Gretchen Fields is the new president of Aberdeen College. She used to be dean of the school's humanities division.

2. I don't care for some of the new cars. They have plastic bumpers.

3. The Lake Ponchartrain Bridge is the longest bridge in the world. It spans twenty-eight miles of water.

4. The nuns used to teach at the Sacred Heart Catholic Girls' School in Glendora. They were replaced by secular instructors.

5. I'd like you to meet Casandra Phillips. She will be running the computer lab at the college this year.

6. Many of the original Van Gogh paintings have been sent to the Louvre in Paris. They used to hang in the J. Paul Getty Museum.

7. The foreign students from Japan will stay in the dorms for two weeks this summer. You were hoping to meet them.

8. A vaccination-type birth-control method will soon be legal in the United States. It is already available in some European countries.

9. My wife was delighted to inherit from my aunt an amethyst ring. Amethyst is her birthstone.

10. I'd like to get to know Ms. Addleman before I decide whether to have Mills Associates do my income-tax preparation. She is the CPA with whom I'd be working.

Free Combining Activity 4

Combine the sentences in the following example to create more interesting and effective ones.

Example

Michael Forbes is the new president of Hall University. He was the chancellor of a private university system in Delaware. He is taking a considerable cut in pay. He is taking a less prestigious job. However, the presidency appealed to him. It wasn't as stressful as his old job. It demanded less time. The campus was a half hour nearer his home. Some people questioned the presidential choice of the University. It was reputedly looking for a young, energetic leader. Dr. Forbes is nearing the end of his career. He is not known for his strong leadership. He is sixty-three years old. Apparently the University opted for experience and stability over youth and leadership. This surprised a lot of people. It didn't surprise me. I am used to the University making unusual decisions.

COMBINING ASSIGNMENT 5: COMPOUND AND COMPLEX COMBINATIONS

Often more than one joining word from the compound or complex sentence lists are used in the same sentence, or words from all lists are used to join different parts of the sentence.

Combine the following groups of sentences by using joining words from all three lists: *and, or, but, so, for, because, when, if, as, while, although, unless, who, whom, which, that,* and so on.

Example

We're driving down to Boise. Aunt Mavis is very ill. We don't expect to stay more than a day.

Combined:

We're driving down to Boise because Aunt Mavis is very ill, but we don't expect to stay more than a day.

1. The price of gasoline rose 5 cents in May. It went up another 5 cents in June. We expect an even bigger increase during July and August.

2. Joseph reported to work on Monday. His office had been cleared out. It was being remodeled.

3. You may not like Dr. Hargrove for a teacher. She certainly knows her sociology. Students who stay in the class learn a lot.

4. The weather keeps warming up. We'll have to keep all the windows open. We can afford to get the air conditioner fixed.

5. The periwinkles are doing very well. I planted them along the east side of the back yard. They get plenty of morning sun.

6. The yard sale on P Street begins at 8 A.M. I'm going to be there by 7:30. I want to make the first offer on the matching sofa and love seat.

7. Hawaii is a beautiful place to visit. It is an expensive place to live. Many Hawaiians live below the poverty level.

8. Evander Holyfield may not be considered a great heavyweight champion by experts. In a lackluster performance, he barely beat Larry Holmes. Holmes was at least ten years past his prime.

9. Iowa farmers were hoping for rain. Mississippi Delta farmers were hoping for sun. The rains were beginning to flood their fields.

10. You need only six more units to graduate. You should consider finishing up in summer school. You could go through graduation exercises in June. You might still have a chance to enter graduate school in the fall.

11. The state's economy turns around next year. Public education will continue to be underfunded. More parents will opt to send their children to private schools.

12. I'm not interested in working at McDonald's this summer. My roommate Teresa may be. Leave the application here. I'll make sure she gets it.

Free Combining Activity 5

Combine the sentences in the following example in the most effective manner.

Example

The cannery in Kingsburg is one of the best local places to work in the summer. It operates only in July and August. Workers get in at least twelve hours a day. They make a minimum of eight dollars an hour. They are paid time-and-a-half for any hours over forty per week. The owners are good people to work for. The working conditions are excellent. The building is air-conditioned. The machinery is in good working condition. The place is clean. It is well-ventilated. You want health insurance for two months. You only have to pay fifty dollars. The coverage includes a free physical examination. It is difficult getting on at the cannery. It is worth the try. You are almost guaranteed to be rehired the following summers.

I've never worked there. I have a number of friends who have. None of them has ever quit.

 **COMBINING ASSIGNMENT 6: GERUND AND PARTICIPIAL PHRASES**

Two useful sentence structures are the gerund and participial phrases, found most frequently at the beginnings or ends of sentences. Gerund phrases begin with *ed*-ending words and participial phrases with *ing*-ending words.

Examples

Bothered by a sore throat and cold, Joanie stayed home from work.

Driving to school on Tuesday, Sal got a ticket for speeding.

The public-transit system broke down on Monday, *leaving* hundreds of commuters stranded.

Over 50 per cent of all U.S. marriages end in divorce, *meaning* the odds are against a particular couple's remaining married for life.

Combine the following sentences by making a gerund or participial phrase out of one of the sentences. Place the phrase at the beginning or end of the new sentence, wherever it fits best.

Example

John caught a six-pound bass at the reservoir. He used a rubber worm for bait.

Combined:

Using a rubber worm for bait, John caught a six-pound bass at the reservoir.

1. Melanie continued helping her son with his math. She was encouraged by the improvement he was showing.

2. Late into the night, Mark finally fell into a troubled sleep. He had been disturbed by break-ins that occurred in his neighborhood.

3. Gertrude threw a surprise party for her parents. It marked the thirtieth anniversary of their wedding.

4. Rescuers put their ears to the east wall of the mine shaft. They listened intently for any sign of life from the trapped workers.

5. Lucille wrote to all of her relatives. She was elated by the news that she had been accepted into Hastings Law School.

6. Clyde rushed out of the dormitory to catch the bus home. He didn't wait to put on his shoes.

7. Mildred's diamond ring wasn't discovered for six months. It was caught in the trap of her bathroom sink.

8. The GDP rose 2 percent in June and unemployment dropped to 6 percent. These findings indicated that the economy was slowing turning around.

9. Brock started with Muller Shoes as a stock boy. He rose to the top management position in the company in ten years.

10. Newark citizens protested at the September city council meeting. They were frustrated by the slow progress of construction on the east-west freeway that was to span the city.

Free Combining Activity 6

Combine sentences in the following example to form more interesting and effective ones.

Example

I drove across the Bay Bridge on a clear day. I got a good view of one of the most beautiful cities in the world. San Francisco rises from the bay. It looks like a bedazzling jewel. Its skyscrapers are white. They are graceful. They shimmer in the morning sky. The bay is a deep green. Its beauty belies the treacherous currents below its surface. The Golden Gate Bridge looms in the background. It is world-famous. It is elegant. It connects the magical city to the sleepy harbor of Sausalito. You climb the mountain road northwest of the Golden Gate. You get a reverse-angle view of the City. It is no less spectacular. San Francisco is a beautiful city. It is an alluring one. It beckons tourists. They come from all over the world.

COMBINING ASSIGNMENT 7: INTRODUCTORY PREPOSITIONAL PHRASES

Another common sentence beginning is the prepositional phrase. The following prepositions can begin sentences: *on, in, to, with, of, behind, under, through, by, from, against, over, into, for, around, throughout.*

Examples

On the third day of October there will be a total eclipse of the sun.

In the interest of time, let's take separate cars so we don't have to wait for each other.

From the looks of that scraggly cat, she should be taken to a veterinarian.

Under the hood of the '55 Chevy in the junkyard John discovered a fully chromed 350-cc engine.

Against the wishes of her mother, Mildred decided to attend a college two thousand miles from home.

With the best of intentions and absolutely no experience, Max began re-shingling his roof.

Combine the following sentences by beginning the new sentence with a prepositional phrase and deleting unnecessary words.

Example

Maria felt like a million dollars. She had her college degree and a physical therapy job awaiting her.

Combined:

With a college degree and a physical therapy job awaiting her, Maria felt like a million dollars.

1. You appear to be well qualified for a lab chemist position. I could tell from the information in your resume.

2. You can always find our cat Chubby sleeping. She'll be behind the television set in the corner of the family room.

3. Let's take a trip to Niagara Falls. Let's go on the third or fourth of August.

4. Leticia was well prepared for the triathalon. She had six months of training behind her.

5. You'll find the remote control. It's on top of the television set behind the VCR.

6. I've told you I don't know where you left your watch. I've told you for the last time.

7. Please take back my library books today. You can do it on the way to the supermarket.

8. Surviving civilizations have learned from their mistakes. This has occurred throughout time.

9. Miriam decided to take a cruise around the world. She decided this at age 85 and against the advice of her doctor.

10. All of the good concert seats will be taken. That will occur by the time we finally get to the Hollywood Bowl.

Free Combining Activity 7

Combine sentences in the following example to form more effective and interesting ones.

Example

Tim made up a very difficult mid-term test for his biology students. He did this for the first college class he ever taught. The test was ten pages long. It had over one hundred questions. It had fill-ins. It had short-answer essays. Tim was pleased with the test. His students were flabbergasted. Most of them did rather poorly. A number of them were ready to drop the class. They were going to do it immediately. However, Tim graded the test on a curve. He did this because he realized the test was tough. He did this to help the students. He did this to keep students from dropping. Now the students know what to expect. They will study harder for the final. It is coming up in five weeks. Tim decided not to make the final any easier. He stuck to his high testing standards. He believed the students could do much better.

COMBINING ASSIGNMENT 8: APPOSITIVES

An appositive is a word or group of words that provides information about the word that precedes it. It functions like a relative clause without the *who, which,* or *that*.

Examples

Florida, *a state known for its sunshine*, gets over twenty inches of rain annually in some areas.

Of the original cast members of "Bonanza," *a popular television western of the 60's*, only one, *Pernell Roberts*, is still alive.

The New York Yankees, *the most dominant baseball team in history*, has struggled mightily the past twenty years.

The triathalon, *an event that includes twenty-six miles of swimming, running, and cycling*, is reputedly the most grueling sporting activity.

Combine the following pairs of sentences by forming an appositive from one sentence and inserting it into the new sentence.

Example

The Pacific pelican lives in and around harbors along the West Coast. It is a large-beaked, ungainly looking bird.

Combined:

The Pacific pelican, a large-beaked, ungainly looking bird, lives in and around harbors along the West Coast.

1. In 1992, Mike McGuire chased Babe Ruth's home run record for most of the season. He is a man of immense proportions playing for the Oakland Athletics.

2. M. C. Hammer rivals Michael Jackson for dancing prowess. Hammer is an internationally renowned rap artist.

3. The word processor has revolutionized the revision process for writers. The word processor is the modern counterpart of the standard typewriter.

4. A dark-horse candidate for the Presidency in 1992 was Ross Perot. He was the only independent candidate to be taken seriously in over one hundred years.

5. American female gymnasts should do well in the 1992 and 1996 Olympics. They are the smallest athletes among the U.S. Olympic contingent.

6. I love barbecued baby-back pork ribs. They are the tenderest, tastiest ribs around.

7. Melissa enjoys shopping at The Emporium and I. Magnin's. They are the two most expensive clothing stores in town.

8. On his plane trip to the Bahamas, Clyde hopes to get a C section seat so he can enjoy the view. C section seats are next to the window.

9. The longest driver on the pro golf tour is not the straightest hitter. His name is John Daly.

10. The Sears Tower dominates the Chicago skyline. The Tower is the tallest building in the country.

Free Combining Activity 8

Combine sentences in the following example to form more effective and interesting ones.

Example

I've got a strange eating pattern. It is one no health expert would recommend. I eat no breakfast. I eat cereal for lunch. I eat a large dinner. I do this instead of having three regular meals a day. I've never had an appetite in the morning. I get up just early enough to get to work. Breakfast doesn't interest me. I don't care much for sandwiches or soup. I do like some kinds of cereal. I eat cereal for lunch. I also get my fiber that way. I've only had four or five hundred calories by dinner time. I'm ready to pig out. I also snack in the evening. That is something I never do during the rest of the day. I eat a big dinner. I eat lots of late-night snacks. I don't gain weight. My total calorie count for the day isn't high for my size. I just pack my calories into the end of the day. My eating habits aren't that healthy. That's what I am told. They work all right for me. I've been eating this way for about fifteen years.

COMBINING ASSIGNMENT 9: SUBJUNCTIVE CONJUNCTIONS

Subjunctive conjunctions, more easily remembered as *transitions*, connect complete sentences and show relationships between the sentences. Since transitions are not "joining words" in the sense of coordinate or subordinate conjunctions, they are preceded by a semi-colon (;) rather than a comma.

Example

Mildred is tired of working the night shift at the IRS; *therefore*, she is going to request a move to day shift before next tax season.

Mildred is tired of working the night shift at the IRS; *however*, she still likes it better than her previous job at the chicken-processing plant.

The following transitions and transitional phrases are used frequently by writers to tie together sentences whose ideas are closely related.

Therefore: Similar to the coordinate conjunction *so*; it indicates that the first sentence influences what happens in the second sentence.

Example

You've been studying very hard for your calculus final; *therefore*, I'll bet you will do well on it.

The warm weather has melted a lot of the snow at Sierra Summit; *therefore*, the skiing conditions will be poor because of the slush.

Other transitional options that are used interchangeably with "therefore" include *consequently* and *thus*. (I'm really tired tonight; *consequently*, I'm not interested in leaving the house for anything. Sarah's new tennis shoes pinch her toes; *thus*, she took them back to Macy's.)

However: Similar to the coordinate conjunction *but*; the second sentence contrasts with the first sentence in some way.

Example

I'm really tired tonight; *however*, I still have to go out and milk the cows.

Sarah's new tennis shoes pinch her toes; *however*, she can't return them to Macy's because she lost her sales receipt.

Other transitions and transitional phrases that are used interchangeably with "however" include *nevertheless, nonetheless, despite that, in spite of that.* (The college basketball team was behind twenty points at halftime; *nevertheless,* they battled back in the second half and won the game. The library will be closed in a half hour; *nonetheless,* we still need to go there and reproduce some articles on pesticide poisoning. Bill Clinton was the fifth leading Democratic contender for President when the campaign began; *despite that,* he became the Democratic nominee and won the presidency.)

Furthermore: means "in addition to." The second sentence usually provides additional information about the subject of the first sentence.

Example

Jacquiline doesn't like eating any kind of red meat; *furthermore,* she won't eat chicken or fish more than once a week.

It's raining hard right now; *furthermore,* the wind-chill factor is below zero.

Other transitions and transitional phrases used interchangeably with "furthermore" include *in addition, on top of that, beyond that, moreover.* (You should take very little luggage on your China trip; *in addition,* you should take mostly casual clothes for touring. Monroe weighed in twenty pounds overweight for the heavyweight fight; *on top of that,* he had been sick for the week before the fight. Marvin is an excellent student; *moreover,* he is a genuinely nice person.)

Combine the following sentences by using an appropriate transition or transitional phrase: *therefore, consequently, thus, however, nevertheless, nonetheless, despite, in spite of, furthermore, in addition, moreover.* Insert a semi-colon (;) after the last word before the transition. Use a different transition for each sentence.

Example

There's a great bargain on throw rugs at Pier One Imports. Let's drop by there on our way home from work.

There's a great bargain on throw rugs at Pier One Imports; *therefore,* let's drop by there on our way home from work.

It's going to be a long drive from Charlotte to Buffalo. We've got to make it in two days.

It's going to be a long drive from Charlotte to Buffalo; *nevertheless,* we've got to make it in two days.

1. It's a twenty-block walk from the wharf to the Civic Center. It's all uphill.

2. Some modern art is so strange that it is difficult to evaluate. Modern art by masters like Chagall and Picasso is interesting and provocative.

3. With our special entertainment booklet coupons, we stayed at the Madison Inn at half price. We had plenty of money left over for hotel valet parking.

4. The Exploratorium by the Presidio is filled with hundreds of fascinating hands-on science exhibits. Visitors need to plan a full day there to see and do everything.

5. The Washington, D.C., subway system is one of the cleanest and most efficient in the country. It is also an expensive means of transportation to most areas of the city.

6. Michigan had the greatest collection of athletes in the NCAA basketball playoffs. They lost to a more disciplined and organized Duke team.

7. American rap music has gone international, with rap groups springing up in Japan and Italy. Unlike in America, rap music is still more of a novelty than a mainstream form of music in those countries.

8. Americans drive more in the summer than any other time. The price of gas always goes up in response to supply and demand.

9. The Lake Ponchartrain Bridge is the longest in the country. The lake itself is too shallow to be of any commercial fishing or shipping value.

10. You have a very light and deft touch on the piano. You play with a passion that is conveyed to your listeners.

Free Combining Activity 9

Combine sentences in the following example in ways that will produce more interesting and effective ones.

Example

Malcolm's ticket out of the poverty-ridden inner city was a basketball scholarship. He practiced long and hard. He did well in school. He showed college coaches the potential to play Division I ball. Several schools offered him tentative scholarships early in his senior year. Then he took the SAT test. His composite score wasn't high enough to be eligible for basketball his freshman year. The Division I colleges lost interest in him. They wanted players who could come in and play immediately. He enrolled at a community college in Texas. He didn't last a year. He didn't like the coach. He didn't like the players' nonchalant attitudes toward the game. He transferred to a California community college. He played there his sophomore year. No Division I school offered him a scholarship. In his junior year, he became a walk-on player at Auburn. Auburn's coach had originally recruited him out of high school. He didn't make the team. There were too many good young players on scholarship. The coach didn't want to invest time on a junior. He didn't want to invest scholarship money. Malcolm dropped out of school. He returned home.

COMBINING ASSIGNMENT 10: COMBINATIONS

Combine the following groups of sentences into single sentences using any of the variety of sentence structures presented. You might use two or three different structures in the same sentence.

Example

John went to Buckingham Palace. Matthew went with him. Pamela also went with them. They went to see the Changing of the Guard. They had to wait for two hours. Their guidebook had the wrong times listed.

Combined:

John, Matthew, and Pamela went to Buckingham Palace to see the Changing of the Guard, but they had to wait for two hours because their guidebook had the wrong times listed.

1. You may like getting a sun tan. A sun tan was a symbol of healthiness in the 70's and 80's. You should be very careful. The sun's rays can damage to your skin. They can be dangerous to your health.

2. Samantha, Teresa, and Maria are sisters. They are all the same size. They are all teenagers. They can wear each other's clothes. They seldom do. Samantha likes grungy clothes. Teresa dresses traditionally. Maria prefers daring outfits.

3. The moon hung outside our porthole. We were on a cruise ship. The moon was full and bright. It cast a shimmering path across the ocean.

4. Street people hung out along Market Street. Some played guitars. Others passed out strange types of literature. Most just stood or sat around. They had cans in their hands. They were waiting for passing tourists.

5. Please don't bother me with your insurance sales pitch tonight. I've got lots of work to do. I'm not in the mood to hear about term life insurance. I'm skeptical about it anyway.

6. John sat patiently in the careers center at the college. He was waiting to hear of job openings on campus for the summer. He was hoping there would be work in the financial-aid or admissions office. He had experience working in both.

7. I hate to inconvenience you like this. However, please take me to the dentist's office this morning. Do it on your way to the bank. My car isn't running well.

8. I'd recommend that you buy a Macintosh home computer. You are looking for a computer that's easy to use. You are looking for one that has great graphics. It is relatively inexpensive. It is light. It doesn't take up much space.

9. The jury only deliberated for thirty minutes. That was a bad sign for William Crowder. His attorney felt it was. Crowder was on trial for embezzlement. They were both surprised by the verdict. They were thrilled by it. Crowder had been acquitted.

10. Cropdusting is a dangerous occupation. It involves pilots flying low over planted fields. There are lots of potential obstacles to avoid. They include power lines. They also include tall buildings. They also include other cropdusters. They are working over adjacent fields.

11. Hector Guzman had quintuple-bypass surgery last year. He was forty-five years old. He was a good friend of mine. The surgery consisted of tying off five clogged arteries to his heart and replacing them with veins from his legs. The surgery was successful.

12. Tax-sheltered annuities are a great way to defer taxes. They don't eliminate them. Many annuities holders are unpleasantly surprised. About 30 percent of their annuity money goes to the government. This happens when it is withdrawn.

12. Oversized tennis rackets were very popular for a while. They allow players to strike balls more solidly. They have lost their attraction. They are too heavy. They slow a person's swing.

14. John finished his term paper just before his 8 o'clock English class. He had worked all night on it. The paper was on the dangers of microwave oven radiation. His teacher was Dr. Freely.

15. Motorists complained about the rough condition of Highway 99. It hadn't been repaved in over thirty years. It was full of narrow bridges. The state did nothing about it.

16. The defense attorney chipped away at the star witness's credibility. The prosecutor objected to his badgering of the witness. She was visibly shaken on the stand.

17. You want to try a new Mexican restaurant. I'd recommend going to Chevy's. It has homemade tortillas. It has great chili verde.

18. The ivory covers on the piano keys were chipping off. It happened from years of heavy use. All of the Williams family played. They were excellent pianists.

19. Those clothes have been sitting in the dryer too long. I can tell from their wrinkled appearance. They need to be dried again. It will only take about thirty minutes. This will get the wrinkles out.

20. You list your teenage son as a secondary driver on the Honda CRX. The car insurance will be less expensive. The CRX is considered a sportscar. Teenage boys in sportscars spell trouble to insurance agencies.

Free Combining Assignment 10

Combine sentences in the following example in ways that will create more effective, interesting ones.

Example

I wish I could take my time with a novel. I wish I could learn to savor it. Instead, I rush through a book. I do it as if every page must be devoured before the book self-explodes. Here is an example. I bought six paperback novels at a bookstore three days ago. I've already finished two of them. I'll start on a third this evening. Six novels would last some people an entire summer. I'll finish them in two weeks. That's thirty bucks of books. My wife reminds me of that. There is another problem. I become obsessed with reading a book. I block out everything else. I block out everyone else. This doesn't make me too popular around the house. I put off my writing. I put off my yard work. I put off my family. I don't do those things intentionally. An interesting book just gets me in its clutches. I'm a goner until I finish.

Chapter Nine

Editing Guidelines

This final chapter covers areas of punctuation, grammar, and sentence structure that give many writers problems. As you edit your drafts during the course, you may want to refer to the section covering those areas where you tend to make errors and work through the activities.

SENTENCE BOUNDARIES

Some writers have a problem setting off complete sentences with a period. They may either run more than one sentence together or insert a period before a sentence ends. In either case, readers can become confused. Once thrown off, they have greater difficulty following the writer's thoughts.

Run-On Sentences

A run-on sentence is an error where two or more sentences are run together without periods separating them. Not surprisingly, most run-ons involve sentences that are closely related in meaning.

Examples

Mildred was late for English class she overslept when her alarm didn't go off.

Our cats don't let us sleep late on weekends they start meowing under our bedroom window by 6 A.M.

In these two run-ons, the second sentence relates closely to the first, and some writers might begin the second sentence without realizing the. first one had ended. The sentences should be punctuated like this:

Mildred was late for English class. She overslept when her alarm didn't go off.

Our cats don't let us sleep late on weekends. They start meowing under our bedroom window by 6 A.M.

Here are some suggestions for identifying and correcting run-on sentences.

1. A sentence expresses a complete thought. A run-on sentence expresses two or more complete thoughts. For example, in the "Mildred" sentence, the first sentence tells what happened (Mildred was late for class) and the second sentence tells why (she overslept). Two separate statements are being made, and each is a complete sentence.

2. Run-on sentences often involve two fairly short sentences, and the second sentence in the run-on often begins with these words:

a. Pronouns: I, you, she, he, we, they, it.

b. Introductory "t" words: this, these, that, those, the, then.

c. Names: Sam, Ruth, Rita, Malcolm, Roberta.

d. "Command" verbs: go, don't, wait, stop, get.

Examples

Marvin is a twenty-one-year-old college freshmen he was in the Marines for three years.

Let's finish cleaning the house today then we can go to the lake tomorrow.

You shouldn't rush your wife while she's shopping find a place to sit down and relax.

I'm not interested in going to the wax museum Sam will go with you.

Don't take the Harbor Freeway after work it will be too congested.

3. To correct a run-on sentence, do one of three things.

a. Most commonly, place a period after the first sentence and capitalize the first word of the second sentence.

Run-on: I might as well go out and mow the lawn now it's not going to get any cooler today.

Corrected: I might as well go out and mow the lawn now. It's not going to get any cooler today.

b. If the sentences are rather short, combine them with an appropriate joining word.

Run-on: My sister Florence is from Houston she'll be with us until Friday.

Corrected: My sister Florence is from Houston, and she'll be with us until Friday.

c. Occasionally, for variety, join closely related sentences with a semicolon (;).

Run-on: The burglar isn't going to hit this block again he's halfway across the state by now.

Corrected: The burglar isn't going to hit this block again; he's halfway across the state by now.

ASSIGNMENT 1

Correct the following run-on sentences by inserting periods, joining words, or semicolons between the two sentences.

Examples

Our family doesn't know where to eat out we only moved to Crescent yesterday.

Corrected: Our family doesn't know where to eat out because we only moved to Crescent yesterday.

For now let's just put all of the old furniture on the back porch later we can decide what to keep and what to give away.

Corrected: For now let's just put all of the old furniture on the back porch. Later we can decide what to keep and what to give away.

1. The rain storm hasn't let up in three days in fact, right now it's raining harder than ever.

2. You used to be a conservative dresser now you wear pretty wild outfits.

3. Dark clouds gathered in the western sky above the mountains then they slowly made their way across the valley.

4. I haven't been to Fresno in twenty years I've heard its population has almost doubled since then.

5. Gwendolyn could write a poem in fifteen minutes and it sounded great she could spend three hours on a poem and it wouldn't sound as good.

6. Fred is getting tired of storing all of his writing projects on floppy discs he is considering putting a hard disc drive in his computer when he can come up with $500.

7. Florence is very tired she was up all night studying for her psychology final.

8. In 1992 Bill Clinton selected Al Gore as his Presidential running mate they formed the youngest duo ever to run for the country's highest offices.

9. I hate spinach I would eat grass first.

10. Felicia's hair hadn't been cut since elementary school it cascaded down her back like a fiery waterfall.

ASSIGNMENT 2

While most writers can identify sentences in run-ons like those of Assignment 1, the task becomes more difficult when the run-ons appear in the more realistic context of a paragraph.

Locate and correct run-ons in the following example paragraph by inserting periods, joining words, or semicolons between sentences.

> The combination of heat and humidity in the French Quarter was oppressive it felt particularly bad when my brother and I came out of our air-conditioned hotel room. After walking a block our clothes were sticking to us and our hair was damp. We couldn't wait to dive into the cooler confines of the next T-shirt shop or art gallery it was like jumping from oasis to oasis. Sadly, the night brought little relief from the heat Bourbon Street at 11 P.M. was still ninety degrees and sticky. We ducked into Preservation Hall for some relief and some jazz, but only one antique fan stirred the thick air as we stood in the back of the packed room. After a half hour we escaped into the welcome cool of a sudden thunder shower unfortunately, it didn't last long, and its lingering moisture turned the street into a steam bath. By the time we got back to our hotel, our clothes were drenched in sweat we were too tired to bathe. The next morning, we steered our car towards the cooler Mississippi Gulf Coast.

Comma Splice

A particular type of run-on sentence called a comma splice has a comma between sentences rather than a period. Apparently the writer understands the need to insert punctuation at that point, but either does not recognize the end of the sentence or feels that a comma is an appropriate way to join sentences.

A comma by itself neither joins nor separates sentences. It is used between sentences *only* when it precedes a joining word like *and, but, or, so, yet,* or *for.* Comma-splice sentences are corrected like other run-ons.

Examples

Comma splice: Your aunt is an excellent cook, I don't care for the spicy Cajun-style food she prepares.

Corrected: Your aunt is an excellent cook, *but* I don't care for the spicy Cajun-style food she prepares.

Comma splice: Hundreds of small sailboats were moored in Chicago's harbor, they looked like a flotilla of toy boats.

Corrected: Hundreds of small sailboats were moored in Chicago's harbor. They looked like a flotilla of toy boats.

Comma splice: James Cochran is my only uncle, he is a forty-year-old bachelor.

Corrected: James Cochran is my only uncle; he is a forty-year-old bachelor.

ASSIGNMENT 3

The following example paragraph contains both regular run-on sentences and comma splices. Correct both types of problems by inserting periods, joining words, or semicolons between complete sentences.

Example

Georgette was fascinated by the Washington, D.C., subway system, a Los Angeles girl, she had never ridden a subway and had heard terrible things about underground travel in New York City. However, as she entered the subterranean world of Washington, she was impressed. The underground tunnels were clean and well-lit, escalators connected the three subway levels. Color-coded signs were everywhere, showing commuters what level to choose and where to stand to reach specific destinations. Georgette had no trouble catching the subway that would make a stop one block from the Capitol building. She was whisked along in smooth silence in a clean, attractive compartment. For the most part, her fellow passengers were well dressed and courteous, there were none of the street toughs and derelicts she associated with New York City subways. Traveling Washington's subways turned out to be one of the highlights of Georgette's three-day stay in the Capital she became quite adept at getting around the city.

Sentence Fragments

Sentence fragments are the opposite problem of run-ons. Instead of running sentences together, a writer will set off part of a sentence with a period, creating a fragment. The following example of underlined sentence fragments are typical of the problem.

Examples

Warren isn't interested in running for a student-body office. <u>Because he doesn't see school government as a vehicle for change</u>.

<u>Although the tide is in all the way</u>. It will be out far enough in two hours to walk around those presently submerged rocks.

Let's take a trolley to Fisherman's Wharf. <u>Unless you'd rather get some exercise and walk the half mile</u>.

I really enjoy talking to Muriel. <u>A woman with a quick wit and unusual ideas</u>.

Our neighborhood is going downhill. Yards not kept up. Broken-down cars in front of houses. Packs of dogs roaming wildly.

I don't enjoy going to Disneyland that much. Especially when you have to wait an hour to go on one ride.

The sink in our bathroom has a slow, constant drip. Which drives me crazy when I'm trying to sleep.

The double feature at Festival Cinema won't be over until 1 o'clock. Meaning we won't get home until at least 2 A.M.

In most sentence fragments like the ones above, the writer places a period at the end of what is structurally a complete sentence, but *leaves the rest of the sentence stranded by itself, creating a sentence fragment.* To eliminate the fragment, the writer needs to attach it to the sentence it goes with.

Examples

Corrected: Warren isn't interested in running for a student-body office because he doesn't see student government as a vehicle for change.

Corrected: Although the tide is in all the way, it will be out far enough in two hours to walk around those presently submerged rocks.

Corrected: Let's take a trolley to Fisherman's Wharf, unless you'd rather get some exercise and walk the half mile.

Corrected: I really enjoy talking to Muriel, a woman with a quick wit and unusual ideas.

Corrected: Our neighborhood is going downhill: yards not kept up, broken-down cars in front of houses, and packs of dogs roaming wildly.

Corrected: I don't enjoy going to Disneyland that much, especially when you have to wait an hour to go on one ride.

Corrected: The sink in the bathroom has a slow, constant drip which drives me crazy when I'm trying to sleep.

Corrected: The double feature at Festival Cinema won't be over until 1 o'clock, meaning we won't get home until at least 2 A.M.

The following guidelines will help you identify and eliminate fragments in the writing.

1. While a sentence expresses a complete thought, a fragment does not. By itself, a fragment does not make much sentence.

Examples

Meaning we won't get home until at least 2 A.M. (What does that mean?)

Which drives me crazy when I'm trying to sleep. (What drives you crazy?

Especially when you have to wait an hour to go on a ride. (Where are you? What happens?)

A woman with a quick wit and unusual ideas. (Who is it?)

Unless you'd rather get some exercise and walk the half mile. (What's the option? Walk to where?)

2. Since most sentence fragments are punctuation problems, to eliminate the fragment, simply attach it to the sentence it belongs with, *which is usually the sentence that precedes it.*

Examples

I'm not enjoying school this semester. Because I have so little free time.

Corrected: I'm not enjoying school this semester because I have so little free time.

Melinda is an attractive woman. Particularly when she doesn't act self-conscious about her 6'2" height.

Corrected: Melinda is an attractive woman, particularly when she doesn't act self-conscious about her 6'2" height.

ASSIGNMENT 4

Identify whether each of the following groups of words is a sentence or a fragment, and add your own words to each fragment to make complete sentences.

Example

Unless the weather clears up. (fragment)

We won't be going to the drive-in tonight unless the weather clears up. (complete sentence)

1. An animal of great beauty, strength, and cunning.

2. Leaving the rest of us only the necks, wings, and backs to eat.

3. Walking to school is Clarence's only exercise.

4. Especially in the springtime and early fall.

5. Because I don't have the money or the time for a vacation.

6. Although my new shoes are a little tight, I'm going to keep them.

7. Golf clubs, a golf bag, golf shoes, balls, tees, ball markers, a towel, a score card, and a partner.

8. Just sit around in the back yard and enjoy the cool weather and the sunset.

9. The price of gasoline is steadily rising.

10. Which is one of the fastest, best built, and most expensive sports cars on the road.

ASSIGNMENT 5

Each of the following groups of words contains one or more sentence fragments. To eliminate each fragment, connect it to the sentence it belongs with.

Example

You really worked hard today. Which means you're probably tired. Therefore, we won't do anything tonight. Unless you absolutely want to.

Corrected: You really worked hard today, *which means you're probably tired.* Therefore, we won't do anything tonight *unless you absolutely want to.*

1. No state employees are getting a raise this year. Because the state is $2 billion in debt. Most employees are accepting the situation. Since the state has guaranteed there would be no layoffs.

2. I've been busy all morning washing the car and truck. While you have been sleeping in. Tomorrow, let's reverse the situation.

3. The New York Knickerbockers had a great year in basketball. They'll even be tougher next year. Especially when you look at the quality of their draft picks.

4. Dr. Freeback decided to grade the biology lab test on a curve. Which means the class didn't do that well overall. I hope he dropped the curve low enough for me to pass. Because I know I didn't get a good score.

5. It was a beautiful day at the park. Mallard ducks swimming in the lake. Couples drifting across the water in rowboats. Oak and maple trees turning bright shades of red and orange.

6. I've never gotten along that well with my brother. However, I really like my sister. A person I can always count on to help out.

7. We need to buy a lot of things for the dinner party tonight. Like chicken, paper plates, styrofoam cups, and ingredients for green salad and pasta salad. We'd better go to the store now. Before it gets crowded with after-work shoppers.

8. I know that Lily will be an excellent waitress. Once she learns to slow down a little. And not get so excited. She has all of the qualities needed. Intelligence, a sense of humor, a good memory, and physical dexterity.

9. I'm going to call for tickets to Saturday's philharmonic performance. As soon as Ticketron has them in their computer. Which shouldn't be more than a couple hours from now.

10. Allison McFall should do well in the upcoming gubernatorial race. Unless the women's vote splits. Giving George Landau an unexpected windfall. And a four-year stay in the governor's mansion.

ASSIGNMENT 6

Eliminate any sentence fragments in the following example by connecting them to the sentences they belong with.

Example

Bench pressing is an unpredictable exercise. Three friends and I try to "bench" at the gym at least twice a week. We are all very competitive. Always trying to outdo one another and increase our maximum life. The trouble is, we never know how well we are going to do. From one day to the next. For example, some days I come in and the weight feels very heavy for no particular reason. On those days I'm lucky to bench press 250 pounds. On another day, the same weight will feel much lighter. Enabling me to lift as much as 275 pounds. I'm beginning to believe in the concept of biorhythms. Where our bodies are more "up" for physical activity on some days than others. However, my good lifting days are so unpredictable that I don't see any pattern that I could chart. I'll just continue going to the gym and pumping iron. Hoping that today's the day that the energy and the strength will be there. However, it seems like those days are getting fewer and further between. Probably because I'm getting older and my recovery time slower.

PUNCTUATION

This section presents some general guidelines for using commas, semicolons, colons, apostrophes, and quotation marks in your writing. The purpose of such punctuation is to help readers move through your writing smoothly and with the greatest possible understanding.

Comma Usage

The most common and useful punctuation mark is the comma. Commas indicate where the reading pauses are in your sentences, helping your audience easily follow your thoughts. While a general guideline is to insert a comma wherever there is a natural reading pause or hesitation in a sentence, the following rules will help you punctuate your sentences most effectively.

1. Commas in a series:
    Whenever three or more words or groups of words are presented in a series, put commas between the words (or groups of words).

    (*Note:* Don't put a comma between two words or groups of words joined by *and*, *or*, or *but*: Sam and Maria enjoy classical music and country/western. You can leave the fruit in the garage or in the refrigerator. I like the brown and yellow linoleum squares but not the blue and orange ones.)

    Example

    Susanne enjoys bike riding, jogging, canoing, white-water rafting, and rock climbing.

    Let's get to the museum by 10, leave at noon, eat at the cafe around the corner, and then shop the rest of the afternoon.

    Getting her BA degree, finding a full-time job, getting married, and buying a house are all in Juliet's plans for the next three years.

2. In compound sentences:
    When two complete sentences are joined by *and*, *but*, *or*, *so*, *for*, or *yet* to form a compound sentence, put a comma after the word before the joining word.

    Examples

    You can enroll in any English course at the college, but it would be wise to take one of the courses the counselors suggest based on your English placement score.

    The wind always comes up along the central coast in the afternoon, so we should take the boat out early and finish our fishing by noon.

    (*Note*: Short compound sentences don't require commas because there is no need for a reading pause: I don't like liver and I'm not going to eat it. You can run but you can't hide forever. I'm leaving now so you might as well ride with me.)

3. Introductory groups of words:
A comma often sets off the following kinds of introductory word groups: the first part of a complex sentence beginning with *before, when, if, as, because, while, since, although, unless,* or *whenever*; a prepositional phrase beginning with *for, in, by, with, to, on, against, through, throughout, behind,* and *under*; an introductory phrase beginning with an *ed-* or *ing*-ending word or *to* plus a verb.

(*Note*: Don't put a comma before words like *because, unless, before, after, if, although* in the middle of a sentence unless the sentence is long and there is a definite pause before the word: Your car is driving rough because you haven't rotated the tires lately. I'm not going on the roller coaster unless you do. You're going to get a ticket if you keep driving without your seat belt.)

Examples

While I finish cleaning up the garage, you can run to the store and buy some milk and cereal.

Unless you have a better plan, I'd suggest we call a plumbing company to unclog your drains.

Against the wishes of her parents, Mahlia chose to attend college halfway across the country.

Throughout the six-month divorce hearing, Beverly and Fred did not speak to one another.

Troubled by a sore knee and elbow, Millicent went to a sports clinic before her next tennis tournament.

Working an eight-hour night shift and going to school full-time, Frederick had little time to spend with his family.

To get to the new art gallery from the college, go straight out Reed Avenue and turn left on Broderick.

4. Relative clauses and appositives:
Put commas before and after relative clauses beginning with *who* and *which* and before and after an appositive (a group of words that modify the word preceding it).

Example

Melanie Griffith, who tried out for the Olympic equestrian team, broke a leg when her horse fell during a hurdle jump.

The top of the The Empire State Building, which is one of the tallest buildings in the world, sways in a stiff wind.

Griffin Keller, a man known for his great strength, once lifted a longhorn steer over his head.

Devil's Sire, a 30 to 1 longshot in the Preakness Stakes, won by three lengths over the favored Mr. Lucky.

(*Note*: Don't use commas with relative clauses beginning with *that*, or with a *who* clause that is needed to clearly identify the word it follows: The plan that you have been working on for Saturday's surprise party sounds great. [The *that* clause identifies the plan.] The women who work at the Dollar Laundry really earn their salaries. [The *who* clause identifies the women.]

5. Ending groups of words:
   Set off ending groups of words, beginning with *ing*-ending words and *ly*-ending words like *especially*, *particularly*, and *usually*.

   Examples

   The last bus left for downtown at 5 P.M., meaning we've got a long walk ahead of us.

   We should be at the concert by 10, especially if we want front-row seats.

   I love chili verde burritos, particularly when they're wrapped in homemade tortillas.

6. Openers and interrupters:
   Set off single-word sentence openers like *fortunately, incidentally, finally, therefore, however,* and *consequently*. Also put commas before and after interrupting groups of words that break the flow of a sentence.

   Examples

   Incidentally, where did you get those jogging shorts that glow in the dark?

   Finally, we finished cleaning the storefront windows and called it a day.

   However, despite their great start in May, the San Francisco Giants often go through a "June swoon."

   August, as you might imagine, is not the best time to visit New York City because of the heat.

Those shoes you're wearing, by the way, resemble the ones that have been missing from my closet.

Gretchen's latest poems, you'll have to admit, are more interesting than anything we've turned in this semester.

John won't be going on vacation this fall unless, of course, he gets that big promotion.

7. Combinations:

Often sentences require a number of commas for different situations. For example, you may have a compound sentence with an introductory group of words, an interrupter, and an ending phrase, all of which may require commas.

Examples

Before you decide on a major, take an aptitude test at the college careers center, but if your test-generated aptitudes don't match your interests, you can always ignore the test and do what you want.

Fortunately, marigolds are hearty flowers, for I've gone weeks without watering the ones in the back yard and, luckily, they've survived.

ASSIGNMENT 7

Insert commas in the following sentences based on two guidelines: the seven rules just presented, and the natural reading pauses in the sentences. Most sentences will require more than one comma.

1. If you want to improve your reading speed I'd suggest looking into the Evelyn Wood Reading Seminar which has helped a lot of people read faster and with greater comprehension.

2. Since it's only July no one knows who's going to win the 1992 Presidential race but in my opinion Perot's support will fade Clinton's campaign won't gather steam and Bush will be the winner which won't excite many people.

3. The last place I'd look for Clarence this time of year is in the library because no matter how many finals he has he doesn't start cramming until the week before.

4. Becky Garcia who is active in the baker's union in Chicago led a picket against the Chicago Unified School District which broke its contract with the union and started buying from outside vendors.

5. Unless this three-year drought lets up there won't be enough water to meet the state's needs and everyone is going to experience forced water rationing which will cause a lot of grumbling.

6. Throughout the build-up to the Iraqi–American war no American political or military leader honestly assessed the great military advantage the United States had meaning the average American was left to worry needlessly about our chances.

7. Gasoline prices as you might imagine go up in the summer and down in the winter in response to consumer demand which is predicated on how much people travel.

8. The latest Gallop Poll on American's sexual activity which was conducted in April revealed that single adults were having fewer sexual partners and less casual sex than at any time in the last fifteen years.

9. My uncle from Salem who owns a millinery shop on R Street hadn't left his home state in twenty years but that all changed when he won the lottery and left for a year's cruise around the world taking his wife and four children with him.

10. If you really enjoy the outdoors are in good physical condition and are an adventurous type consider hiking one of the trails across the Adirondack Mountains which will take you about three months.

ASSIGNMENT 8

Insert commas wherever needed in the following essay.

Fishing Woes

I'd always wanted to fish one of the secluded lakes in the high country of the Sierras and I finally got my chance when my friend Jim invited me. After driving as far as we could in his jeep we hiked a mile across a meadow and then began our mountain ascent to Jackass Lake. It was a three-mile hike up the mountain and I was exhausted when we finally reached the lake.

Jackass Lake is a beautiful sight. Its deep turquoise waters are nestled among thick pine trees with a sparkling granite cliff framing its east side. There was no one at the lake but Jim and me and the utter stillness and silence seemed in reverence to the beauty of the place.

I couldn't wait to start fishing imagining the beautiful golden trout lurking beneath the surface. Although we didn't get a bite the first half hour I was perfectly content to enjoy the tranquillity the beauty of the surroundings and my friend's company. However after an hour without a bite we grew a bit restless and moved to another spot on the lake. An hour later we were still without a fish and I was beginning to wonder what the problem was.

All of a sudden we started getting bites but they weren't the kind we expected. The cathedral-like silence was broken by an ominous buzzing sound and the warming summer air was soon thick with mosquitoes who quickly discovered their blood-filled prey. In seconds our limbs were covered with the pesky diners and we didn't have enough hands to ward them off. Quickly growing tired of slapping mosquitoes and trying to fish we left our poles and retreated into the trees to eat lunch scratching itchy mosquito welts between bites of scrambled egg sandwich.

Our next surprise was the sound of human voices through the trees and soon a troop of Boy Scouts stood at water's edge. While under other circumstances I would have been upset at other humans' invading our pristine territory I was glad to see them. Since the Scouts' oath is "always be prepared" I figured they'd have some mosquito spray we might borrow and luckily I was right. We sprayed our limbs and face and thanked the scouts who soon continued on their nature hike pleased to have done their good deed for the day.

Freed from the torment of mosquitoes we continued to fish for a couple more hours but our luck got no better. This was one of those days when the fish had no interest in anything we dangled before them including worms grubs salmon eggs crickets dough balls and lures. We knew there were fish in the lake because occasionally one would leap into the air sending gentle ripples across the glassy surface. They were beautiful to watch but that was as close as we'd get to one that day.

Finally we packed our gear and headed down the mountain. The descent was much easier than the climb and took half as long. Then we crossed the meadow loaded the jeep and took off for the nearest gas station which was five miles down the road. When I went inside the station I saw Polaroids of fishermen on one wall their strings of golden trout dangling proudly before them. All the fish had been caught at Jackass Lake the past month and I silently vowed to return one day soon armed with a large can of mosquito spray.

Colons and Semicolons

Though used less frequently than commas, colons (:) and semicolons (;) are useful in certain writing situations. While I use both of them from time to time in my writing, I don't depend heavily on either.

Though similar in looks, colons and semicolons have very different functions. These are the most common.

1. Semicolon:

    a. A semicolon joins two closely related sentences. The semicolon provides an option other than inserting a joining word or separating sentences with a period. (*Note*: The following words are often preceded by a semicolon: *however, therefore, nevertheless.*)

        Examples

        The last ferry to Victoria Island left fifteen minutes ago; there won't be another until tomorrow morning at 9 A.M.

        Your necklace goes great with that outfit; your earrings, unfortunately, don't seem to match.

        Clyde didn't save his file before turning off the computer; therefore, he lost everything he had typed.

        There are no free bytes left on that floppy disc; however, you can delete one of the files to give yourself room.

    b. A semicolon sets off series of words when using commas may cause confusion.

        Examples

        We can start putting $50 a month in a tax-sheltered annuity, which would reduce our income tax; put it in the bank, drawing 5 percent compounded interest; purchase mutual funds, which are a tax-sheltered form of stock; or spend it on entertainment.

        (*Note*: If commas were used instead of semicolons, the four options would not stand out as clearly to readers—especially because there are commas within each option.)

        Jonalyn has lived in Fairbanks, Alaska; Genoa, Italy; Kyoto, Japan; Maui, in the Hawaiian Islands; and four Central American countries.

        (*Note*: If commas were used instead of semicolons, some readers could get confused about what cities went with what state or country.)

        For the vignette assignment in my computer class, I have to set up an ethical problem dealing with computer use in classrooms; invent four employees with different perspectives on the problem;

generate questions that they should discuss in a hypothetical meeting; and write a script of dialogue for their discussion.

(*Note*: A series of long clauses are often set off with semicolons.)

2. Colon:

a. A colon is used to indicate that a series of specific examples will follow. A colon is always preceded by a complete statement.

Examples

For the Fourth of July picnic we will need to take the following items: paper plates, cups, napkins, chicken to be barbecued, and soft drinks.

The Hyatt Hotel has everything you need for your September convention: a large room for general assemblies, a dining room that seats five hundred, a dozen meeting rooms for break-out sessions, and four hundred rooms reserved for convention delegates.

Marti has all the qualities of an effective college counselor: good listening skills, a concern for the student's welfare, a pleasant personality, common sense, and the knowledge to help students plan their schedules.

(*Note*: Do not use a colon when a series of examples is preceded by *like* or *such as*: To clean up the back yard, we'll need tools like rakes, shovels, pruning shears, electric bush clippers, hula hoes, and chain saws. I like listening to rock stars from the fifties such as Chuck Berry, Little Richard, Elvis Presley, and Buddy Holly.)

b. A colon is used to set off and emphasize one important point in a sentence.

Examples

There's only one important thing lacking in your diet: regular intake of Vitamin C.

Gretchen has a rare quality many marathon competitors lack: the fortitude to keep going when she's on the brink of exhaustion.

I'll tell you what this room needs more than anything else: some comfortable places to sit.

ASSIGNMENT 9

Insert colons and semicolons where they are needed in the following sentences. Some sentences will require no additional punctuation.

1. George Monroe doesn't appear ready for his upcoming fight he's overweight and clearly out of shape.

2. Successful talk show hosts have a number of common traits inquisitive minds, good senses of humor, stamina, a touch of humility, and a genuine enjoyment of their jobs.

3. A number of countries have higher standards of living than the United States such as Sweden, France, Switzerland, Denmark, and Belgium.

4. One thing Fred strived for much of his adult life financial security.

5. Americans are migrating primarily in three directions: from colder to warmer climates, from rural areas to city suburbs, and from expensive property areas to more affordable ones.

6. Your St. Bernard has one bad habit pouncing on anyone who comes through the door.

7. I'm not saying that vaccinating chickens and turkeys is a terrible job I just don't think you would be interested in it.

8. In the middle of the Diana Ross concert in Central Park it started raining heavily nevertheless, Diana kept on singing and the huge crowd roared its approval.

9. There is one thing you didn't anticipate when you drove to the airport the typical 5 P.M. traffic jam on Interstate 405.

10. You need to take a few things to the computer lab like your floppy disc, a rough draft of your essay, a pocket dictionary, and your Word Perfect instructional handbook.

11. Sometime in the next month I need to wax my car, which I haven't done since I bought it three years ago rotate the tires, repair the right front fender damage, the result of someone backing into my parked car shampoo the carpets, which are full of ground-in dirt and have the car completely serviced by the dealer.

12. As a career military officer, Cassandra has had a lot of "home" addresses in the last five years 21 Elm Street, Selma, California 3232 DePaw Avenue, Phoenix, Arizona 301 Route 32424, Nashville, Tennessee 12 Ivan Road, Tuelle, Utah and 4242 Westmont Drive, Westmont, California.

ASSIGNMENT 10

Insert colons and semicolons wherever needed in the following.

Example

When I get to school on Thursday, there is one person I need to see immediately Laverne. She borrowed my sociology notes last Thursday and was supposed to return them on Tuesday however, she didn't come to class. We've got a sociology test at 3 P.M. today, and the questions will come from three sources the textbook lecture notes and filmstrips. I've studied the book and the filmstrips, but if I don't have a couple hours to review my notes, I'm in trouble. Laverne usually goes to the cafeteria around 9 A.M. I'll be there waiting for her, and she'd better have my notes. One thing I've learned from this experience don't lend out my notes a week before a test!

ASSIGNMENT 11

You may have had little experience using colons and semicolons. For practice, write a paragraph on a topic of your choice, and insert some colons and semicolons in your sentences in appropriate places. Include the four different sentence situations in which colons and semicolons are used.

Apostrophes

There are two situations in which writers use apostrophes: in contractions and in possessive words. While most writers have little trouble punctuating contractions correctly, some have a problem remembering to punctuate possessives. Here are the basic rules for apostrophe use.

1.   In contractions:
Whenever two words are joined to form a contraction, an apostrophe (') is inserted in place of the omitted letters.

Examples

he is	he's	does not	doesn't
it is	it's	have not	haven't
they will	they'll	there is	there's
we have	we've	we are	we're

2.   In possessive words:
To show that a word "possesses" the word that follows it, you add either 's or s':

Singular possessive: add 's (dog's collar, Mary's blouse, wind's ferocity, city's skyline, newspaper's headlines).

Plural possessive: add s' (six boys' lockers; the cities' common problems, your grandparents' love; all of the teams' mascots).

Plural possessive exception: add *'s* if the possessive word forms its plural without adding *s*: men's room, women's support; children's games; oxen's yoke.

Possessive pronouns: Possessive pronouns do not require an apostrophe: yours, ours, hers, his, theirs, its.

ASSIGNMENT 12

Write the correct contractions and possessive forms for the following.

Contractions:

you are	should have
he is	there is
they are	we have
does not	should not
do not	he will
will not	could have

Possessives:

the bone belonging to the dog

the bracelet belonging to the girl

the cats belonging to the sisters

the arsenal belonging to the navy

the bias belonging to all newspapers

the enthusiasm belonging to Ralph

the work belonging to the day

the cause belonging to the women

the outrage belonging to the citizens

ASSIGNMENT 13

In the following example, insert apostrophes where needed in contractions and possessive words.

Example

Michael Jordan is a magnificent athlete. As a basketball player, hes in a class by himself, and he may be the greatest of the worlds athletes. Most people know of Michaels basketball talents: his great leaping ability, body control, shooting talent, defensive skills, and passing adeptness. He is head and shoulders above the rest of basketballs superstars. What many people dont know about, however, is his athletic versatility. He is also an excellent golfer, baseball player, and football player. It seems theres no sport that Michael

couldnt have excelled in professionally if he had chosen to. Fortunately, he chose basketball, where his combination of grace, speed,
and skill are best displayed to Michaels admiring legion of fans.
Michael Jordan is regularly acknowledged as the greatest player
ever to play basketball, whether it be a coaches poll, a players poll,
or a newscasters poll. Beyond that, perhaps he is the greatest athlete
ever to play any game.

Quotation Marks

Quotation marks to indicate a person's spoken words are an important
part of any writer's punctuation arsenal. A few simple rules enable
writers to use quotations effectively.

1. Place the words of the speaker within quotation marks.

> Mavis said, "I'm going to spend more time with my younger
> sister."

> Her younger sister Gayle replied, "It's about time."

2. Place the ending quotation mark outside of the end mark.

> The bailiff said, "The court is now in order." (end quotation
> mark outside of period)

3. Always identify the speaker in some manner.

> My neighbor wondered, "Who or what is eating my prize
> roses?"

> "I'm astounded by how young you look," Fred told his former
> classmate.

> Matthew said, "It's going to be a long, cold, wet night."

4. When your speaker reference ends this sentence, put a comma after
the quotation instead of a period.

> "I'm not going to go anywhere this summer," replied Claire.

> "The IRS is going to question your deduction for chewing
> gum," said Hal.

5. If your speaker reference comes between quoted segments, punctuate your sentence(s) like this.

a. The reference divides one quoted sentence.

> "I do believe," said Melissa, "that I was next in line for tick-
> ets." (quotation marks before and after the speaker reference,
> a comma after the speaker reference, and a lower-case letter
> to continue the sentence after the speaker reference)

b. The reference divides two separate quoted sentences:

"You'll have to excuse the way my brother looks," said Henry. "He's been working on a broken water pipe and hasn't had time to clean up." (quotation marks before and after the speaker reference, a period after the speaker reference to end the first sentence, a capital letter to begin the new quoted sentence)

6. Do not use quotation marks with an indirect quotation, where the actual words of the speaker are not used:

Mary told me that I should apply for the waitperson job at the new restaurant downtown.

I told her that I would like to apply but that I didn't have any waiting experience.

She said for me just to go in anyway and fill out an application. I told her I'd do it, but that I was probably wasting my time.

ASSIGNMENT 14

Correctly punctuate the following sentences, most of which include direct quotations.

1. I don't feel well enough to go to church today said Harold.

2. Sarah replied You felt well enough to drink a bottle of wine last night.

3. Last night said Harold has nothing to do with how I feel this morning.

4. I think it has everything to do with it said Sarah When you drink like that, you always have a hangover.

5. Harold said I don't have a hangover. I think I'm coming down with a cold.

6. I really don't care what you think said Sarah I'm going to church with or without you.

7. Harold told her to do what she wanted to.

8. Sarah told Harold that he had a problem.

ASSIGNMENT 15

Write your own conversation between any two people who are having some type of disagreement. Use quotation marks to set off the speakers' words, and put your speaker references in different places: at the beginning, in the middle, and at the end of your quotes.

GRAMMAR

This section covers four areas of grammar that tend to give writers problems: subject-verb agreement, irregular verbs, pronouns, and comparative and superlative adjectives.

Subject-Verb Agreement

Subject-verb agreement problems arise most frequently in sentences where the subject and verb are some distance apart in the sentence, or where the subject-verb order is *inverted*, with the verb coming before the subject.

These basic rules apply to all subject-verb agreement situations.

1. Agreement is only a problem with present-tense verbs. Past- and future-tense verbs do not change form depending on the subject.

   Exception: Only two past-tense verbs—*was* and *were*—change their form like present-tense verbs.

2. If the subject of a sentence is **singular**, the present-tense verb ends in *s*:

   John *walks* to school.

   The theater *is* a block away.

   Your sister *behaves* strangely sometimes.

   Exceptions: The subjects *I* and *you* do not take an *s* ending.

   I *am* tired of school.

   You *look* radiant this morning.

   I *believe* it's going to snow today.

   (See the following rule for an explanation.)

3. If the subject of a sentence is **plural**, the present-tense verb does *not* end in *s*:

   The boys *walk* to school.

   The theaters *are* a block away.

   Your sisters *behave* strangely sometimes.

   Exception: Present-tense verbs end in *s* only in words like *press*, *dress*, *impress*, and *caress*.

(*Note*: The subjects *I* and *you* are considered plural for determining the proper present-tense verb form.)

Troublesome Situations

The following subject-verb situations present the most agreement problems for writers.

1. Separated subjects and verbs. Sometimes the subject and verb in a sentence are separated by a group of words that may erroneously influence the writer's choice of verb forms. As a general rule, *ignore any words between the subject and verb of a sentence when making agreement decisions.*

    Examples

    One of the brothers *looks* just like his dad. (The subject *one* is singular, so the verb ends in *s*).

    The dogs that constantly roam around our neighborhood *need* to be put on leashes. (The subject *dogs* is plural, so the verb does not end in *s*).

    The aroma of barbecuing steaks *tantalizes* Frederick. (The subject *aroma* is singular, so the verb ends in *s*).

    On most days, the mountains to the east, which you can see so clearly today, *are* barely visible because of the valley smog. (The subject *mountains* is plural, so the verb does *not* end in *s*).

    Exception: Certain subjects like *some*, *all*, *half*, and *a lot* may be singular or plural depending what follows them. With these subjects, look into the phrase following the subject to determine the correct verb form.

    All of the *cake is* gone.

    All of the *girls work* in the admission's office.

    Some of the *waste is* the fault of the city.

    Some of our best *actors are* out of work.

    Half of the last month's *rent is* still due.

    Half of the *clams are* too small to keep.

2. "There + verb" sentences. With sentences that begin *There is, There are, There was,* and *There were*, ignore the *there* and locate the subject *after* the verb in making your agreement decision.

    There are several *ways* to cook duck.

There is only one *way* to cook duck with red wine.

There were many *hitchhikers* along the coast highway.

There was only one *hitchhiker* between Stockton and Modesto.

3. Compound verbs. If two or more present verbs joined by *and* have the same subject, they must all agree with it.

Joan *enjoys* performing with the philharmonic youth orchestra in the summer but *dislikes* all of the travel the concerts entail. (*Enjoys* and *dislikes* agree with the singular subject *Joan*.)

My children's grandfathers *are* very different in looks, personalities, and status but care equally about their grandchildren.

4. Singular subjects. The following subjects are singular and agree with *s*-ending verbs: *one, each, either, neither, someone, somebody, everyone, everybody, nobody, no one.*

Each of you *gets* a new deck of cards with your gasoline purchase.

Either John or Marsha *has* to represent the family at the hearing.

Everyone in the play *needs* to be at the theater an hour before the performance.

ASSIGNMENT 16

To handle all agreement situations in your writing, it certainly helps to be able to identify subjects and verbs in your sentences. For practice, underline the subjects and circle the verbs in the following sentences. The subject is the main word that the sentence focuses on, and the verb tells what the subject is doing, thinking, or feeling. Some sentences will have more than one subject and verb. (*Note*: The following forms of *to be* are always verbs: *am, is, are, was, were.*)

Examples

The kitchen faucet leaks from the top and covers the drain board with water.

I enjoy working with my hands, but my sister Clarita prefers mental challenges.

1. Saint Bernards belong in a much cooler climate than southern Florida.

2. Garden snails eat my marigolds as fast as I plant them.

3. Since there is no longer a Soviet military threat, the United States needs to cut its military spending drastically.

4. The sound of dripping water annoys Herbie, but his brother Wallace finds it soothing.

5. Descendents of the original pilgrims still live in the Cape Cod area, and some of their modern-day feuds stem from centuries-old differences among families.

6. In the yard behind my house, a family of gophers lives in an underground labyrinth, which I regularly flood.

7. If you believe that your chances of winning the state lottery are good, you are misguided.

8. The problem with the blueprints for Sarah and Jake's house is that there is no weight-bearing interior wall in the second story.

9. Your aunt from Chicago looks much like your mother although I know that they are in-laws.

10. Swallows return to the mission at Capistrano every year, but they continue to arrive in smaller and smaller numbers.

11. The trees along Crawford Boulevard are rather sickly because skyscrapers cast shadows on the street all day and block the badly needed sunlight.

12. I am very happy with the city's renovation plans for my old neighborhood, but many older residents doubt the sincerity of the city's intentions.

13. Most of my friends enjoy eating at the Golden Corral because the salad bar is a meal by itself, and no one goes home hungry.

14. European countries allow certain drug treatments for cancer and AIDS that the United States continues to ban, so some Americans in search of hope fly to Europe for treatments.

15. Winter and summer are the seasons with the highest crime rates, and there are many theories as to why.

ASSIGNMENT 17
Fill in the blanks in the following paragraph with appropriate present-tense verbs that agree with their subjects.

As the level of water in reservoirs _____ to drop,

Californians _____ to the skies for some relief from

the drought. After five years of below-average rainfall, the snow-

pack in the mountain ranges _____ small, lakes

throughout the state _____ low, and underground water supplies for agricultural and public use _____ dwindling. Although people in every county _____ on government-recommended water rationing schedules, there _____ fears that the water supply _____ not sufficient to meet agricultural needs for the summer. Rivers and canals in the agriculturally rich Central Valley _____ water to hundreds of thousands of acres of farmland, but once the water level in the major reservoirs _____ below dam release level, irrigation sources _____ to a trickle, and a lot of cropland _____ in serious danger. _____ Meteorologists from the state university system _____ a wetter fall and winter than those of the past five years, but people _____ whether one good year of rainfall _____ up for years of drought. With the widespread fear that the greenhouse effect caused by air pollutants _____ changing national weather patterns, many residents in the state _____ a calamitous situation at hand, one that in some experts' eyes _____ the economic future of the state and the well-being of its citizens.

ASSIGNMENT 18

Proofread the following two paragraphs for verbs that do not agree with their subjects. Correct those verbs to eliminate all agreement problems.

My daughter enjoys shopping in the city's garment district. One of her greatest pleasures are spending a day in one of the rundown multi-story buildings where hundreds of outlet stores for brand-name clothing, shoes, and jewelry is housed. The great attractions of these stores is that all of the merchandise is sold at cut-rate prices and both the volume and variety of goods is tremendous. On a Saturday my daughter spends a good eight hours in the garment district, and I always worry a little until she gets home. All of the old buildings in the garment district is firetraps. There is no indoor sprinklers, the stairways are narrow and cramped, and the wooden exteriors are a tinderbox. If a fire in any one of the buildings break out, no one on the upper floors get out alive, and the fire quickly spreads to other buildings. One of the reasons that the merchandise is so reasonably priced are that the leases for the buildings is very reasonable.

Irregular Verbs

Some verbs do not form their *past* tense with the regular *-ed* verb ending. Instead, they form their past tense in different, *irregular* ways that involve changes within the verb instead of the addition of an ending. Although there are groups of irregular verbs that form their past tense in similar ways, there are no rules to follow (like the *-ed* rule for regular verbs); therefore, *irregular verb forms* need to be memorized.

The following is a list of frequently used irregular verbs whose forms are often confused. The verbs with similar forms are grouped as much as possible. The last column, "Past Participle," contains the irregular verb forms used with *helping verbs* such as *has, have, had, was,* and *were*. Here are examples of sentences containing the past tense and past participle verb forms:

John *flew* cross country in a single-prop Cessna. (past tense, action completed)

John *has flown* cross country many times. (past participle + helping verb *has*; action continuing into the present)

Lillie *sang* beautifully at the graduation ceremony. (past tense, action completed)

Lillie *has sung* at many graduation ceremonies. (past participle + helping verb *has*; action continuing in present)

Lillie *had sung* at many graduation ceremonies. (past participle + helping verb *had*; continuing action completed in the past)

Present Tense	*Past Tense*	*Past Participle*
become	became	become
come	came	come
run	ran	run
begin	began	begun
drink	drank	drunk
ring	rang	rung
sing	sang	sung
swim	swam	swum

Present Tense	Past Tense	Past Participle
fly	flew	flown
grow	grew	grown
know	knew	known
throw	threw	thrown
burst	burst	burst
cut	cut	cut
quit	quit	quit
set	set	set
choose	chose	chosen
drive	drove	driven
eat	ate	eaten
get	got	got, gotten
give	gave	given
rise	rose	risen
speak	spoke	spoken
take	took	taken
write	wrote	written
bring	brought	brought
build	built	built
catch	caught	caught
has	had	had
lead	led	led
sit	sat	sat
do	did	done
go	went	gone
see	saw	seen
lay	laid	laid (to place or set something down)
lie	lay	lain (to recline or rest)

ASSIGNMENT 19

Fill in the blanks with the correct past tense and past participle forms of the irregular verbs in parentheses. Use the past participle form when a helping verb (such as *has, have, was, were*) comes before it.

Examples

(get) She has gotten good grades on her math quizzes.

(run) George ran into a brick wall.

1. (write) Ted has _____ more this semester than ever before.

2. (lead) The winding path _____ to a gazebo among the pines.

3. (drive) You have _____ me wild with your accusations.

4. (sit) Grace _____ on a stump contemplating her future.

5. (eat) Have you _____ the stuffed peppers in the cafeteria?

6. (build) Ted has _____ model planes since he was in grade school.

7. (begin) It has _____ to drizzle outside.

8. (throw) Mia _____ her back out in aerobic dance class.

9. (know) Hal has _____ some very strange people.

10. (set) Judy _____ her collection of figurines on the mantel.

11. (fly) We've _____ with six different airlines.

12. (drink) You have _____ enough coffee to last you a month.

13. (see) No one _____ or heard from Ezekiel for over two months.

14. (choose) You have _____ the most expensive brand of panty hose.

15. (come) By the time Ames had _____ home, everyone was asleep.

16. (become) You have _____ very proficient at archery.

17. (go) Mattie has _____ to collect dry firewood by the lake.

18. (bring) Grover _____ swamp mud in on his shoes.

19. (give) Reading has _____ Louise great pleasure for years.

20. (swim) Have you _____ across the lake by yourself yet?

21. (lie) Yesterday I _____ down at noon and awakened at 6:00 p.m.

22. (lay) Where have you _____ your pipe?

23. (lie) Have you ever _____ in a hammock?

24. (lay) The construction crew _____ five miles of asphalt in a day.

25. (see) Has anyone _____ my red pajamas?

Here is more practice using irregular verbs. Write sentences using the following irregular verbs in the tenses indicated. Then share your sentences with a classmate and check each other's verb forms.

Examples

run (past)   Last night John ran past my house at 3 A.M.
eat (past participle)   You have eaten all of the cherries I was saving
                    for the picnic.

1. fly (past participle)

2. burst (past)

3. choose (past)

4. fly (past participle)

5. drink (past participle

6. write (past participle)

7. set (past)

8. rise (past)

9. take (past)

10. see (past)

11. lie (past participle)

12. swim (past participle)

12. drive (past participle)

14. become (past participle)

15. ring (past participle)

16. bring (past)

17. lead (past)

18. lay (past)

19. throw (past participle)

20. drive (past participle)

Pronouns

The two pronoun situations that give writers the most problems are *subject pronouns* and *pronoun-antecedent agreement*. However awareness of a few basic rules helps most writers use pronouns correctly.

The following guidelines will help you use pronouns effectively in your writing.

1. Rather than repeating a word unnecessarily, replace it with a pronoun or pronouns.

Without pronouns: John took John's mother to John's house so that John could show John's mother John's slides of Mexico.

With pronouns: John took his mother to his house so that he could show her his slides of Mexico.

2. The following pronouns are always used as subjects: *he, she, it, you, we,* and *they.* Do not use the object forms *him, her, us,* or *them* as subjects. When a pronoun other than *I* shares the *subject* with a name or other noun, the pronoun always comes first.

Wrong: Fred and me are planning to open a boutique together.

Right: Fred and I are planning to open a boutique together.

Wrong: Julie's mother and her are best friends.

Right: She and Julies' mother are best friends.

Wrong: The Garcias and them usually car pool to football games.

Right: They and the Garcias usually car pool to football games.

Wrong: I don't think that the Joneses and us have much in common.

Right: I don't think that we and the Joneses have much in common.

Wrong: Your sister and him seem to be quite compatible.

Right: He and your sister seem to be quite compatible.

Wrong: Him and me have been competitors since the fifth grade.

Right: He and I have been competitors since the fifth grade.

3. When a pronoun replaces a word (its antecedent), it must *agree with the word in number and gender.*

   a. Replace singular masculine words (man, boy, Joe, Herb) with *he, him, his,* and *himself.*

   The young boy played by himself in his back yard.

   Replace singular feminine words (girl, sister, Freda, woman) with *she, her, hers,* and *herself.*

   Freda doesn't think that she can color her hair by herself.

   Replace singular neutral words (roof, book, chair, tree) with *it, its,* and *itself.*

   The hurricane began losing its force over the Gulf waters, and it hit the Southern coast rather meekly.

   Replace plural masculine, feminine, and neutral words (boys, girls, athletes, cars, books, chairs) with *they, them, their, theirs,* and *themselves.*

The teachers hired their own attorney to settle the back pay issue for them.

Replace plural references that include yourself (John and I, my classmates and I, the other pianists and I) with *we, us, our, ours,* and *ourselves.*

My sister and I have $50 between us, and we are going to spend it on concert tickets for ourselves and our husbands.

Use the following pronouns to refer to yourself: *I, me, my, mine,* and *myself.*

I don't have any current plans for Easter break, but I don't want to spend it by myself doing nothing.

b. The following words always require singular pronoun references: *one, each, every, either, none, everyone, no one, someone, everybody, nobody, somebody.*

One of the boys lost his watch.

Everyone in the private girls' school bought her own uniform.

Every house on the block lost its roof in the tornado.

Nobody on the men's basketball team had his sneakers stolen.

c. Singular words that refer to both males and females (student, person, politician, writer, everyone, someone, nobody) are replaced by *he or she, his or her, his or hers,* and *himself or herself.*

A person should do his or her best to help the less fortunate.

A writer sometimes takes for granted familiar things that his or her readers may know little about.

A student needs to take his or her time in deciding on a major and make the final decision by himself or herself.

Everyone in Olympic Stadium rose to his or her feet when the athletes paraded in.

Nobody should go through life shouldering burdens all by himself or herself.

Not one of the students brought his or her student body card to the hockey game.

ASSIGNMENT 20

Insert correct pronoun forms in the blanks in the following example paragraphs. (The writer is referring to herself throughout the paragraphs.)

Melinda Jones and _____ had been best friends since _____ were in five years old. _____ and _____ lived in the same neighborhood and played together constantly. _____ both had brothers whom _____ hated because _____ would gang up on _____ and make _____ lives miserable. _____ and _____ ran home crying to _____ mothers more than once after the boys attacked _____ with a garden hose or pulled _____ hair.

Melinda and _____ often went shopping with _____ mothers, and _____ would immediately ditch _____ at the mall and head straight for our favorite hang-out: the arcade. Each of _____ would bring a handful of quarters, and _____ would play arcade games until _____ mothers hauled us out. Neither of the mothers ever lost _____ temper with _____ , probably because _____ knew _____ were very good at taking care of each other.

Growing up, a child usually takes _____ best friend for granted. That was the case with _____ until Melinda suddenly moved away with _____ mother to upstate New York. _____ was depressed for many months, and even as _____ grew accustomed to not having Melinda around, there was still a void in _____ life that no one could fill. When a child loses _____ best buddy, a replacement seldom miraculously appears.

Five years later Melinda moved back to town and started going to

_____ junior high school. _____ was now a foot taller than _____ was, wore makeup, and appeared more interested in boys than in _____ childhood chum. One of _____ took a similar interest in Melissa, and _____ were soon in a world by _____ , going around school holding hands and sighing. Melissa and _____ were obviously at different stages in _____ lives, and _____ soon realized that things wouldn't be the same between _____ as when were children. _____ still missed the Melissa of my childhood, but the new Melissa was almost a stranger. _____ and _____ situation made me more aware of the fragility of special friendships as well as the special magic that _____ hold.

ASSIGNMENT 21

Proofread the following example paragraphs and correct any errors in subject pronouns or pronoun-antecedent agreement.

On the whole, today's typical college student is taking longer to graduate than ever before. This doesn't mean that they are lazier or less intelligent than their counterparts of years past. Their circumstances are just different.

First, many of today's college students are older. His or her average age is about twenty-eight. Older students often have more responsibilities, including full-time jobs and families to support, so he or she can't take as many units per semester as younger students. Consequently, it takes them longer to complete their majors' requirements and to graduate.

Second, getting good grades in college is more important today than ever. If a student doesn't have an A/B average in college, they may not get into a graduate school to get the advanced degree they need for employment. Consequently, to keep their grade points up, students frequently drop classes in which they aren't doing well or retake courses where they got a C or worse. In both cases, the amount of time spent in undergraduate studies lengthens.

Third, students are changing majors more often than before. This occurs for three reasons. First, with the job market changing as rapidly as they are, a major that seemed promising in a student's freshman year could hold little promise for employment by their junior year. Second, with students staying in school longer, he or she has more time to rethink the major decision he or she may have hastily made their freshman year. Third, a typical student is more concerned than ever with getting into a profession that they are suited for and that will bring them professional satisfaction, which may require reassessing and changing majors. Whatever the reason, changing majors results in most students having to stay in school at least one additional year.

My friends Marcus and Marjorie and me are three good examples of the current trend. Him and her are married, and both are going to school and working. Neither can take more than twelve units because of their work schedule. Both Marcus and me have changed majors once, and we lost at least a semester of courses that won't apply to our new majors or our general education requirements. Marcus and Marjorie figure it will take them at least six years to get their degrees, his in social work and hers in nursing, and it will take me at least five. Our situations are similar to many of the people with whom we go to school.

Comparative and Superlative Adjectives

Since writers frequently use comparisons to clarify points and draw conclusions, they need a good command of comparative and superlative adjectives. *Comparative* adjectives compare *two subjects* while *superlative* adjectives compare *three or more subjects*.

Comparative: John is a *harder* worker than his sister Thelma.

Superlative: John is the *hardest* worker in his family.

The following rules for using comparative and superlative adjectives will serve you well, both in writing and conversation.

Comparative Adjectives

1. Comparative adjectives compare *two* subjects.

2. If the adjective has one syllable, add *er* to form the comparative.

Martha is *taller* than Louise.

Mannie is *wiser* than his father.

3. If the adjective has two or more syllables, add *more* in from of the adjective.

Martha is *more* assertive than her cousin Meg.

The Giants are *more* aggressive on offense than a year ago.

4. *Exceptions:* Two-syllable adjectives ending in *y* or *w* require the *er* ending instead of *more*.

I am *hungrier* this morning than I was yesterday.

Thelma is getting *angrier* by the minute.

Let's use the *shallower* end of the swimming pool.

5. Never use the *er*-ending and *more* together.

Wrong: Washington, D.C., is more hotter in the summer than Chicago.

Right: Washington, D.C., is *hotter* in the summer than Chicago.

Wrong: Juanita is a more gracefuler ballerina than her sister.

Right: Juanita is a *more graceful* ballerina than her sister.

6. The comparative word *than* is found in sentences using comparative adjectives.

Japan's bullet train goes faster *than* any American train.

Cicily seems more cordial towards her in-laws *than* she used to be.

7. The comparative form of "good" is *better*; the comparative form of "bad" is *worse*.

Malcolm scored *better* on his SAT test his junior year than he did his senior year.

Your cold appears no *worse* than it was yesterday.

ASSIGNMENT 22

In each of the following sentences, fill in the correct comparative form of the adjective in parentheses.

Examples

(swift) The Jaguar is *swifter* than the leopard.

(interesting) The Picasso paintings are *more interesting* than the Dali's.

1. (quick) Martina Navratilova has a _____ serve than Monica Seles.

2. (adept) Eight-year-olds are _____ at social relations than five-year olds.

3. (determined) Angelica is _____ to do well in school than she was last semester.

4. (sharp) Indian arrowheads were _____ than Chinese arrowheads from a similar time period.

5. (industrious) Ants are _____ insects than flies.

6. (pretty) The flower arrangement on the kitchen table is _____ than the one in the living room.

7. (tall) In general, each generation of Americans has been _____ than their parents.

8. (yellow) The white clothes looks even _____ than before they was washed.

ASSIGNMENT 23

Insert your own comparative adjectives in the following sentences. Use both one-syllable and multi-syllable adjectives.

Example

The knives in the drawer are *duller* than the ones on the counter. Male children are *more aggressive* than females.

1. The Sunday crossword puzzle in the *Examiner* is _____ than the weekday puzzles.

2. Bran flakes are _____ than rice crispies.

3. The Sears Tower in Chicago is _____ than New York's Empire State Building.

4. Gwen seems _____ of the things people do for her than she used to be.

5. Frances is _____ than ever about the fragile condition of her prize rose bushes.

6. Thanks to the movie *Jurassic Park*, dinosaurs were _____ in the United States in 1993 than they'd ever been.

7. Gretchen has a much _____ piano-playing style than her brother.

8. Because of their long legs, baby ostriches seem _____ than they actually are.

Superlative Adjectives

1. Superlative adjectives compare two or more subjects.

2. If the adjective has one syllable, add *est*.

    Tabor Hall is the *tallest* building on campus.

    The *quickest* way to the cafeteria is the path along the lagoon.

3. If the adjective has two or more syllables, add *most* in front of the adjective.

    Cypress 3X is the *most reliable* software program for personal income-tax preparation.

    Samantha's *most noticeable* characteristic is her inimitable laugh.

4. Exceptions: Two-syllable adjectives ending in *y* or *w* require the *est*-ending rather than adding *most*.

    Sarah is one of the *luckiest* bowlers I've ever bowled with.

    Cloud Bay is the *shallowest* entrance to Fortuna Island.

5. Never use *est* and *most* together.

    Wrong: Greg is the most handsomest guy on the soap opera *Raven*.

    Right: Greg is the *most handsome* guy on the soap opera *Raven*.

    Wrong: VanDyke makes the most hardest catches look easy.

    Right: VanDyke makes the *hardest* catches look easy.

6. The word *the* precedes superlative adjectives.

    Florida is *the* most popular southern state for tourists.

    You have *the* most unusual-looking hamster.

    Slade is *the* weirdest character in the neighborhood.

7. The superlative form of "good" is *best*; the superlative form of "bad" is *worst*.

Those were the *best* dumplings I've ever eaten.

John has the *worst* table manners of anyone in his family.

ASSIGNMENT 24

In each of the following sentence, fill in the superlative form of the adjective in parentheses.

Examples

(smart) The gorilla is the *smartest* of the Simian species.

(beautiful) That was the *most beautiful* sunset of the week.

1. (devious) You are the _____ poker player I've ever played against.

2. (stout) Uncle Manuel is the _____ of my relatives.

3. (short) The _____ distance between two points is a straight line.

4. (imaginative) (distracted) The _____ child in a class can sometimes appear the _____ .

5. (angry) The _____ I've ever seen the President was at a rally in Columbus where he was heckled by Girl Scouts.

6. (bad) *Angry Nights* was the _____ movie of the summer.

7. (loathsome) Square Pegs is the _____ punk rock group in the Seattle area.

8. (sharp) Matilda is the _____ dresser in the church choir.

ASSIGNMENT 25

Insert your own one-syllable and multi-syllable comparative adjectives in the following sentences.

1. Of all his fraternity brothers, Siegfried is the _____ .

2. You are the _____ person around young children.

3. The Japan Tower is the _____ building in Tokyo at night.

4. Aunt Mavis is the _____ cook in the family.

5. The _____ part of the movie was when the crooks backed their getaway car into the police station parking garage.

6. Jack the Ripper was the _____ criminal in London's history.

7. That is the _____ -looking pillow case I've ever seen.

8. Frank is the _____ person to be around for long periods of time.

ASSIGNMENT 26

Fill in the following example paragraph with appropriate comparative and superlative adjectives.

The _____ building on campus is Filmore Dormitory. It is one story _____ than Santa Rosa Hall. However, the _____ structure on campus is the new adminis- tration building, which is even _____ than the much-acclaimed library building. Overall, the campus is much _____ than it was twenty years ago when I was a student. The trees and shrubs are _____ , the newer buildings are _____ , and the formerly barren area along the river is _____ . Today, the campus is one of the _____ in the state, whereas it used to be one of the _____ .

Index